THE JAZZ
GUITARISTS

THE JAZZ GUITARISTS

Stan Britt

BLANDFORD PRESS
POOLE • DORSET

First published in the U.K. in 1984 by Blandford Press,
Link House, West Street, Poole, Dorset BH15 1LL.

Distributed in the United States by
Sterling Publishing Co., Inc., 2 Park Avenue, New York, NY10016.

British Library Cataloguing in Publication Data

Britt, Stan
  The Jazz guitarists.
   1. Jazz musicians—Biography
   2. Guitarists—Biography
   I. Title
   787'.61'0922   ML399

ISBN 0 7137 1511 1

Designed by   Stuart Keen Mike von Joel
Conceived and Produced for Blandford Press
by Ziggurat Books, an imprint of AGP Newspapers Ltd.,
1/3 Garratt Lane, London SW18
Typeset by. AGP Newspapers Ltd., London SW18
Printed in Great Britain by by JB Offset Ltd.,
Marks Tey, Colchester.

Contents

Introduction

THE BASIC premise of **The Jazz Guitarists** is to cast a wide net to catch a more-than-reasonable selection of gifted players who have made definite personal contributions to a genre that hasn't been always too well documented through the years.

Certainly it does not attempt to include anywhere near the full total of jazz guitar players who have appeared during the past 50-odd years. That would require something considerably more expansive than this particular volume.

Making a final selection of such artists from a not exactly inconsiderable total of half-a-century's worth of guitarists is in itself no easy task; for each musician included, one regrets the omission of at least one other. All the author can hope to have achieved is, first, to have chosen those performers whose presence is absolutely essential for any book like this one and, second, to have produced an overall listing that brings together as many of the facets and styles of jazz guitar playing as possible.

It is true, however, that any list purporting to represent the **Top Twelve Greatest Jazz Guitarists** is going to be slightly more controversial, most especially amongst the real aficionados. Be that as it may, the author feels no guilt at his final choices... except, perhaps, for a slight twinge of regret that no room could be found, ultimately, for the eminently-gifted Jimmy Raney.

Acknowledgement, at least, is made during **The Jazz Guitarists** of the parallel development of blues guitar — and rightly so. Sadly, of necessity, acknowlegement is just about all there is room for. That particular field deservedly requires a comprehensive documentation all its

own — and, after all, this publication is concerned basically about **jazz** and **jazz** players. It is hoped the reader's appreciation will be stimulated by the close attention paid to the discographical aspect of jazz guitar. With particular regard, of course, to more recent newcomers to this field, but not forgetting those of us too young to have witnessed any of the great pioneers in actual live performance. In any case, whether our guitar favourites happen to be alive or dead, it's always good to have around the house as many recordings as possible by as many of those who have helped to contribute to the noble art. And for those who are interested in the thoughts and opinions of the musicians themselves, there should be much interest in the perceptive comments to be found elsewhere by one of the finest guitarists in jazz to-day George Benson. Illustrations in this book are often from rare archives or original and contemporary promotional material, and the quality of reproduction in this book suffers accordingly.

Acknowledgements

In compiling a book like **The Jazz Guitarists,** the author has been beholden, on numerous occasions, to an impressive list of persons.
My deepest thanks go to the following who between them have provided me with sterling assistance and no little expertise:
Mike Carr, Larry Coryell, Ian Cruickshank, Fred Dellar, Eddie Durham, Brian O'Connor, The Record Centre (Birmingham), Bill Skeat, Frank Smith, Dick Spencer (Kingston Jazz Record Society), Rowland Williams. And for special help and real inspiration, above and beyond the call of duty, it would be singularly unforgivable to omit special mention of Charles Alexander, Jim Mullen, Chrissie Murray, Nevil Skrimshire, Judy Reynolds (Import Music Service)
In pursuance of extensive research, the author has had cause to be grateful for ready access to the following respected publications:
New Edition: **The Encyclopedia of Jazz** Leonard Feather/**Encyclopedia of Jazz In the Sixties** Leonard Feather/**Encyclopedia of Jazz In the Seventies** Leonard Feather & Ira Gitler/**Who's Who of Jazz (From Storyville To Swing Street)** John Chilton/**Guitars: From the Renaissance To Rock** Tom & Mary Anne Evans/**The Jazz Guitar** Maurice Summerfield/**60 Years of Recorded Jazz (1917-1977)** Walter Bruyninckx/**Guitar Player Magazine**

History & Evolution

RIGHT FROM the outset, the guitar has had to really fight for recognition and acceptance as a solo voice in the world of jazz, and thus claim a rightful place in the evolution of music. Only at odd intervals in jazz history has the guitar become anywhere near to being an inordinately fashionable instrument — and then primarily because of the out-of-the-ordinary talents of a mere handful of the truly innovative players who have produced their own unique contributions to the genre.

In fact, the jazz guitar doesn't seem to have aspired to the kind of super-star-type all-round popularity of its rock counterpart. Rare indeed has been the jazz guitarist who has succeeded in rousing a mass audience (or a small one, for that matter) to the kind of frenzy the rockers have induced — neither can it be said that jazz guitar players have attained a reputation for taking an overtly sexual stance, like many rock, and some blues, performers. Indeed, restricted for the most part to a basic job of playing rhythm guitar within the framework of a rhythm section, the embryonic jazz guitarist had difficulty in actually being heard, let alone making any kind of individual statement of his own. With a classic early-jazz front-line, of say, trumpet, trombone and clarinet roaring away, complemented by strenuous accompaniments from drums, brass bass and piano, the efforts of the guitarist were made more or less null and void.

The guitar, as a jazz instrument, had to wait a while for final, maybe even grudging, recognition — as a solo contributor to the music anyway. Even though there is photographic evidence of acoustic guitar within the ranks of jazz' first legendary figure (trumpeter Buddy Bolden) as early as the late-1890's, because of the insurmountable sound problem, the instrument had to take a temporary backseat to the tenor banjo. For the banjo, with its clanking, metallic sound, there wasn't too much of a problem in cutting through the overall ensemble noise, making it an especially emphatic member of any rhythm section. Not surprisingly, then, most if not all the early jazz guitarists used banjo at first. Later, with improving club amplifica-tion and record-making facilities, nearly all the banjo-plunkers transferred their affections to, and stayed with, the flexibly superior, and aurally more pleasant guitar.

If the guitar tended to remain mostly in the wilderness during jazz' earlier years, it was to be the premier instrument for a host of emerging country blues musicians — more often than not, singers too — whose own unique art form was developing on parallel lines to jazz. It was these itinerant players, with their subtle, apposite self-accompaniments and dexterous, feelingful solo work, who were first to bring the guitar to a wider audience. Indeed, when listening to recordings by such marvellous blues guitar-players of the 1920's and 1930's, like Blind Willie McTell, Big Bill Broonzy, Scrapper Blackwell, Blind Lemon Jefferson, Robert Johnson, Blind Boy Fuller, Blind Blake, Mississippi John Hurt, and many others, there is ample evidence to support any logical argument that not too many jazz players have surpassed their musical-artistic achievements. Considering that, almost inevitably, these performers were mostly self-taught, the extraordinary intuitive skills produced by McTell, Hurt, Blake, et al, is little short of amazing. And, of course, the feeling and depth imparted by these blues virtuosi more often than not was intensely moving.

It should come as no surprise, then, to find that the first great jazz guitarist was ostensibly a blues performer. In fact, Lonnie Johnson, a black musician-singer from New Orleans, Louisiana, might be said to have been the first-ever cross-over artist — half-a-century or more before that expression entered our regular musical vocabulary. Johnson's enviable flexibility allowed him to move naturally and impressively between the two allied genres at all times. Johnson combined a natural blues warmth and feel with a definite jazz-like approach to his picking.

As a recording artist, Johnson's name is eternally linked with that of Eddie Lang, another superlatively-gifted white guitarist, with whom he was to record a series of 10 guitar duets (including a session featuring also the great trumpeter King Oliver) that remain absolute classics of their kind. Lang's premature death, aged less than 30 — in 1933 — was a terrible loss for the development of solo jazz guitar. Johnson, thankfully, lived on until 1970. He was to become an even more popular figure later still, thanks mostly to his singing. In his middle-to-late years, he operated with particular success in a more overtly rhythm-&-blues field.

During the early portion of the 1930's, the trail-blazing by Johnson and Lang inspired a succession of eminently talented jazz guitarists. Including Teddy Bunn, a mellifluous, warm, blues-touched player with his own distinctive sound and style, and three white musicians — each an avowed disciple of Lang, but with his own method of carrying on what was fast becoming a great tradition: George Van Eps, Dick McDonough, Carl Kress.

But it was to be a remarkable European gipsy, named Django Reinhardt, whose totally individual approach was to fire the imagination, and cause most sparks at this time. Indeed, Reinhardt's electrifying, freewheeling solo brilliance threatened to upstage the total American domination of jazz guitar thus far. Through the succeeding years, right up to date, Reinhardt has remained a legend — especially, of course, amongst fellow guitarists. There can hardly be a post-1930's guitarist, living or dead, who has not responded enthusiastically to his almost unnaturally natural talent. The gifted Larry Coryell, for example — born just over 10 years prior to Reinhardt's death — is just one contemporary player who reacts with excess enthusiasm to the Romany's playing:

'I love Django! Django was the most important force on the European Continent, besides Churchill, besides Dunkirk. Would I have loved to jam with him? Actually, I think I would have been afraid. Oh man, this cat was all over the guitar. If you listen to his phrasing on *Minor Swing*, for instance... I can't possibly duplicate it. I am so impressed that it was done at that particular time. You see, that gives me a little insight as to what life must have been like, then...'

The esteemed Barney Kessel — Coryell's senior by almost 20 years — reacted favourably to Reinhardt's utterly individual approach to jazz guitar comparatively later in his development than most. Strangely, perhaps, but he remains not at all totally convinced of Reinhardt's real greatness as a jazz soloist.

'To me, what he played was improvised gipsy music. But it definitely has its place alongside jazz... Django was a great individualist... what he played was Django. I think it was beyond jazz.'

For most other guitarists, though, Django Reinhardt represents one of the all-time peaks of jazz-guitar supremacy; a talent that constantly bordered on, and sometimes achieved, a state of pure genius...

Reinhardt's dramatically emerging talent, might have temporarily distracted attention from the development of the guitar in jazz in the United States during the first half of the 1930's. But when a young Texan called Charlie Christian appeared on the North American scene during the same decade, the pendulum swung decisively

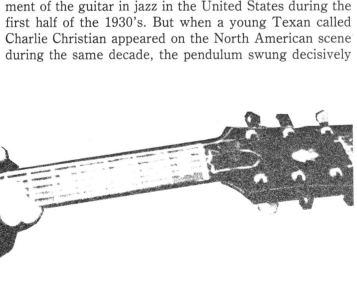

Tal Farlow

back to the birthplace of jazz. After establishing an impressive local reputation in the Midwest, Christian's youthful genius crystallised before a wider audience after he had become a member of the Benny Goodman aggregation in 1939. His basically linear approach to solo guitar-playing, his intense rhythmic vitality — combining impressive drive with a very personal subtlety — explored new and fresh avenues of expression.

Christian, who had been experimenting with a fairly primitive form of amplification for some time before his Goodman tenure, was to become a seminal figure in the transition from the swing era to the jazz revolution of the early 1940's called bebop. But initially it was his use of an amplified instrument that in itself was to play an integral role in another revolution — that of the jazz guitar itself.

In hindsight, it could be said that the amplifying of

the guitar was inevitable. For whereas the acoustic guitar — whether as a solo instrument or as a member of a small combo — had managed to gain a seemingly permanent foothold amongst the rest of jazz' solo instrumental voices, in one area at least, it was experiencing still some difficulty in asserting itself. With the rapid growth of the big bands in jazz during the Thirties, and the surging power and volume that often emanated from outfits that ranged in size from 10-18 pieces, the acoustic guitar, once again, tended to be relegated to a position of near-inaudibility. And its status within the more rip-roaring, extrovert smaller groups was all-too-often that of a second class citizen.

Left to Right: Joe Pass, John McLaughlin,
Jim Mullen, Larry Coryell,
Barney Kessel

Eddie Durham, also gifted as trombonist, composer, and arranger, actually preceded Charlie Christian in the early evolutionary period of the electric guitar in jazz. He ranks amongst the very first to solo on the instrument, on record, an event which took place in 1935, when he was a member of the Jimmie Lunceford Orchestra. Durham, still active as a performer in the 1980's, remembers first hearing Christian play guitar in Oklahoma City.

'Yeah, I was impressed. I told him: "You sound just like Buster Smith!" (an alto player with whom Christian had played). The guitar sounded like an alto... but I never heard him play with a band until somebody said he was goin' with Goodman. I used to advise him 'bout playin' his way with a down stroke — Charlie could never play "up", he always came down. But, you know, I thought that on some of those records with Benny, he sounded jes' like me! He was doin' some of the things that I'd been doin'. He put the guitar on the market, because he was with Goodman... he was great on the instrument. A lot of it was natural.'

When listening to certain Durham recordings of the 1930's — most especially the classic Kansas City Six date for Commodore in 1939 — it is easy to appreciate that he might well have exercised some little influence at least on Christian's development. But there is little doubt that it

was to be the latter, whose basic approach to playing solo guitar corresponded intriguingly with that of tenor-saxophonist Lester Young, who was to be the performer who would exercise the most profound influence on his fellow pickers. Practically every player who followed him, not forgetting many of his direct contemporaries, was touched by his brilliant, innovatory work. It was something of a major tragedy that, like too many other jazzmen, he was to die so young, at age 26. The effect his playing had on other guitarists can be summarised by the brief comment by Jimmy Raney — one of the principal players to emerge from the 1940's:

'When I heard *Solo Flight* (Christian's showcase with the Goodman Orchestra) I almost fainted...'

Christian and Durham apart, other guitar players to make their mark during the 1930's included those who often preferred to restrict their activities to a strictly unamplified role as 'rhythm guitarist', with bands of varying size and style. From a purely rhythmic-plus, non-solo approach, 1937 will remain for all time as a milestone. For that was the year in which a 25-years-old, practically

Joe Pass

Martin Taylor

John McLaughlin

unknown guitarist from Charleston, South Carolina, brought his acoustic instrument into the ranks of the Count Basie Orchestra — and forthwith proceeded to define what amounts to the ultimate in metrononomic, four-in-the-bar rhythm guitar; setting a standard in performance, that was, and remains, beyond reproach. There were other distinguished rhythm guitarists who came to prominence during the 1930's — including Bernard Addison, Allan Reuss, Eddie Condon — and others who followed — like Steven Jordan, Irving Ashby — but no other player is likely to supersede Freddie Green as the ace performer in this specialist area. Al Casey, a soloist, but most often a rhythm player with the Fats Waller Band, is another fine musician whose talents came to fruition in this era.

That amplification of the guitar was to become the instrument's own revolution in jazz seems, in retrospect, to be little more than an obvious truth. Even allowing for the opinion of those who must have viewed — as indeed some must still feel today — the prospects of amplifying an essentially acoustic instrument with horror, that innovation had to come.

The pioneering Eddie Durham, a big-band sideman of some experience, has no doubt as to how he felt about the matter, and the basic reason for adding an amp to his batch of personal instruments.

'The bands were *loud*! They were stronger, then, than now. 'Specially with someone like Louis playin' his trumpet so strong. I just knew that I had to be loud, too. Got my first amplification from the piano mikes — same way as Stuff Smith got his first pick-up for the violin. I did that for a while. Of course, there were times when it wasn't successful. You could blow out the whole sound system — even the lights — in the hall... in the middle of a gig! You might sound like an organ if you got too much volume. And you couldn't play rhythm — you couldn't get the effect of the beat. Then, I got a National guitar. That had a metal resonator. That was much better. When I played that, lots of people preferred that sound. But it was artificial. With the National, I got a sound in between the banjo and the guitar. Kept that one for a long time. Did a lotta recording with it. I just started workin' on 'lectric guitar for myself. Finally, they started improvin' with De Armond pick-ups, things like that. Later than that, they started movin' pretty fast with the more sophisticated equipment...'

Other guitar players who began to use pick-ups with some real effect during the later part of the 1930's included the extrovert Floyd Smith. And it was his showcase number as a member of the Andy Kirk Orchestra — the decidedly raunchy, very electric *Floyd's Guitar Blues* — that not only threw extra spotlight on amplified guitar, but also brought his name to a wider record buying public. Other late-1930's/early-1940's guitarists to make their mark in the wake of Charlie Christian's accelerated popularity included such as George Barnes, John Collins, Dave Barbour, Tiny Grimes. Each was to use both acoustic and electric at some time during their careers.

With the dramatic birth and rapid growth of bebop, fresh and exciting avenues of jazz guitar-playing emerged. Fresh challenges presented themselves — harmonically, melodically, rhythmically. And with the advent of bebop, new and talented players appeared to add their individual contributions to the continuing story of the jazz guitar. Players of the calibre of Billy Bauer, Bill DeArango, Tal Farlow, Herb Ellis, Barry Galbraith, Arv Garrison, Barney Kessel, Oscar Moore, Jimmy Raney.

Of these, arguably the greatest is Farlow, whose incredible all-round technique lifted jazz playing to fresh levels of creative skill and sheer artistry. Right from his earliest general acceptance, at the end of the 1940's, he became a living legend amongst guitarists. It's a situation that lasts to-day, with successive generations of performers only too willing to worship at the Farlow shrine. Amongst contemporary guitarists, Jim Mullen remains an implacable devotee of the big man from North Carolina — Farlow was his first major influence.

'The thing I love about Tal Farlow is that he is such an *exciting* player. Tal had his own unique sound, always. It was very full, very expressive. Every bit as powerful as a horn, in terms of expression, with a lot of variety of sound to it. But he also used the whole range of the guitar, and beautiful long lines. Wonderful articulation — in a class of its own. Always very relaxed — another quality he has in abundance. You never feel he is under any pressure. He wasn't afraid to try all kinds of things — I don't know anybody who can play harmonics quite like Tal. You can hear the influence of the saxophonists in his playing... on his records, for instance, you can hear him play solos using different techniques. Everybody else is struggling to get off one solo using just one technique — never mind using, like Tal, two or three techniques. But he's such a great creative player that he can use everything that he knows — it just seems to fall under his fingers when he requires it...'

Though bebop was to remain a prime motivation for Falow & Co., its influence never totally obscured the immense debt they, and others, owed to Charlie Christian.

Derek Bailey

Barney Kessel

Joe Pass

During the 1950's, a further slew of top-flight guitarists continued to add further lustre to the genre. Amongst the most talented of these were superbly-gifted performers like Kenny Burrell, Jim Hall, Howard Roberts, Rene Thomas... and Wes Montgomery. Of all these, it was to be the last named — yet another jazz musician to die much too young, in 1968 — who was to make the most lasting impression, during both this and the succeeding decade. Possessor of a warmth not evidenced by many of his contemporaries, a basic, natural drive, Montgomery's idiosyncratic use of a potent right thumb (in place of a pick) alone made him somthing of a marked individualist. In addition, his adroit use of octaves added immensely to

John McLaughlin

untypical, sadly, but some of the jazz fraternity never forgave him for becoming, for a jazzman, almost un-naturally popular as a recording artist, selling impressive quantities of albums; and with one single release — his distinctive treatment of *Goin' Out of My Head*, a fine pop song of 1964 — attaining a very high position in the US pop charts. For Montgomery's fellow guitarists, though, invariably there is nothing but the highest praise, in whatever context his artistry was to be found. Jim Mullen — an unashamed 'life-long, Number One fan of Wes',

Al DiMeola

George Benson

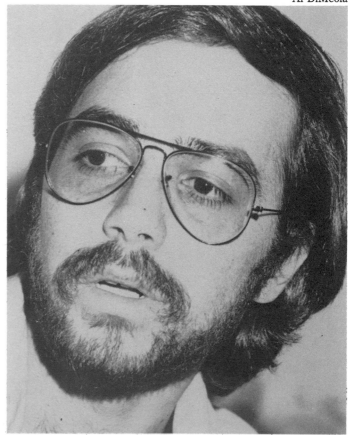

easy identification; only Django Reinhardt's experiments with parallel octaves, years before, are in any way com-parable to Montgomery up to the time of his appearance on the 'big-time' jazz scene at the end of the 1950's. (Mon-tgomery, rather retiring by nature, had preferred to stay and play in his native Indianapolis, for years before becom-ing something of a celebrity, apart from a two-and-a-half year stint touring with the Lionel Hampton Orchestra).

It was thanks to Wes Montgomery's recordings for the Verve label, that jazz guitar was brought to much wider audiences during the latter years of his life. Nothing

that's for sure!' — makes a personal assessement of his contributions to jazz guitar:

'Mostly, I feel, his fire. He was a *burning* player. And, of course, that *wonderful* sound. Very distinctive. I think that, in many ways, Wes was probably the first really great all-round player. It seemed to me he had no limitations. He could really tackle anything he wanted. Because he had everything. Including also great ideas, wonderful rhythmic power — he brought all the authority of the major saxophonists and trumpeters to his playing... finger-bustin' lines... octaves... chords... Wes had the lot'.

With the overpowering influence of rock during the 1960's, it was obvious that the new guitar player of that decade (and indeed for years thereafter) would in some ways at least be influenced by its unrelenting dominance. Something which, as events were to prove, indeed came to pass. With the often terrifyingly exciting Jimi Hendrix reigning as the premier overall influence. Which, in turn, meant that most young players paid scant attention to acoustic guitar, being pre-occupied with expanding the ideas and techniques that involved principally the use of electronics. Even so, the urban black blues guitarists managed to exercise their own important influence, with top names such as B.B. King, Albert King, Freddie King,

Buddy Guy, Muddy Waters, Albert Collins, *et al*, offering a healthy counter-balance to the sheer volume of the sound-only deliberations of the rockers. The cataclysmic offerings of Hendrix, succeeded in bridging both approaches in a way that remains totally unsurpassed...

Featuring prominently amongst the new wave of young players to stake their personal claims during this hectic period of music-making (in its widest sense) were the likes of John Abercrombie, George Benson, Jay Berliner, Larry Coryell, and two Hungarians Gabor Szabo and Attila Zoller. The 1960's arrivals were also often much influenced by the so-called avant-garde jazz movement in general. So, too, were the newcomers from the 1970's — excellent musicians such as Derek Bailey (himself a total individualist, and one who offered a complete re-definition of jazz guitar thinking), Pat Martino, Pat Metheny, Terje Rypdal, Ralph Towner, John Tropea.

But if one single figure can be said to have dominated this overall period — particularly during the whole of the 1970's — it is undoubtedly John McLaughlin. Whether involved with more conventional jazz happenings, or with basic R&B, or with rock, or with the more experimental aspects of jazz, McLaughlin's incandescent brilliance elevated his personal contribution to modern guitar playing above his rivals.

A catalyst supreme in whatever musical circumstance he was to be found, McLaughlin set further new standards of guitar playing; together with his own bands (Shakti, One Truth Band but, most notably, Mahavishnu Orchestra), or in the company of such luminaries as Miles Davis and Tony Williams. As equally fluent and expressive on acoustic as electric guitar, McLaughlin was to forsake the latter completely by the end of the Seventies, seemingly for good. Larry Coryell, a notable contemporary of McLaughlin's, and who has

Barney Kessel

George Benson

worked and recorded with him on numerous occasions, offers his own definition of the man's greatness:

'He's probably got the best picking technique of anybody alive. He can play faster than anybody — and say something. And he has this real spirituality. I have to emphasise that he's really the only Western player that really got inside Indian music, brought it back here and played it *exactly* like they do. Especially, of course, with Shakti. John? He's dedicated, utterly, to his art...'

To-day, the interest in jazz guitar remains as continuous as in previous decades. The collapse of the all-dominating rock world has switched the public's interest away somewhat from the equally powerful rock-guitar superstar syndrome. Which, since the beginning of the 1980's, has meant a renewed interest in jazz guitar-playing. Which, in turn, has meant more regular work — and that doesn't mean just boring studio-bound professional occupations — for most if not all the established jazz players. And it has meant for the more recent performers — amongst them Emily Remler, Kevin Eubanks, Christian Escoudé, and the precocious Birelli Lagrene — the kind of breakthrough for their talents that eluded many of their predecessors.

The worldwide resurgence of interest in jazz *per se*, especially from amongst a new, decidedly youthful audience has helped, too. Indeed, the future for the guitar in jazz is at least as promising as at any comparable period during its altogether fascinating and rewarding history...

The Mahavishnu Orchestra

The Top Twelve

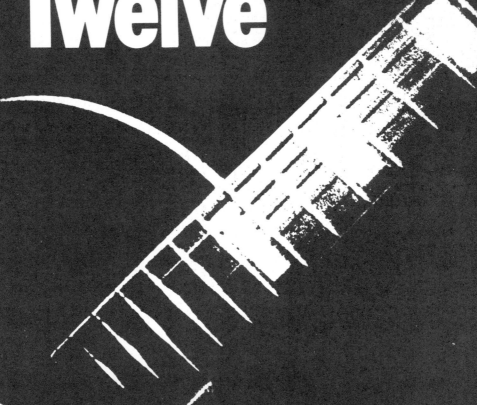

George Benson

George Benson: Born Pittsburgh, Pennsylvania, 1943. Stepfather, a guitarist, taught him ukulele, at same time playing Charlia Christian (q.v.) records for the youngster. By eight, was playing ukulele on street corners for money. Also played with stepfather at local after-hours clubs where young Benson also sang and danced. Known then as Little Georgie Benson. Began studying guitar (1954); same year, recorded four sides for X record label — as singer. During high school days, stepfather made him a guitar. Played with cousin's rock 'n' roll band. Then, at 17, formed own rock group. But having heard altoist Charlie Parker and fellow guitarist Wes Montgomery (q.v.), switched his affiliations emphatically to jazz.

Big break, jazz-wise, came with an offer, at 19, to work with organist Brother Jack McDuff's combo. Toured, recorded extensively with McDuff for about four years. Back to Pittsburgh (1965) for three-months spell as leader of own group — then, back to McDuff, this time for much shorter spell. After which, concentrated exclusively on fronting own small bands. During latter half of 1960's, became popular recording artist in jazz field. But it was the following decade that Benson attained the kind of wide popularity that comes the way of very few jazzmen.

Benson had sold well with CTI and A&M, but it was after signing with WARNER BROS. that he achieved international recognition of enormous proportions, in a combined rock-cum-pop-cum-soul area. *This Masquerade*, from a

hugely-selling first WARNERS LP (19) became his first, smash hit, single (1976) — and the fact it was the only vocal track on an otherwise all-instrumental album was an omen of things to come. Further hits — including *Nature Boy, On Broadway, Give Me The Night, Turn Your Love Around* — together combined to make he something of a pop superstar, helped further by a series of huge selling LPs like (21), (21), (22).

During the past 20-25 years George Benson has continued to develop into one of the most complete guitar players that jazz has known. His swing and drive are comprehensive at all times, and natural adjuncts to a basic guitar technique that is as good as practically any other. His tone is something of real beauty. And his creative fire is a legend in the genre.

Benson's emergence from Pittsburgh came through extensive ground work with Brother Jack Duff. Aural reference to the first recordings he made with the organist — especially studio dates like (1), (6), the latter the first date under his own name — show that his tone, then, was under-developed, and solo-wise, he was only just beginning to produce some kind of real individualism. But the McDuff period was invaluable for the youngster; as much as anything, it helped bring forth a natural affinity with the blues.

Benson's improvement in the years following the McDuff tenure has been little short of astonishing — and

in every way. That swift progress can be traced to a series of record dates for Columbia during 1966-1967. Apart from the obvious tonal quality, Benson's playing throughout (8) is wholly exceptional. He plays finger-busting, bebop-influences lines on *Big Fat Lady,* plays an excellent series of blues choruses on *Slow Scene,* and he positively leaps into the aptly-titled *The Cooker,* producing a solo that is perhaps most notable for its sinewy attack.

A&M RECORDS endeavoured to bring Benson into a more widely-acceptable market, (13/14), by surrounding him with large studio orchestras, including strings. But it took CTI to really present Benson's name to a wider-than-jazz audience. Here, his playing — and sometimes, significantly, his singing too — proved commercially viable. Despite critical sneering from some reactionary jazz circles, Benson's general acceptance increased... without the slightest diminution in artistic endeavours. Indeed, his playing on such LPs as (10), (12), and the widely-popular (26) is never less than excellent, invariably much more so. And with CTI, Benson's particular brand of artistry illuminated recordings by such other label instrumentalists as trumpeter Freddie Hubbard (18), and

tenorist Joe Farrell (17). Best of all CTI's, though, is (16), with Benson's playing benefitting immensely from being recorded before a live — and receptive — audience. He swings hard and hot during *Octane,* and builds a long, always interesting solo — mixing single-string with Montgomery-like octaves — on *Gone.*

From the latter part of the 1960's, there is much to admire on a variety of tracks which comprise the contents of (9), including some blistering bebop *(Billie's Bounce),* some basic blues (*Low-Down & Dirty; Doobie, Doobie Blues*), a sensitive piece of superior ballad-playing (*What's New*). and a poignant, melodic tribute to Wes Montgomery, a major Benson influence, of which he is also the author (*I Remember Wes*).

Despite his pop-type triumphs, involving mostly his vocal excellence, George Benson's importance to the jazz guitar remains an undisputed fact. A youthful veteran of the field, whose tremendous skills will undoubtedly be adding significantly to its continued development during the present decade and thereafter... irrespective of whether or not he maintains his list of successes thus far in a strictly pop vein.

SELECTED DISCOGRAPHY

1 George Benson/Jack McDuff PRESTIGE
2 Brother Jack Alive! At the Jazz Workshop (with Brother Jack McDuff) PRESTIGE
3 Cookin' Together (with Red Holloway, Brother Jack McDuff) PRESTIGE
4 The Concert McDuff PRESTIGE
5 Hot Barbecue (with Brother Jack McDuff)PRESTIGE
6 New Boss Guitar (with Brother Jack McDuff) PRESTIGE
7 Red Soul (with Red Holloway) PRESTIGE
8 Stormy Weather CBS/EMBASSY
9 Blue Benson POLYDOR
10 Body Talk CTI

11 Bad Benson CTI
12 Beyond the Blue Horizon CTI
13 Shape of Things To Come A&M
14 Tell It Like It Is A&M
15 Space CTI
16 In Concert — Carnegie Hall CTI
17 Benson & Farrell CTI
18 Straight Life (Freddie Hubbard) CTI
19 Breezin' WARNER BROS
20 Livin' Inside Your Love WARNER BROS
21 Give Me The Night WARNER BROS
22 Weekend in L.A. WARNER BROS
23 Miles In the Sky (Miles Davis — one track only) CBS
24 Gotham City (Dexter Gordon) CBS
25 Off the Top (Jimmy Smith) ELEKTRA-MUSICIAN
26 White Rabbit CTI

Play in the style of George Benson

Chris Watson notes: Here George Benson plays complex 'be-bop' over a funky back beat. He is such a strong player that if you remove the melodic content of the phrase and beat it out rhythmically it could stand up as a drum break. Notice the use of an E minor laid over an A minor chord on the first beat of the second bar.

Teddy Bunn

Theodore 'Teddy' Leroy Bunn: Born Freeport, Long Island, 1909. Brother Kenneth, violinist; mother played organ, father accordion. First professional work was as accompanist to a *calypso* singer. Became interested in guitar — and jazz — from an early age. By mid-1920's, was fast establishing himself on jazz scene as young player with distinctive style and admirable versatility. So much so, that by 1929, was recording with the Duke Ellington Orchestra, (2), (3) — indeed, around the same period and when Ellington's regular banjoist/guitarist Fred Guy was ailing, Bunn worked with the band for six months. Appeared regularly with the Washboard Serenaders combo during early 1930's, before joining Ben Bernie's Nephews. Band moved to New York, to play long residency at Chick Groman's Stables. There, changed its name to Spirits of Rhythm, with Leo Watson, drummer-singer, its nominal leader for a while. Spirits of Rhythm attained enviable reputation, playing lengthy residencies at top NYC jazz spots like the Onyx, and Nick's; it also toured outside the Big Apple with much success, especially in Philadelphia, Chicago.

Bunn left in 1937, staying briefly with new John Kirby Band (1937); then, led own trio, duo at various New York clubs. Rejoined Spirits of Rhythm (1939). After appearing at New York's World Fair, group moved to California where, for 10 years, it disbanded, reformed fairly regularly. Bunn himself was briefly away from the music scene for a spell ('42). And in 1944, led own Waves of Rhythm. Later, was to front other small combos for gigs in California in general, Los Angeles in particlar.

During 1940's/1950's, worked occasionally with Edgar Hayes (recording with pianist in '48). Gigged for several months in Honolulu, with tenorist Jack McVea's band (1954). Returned to LA, for more work with own groups. Made appearances briefly with Louis Jordan (1959), and late in 1950's toured with rock 'n' roll package shows. Played much less regularly in Sixties primarily because of illnesses (though he did get to work in Hawaii, '69). Regrettably, in 1970 Bunn suffered a mild stroke, followed by three heart attacks, all of which caused almost complete blindness and partial-paralysis. He was able to recover more or less from the latter, but never played publicly again. He died in July, 1978.

Teddy Bunn's beautiful tone, together with his unerring swing and an overall technique that was high on subtlety, enabled him to stand out at all times, even in the most distinguished company. Bunn never lacked an ability to project his talent, yet his work was notable at all times for its laid-back approach. His playing epitomised the ultimate in relaxation — a rare gift when, like Bunn's, it was so highly-developed; ironically, it also meant that delectable performer could sometimes be overlooked by those who were less inclined at most times to listen more keenly to his brand of guitar-playing subtlety.

As an accompanist, Bunn was always discretion itself, yet wholly contributory to proceedings. It is instructive, therefore, to hear his backing comments to jazz greats as diverse in style as Big Joe Turner (13), Sidney Bechet (8), Hot Lips Page (11), and Johnny Dodds (6). That delightfully cloudy sound provides a perfect contrast — and complement — to Page's brash mellophone playing and warm, sandpaper vocals during (11), where the accent is mostly on the blues. As a blues player, Bunn lacked nothing; his approach to the blues was very much, again, of the laid-back variety. On *Do It, If You Wanna*, for instance, his playing combines firmness with tenderness as he unwinds a solo that is notable also for his sheer logicality and real warmth.

Bunn's economic single-string-cum-chordal style might be said to be something of a useful lesson to the more multi-noted performers. With Bechet (8), his rhythmic presence is felt as much as heard though, regrettably, his solo opportunities — as on numerous other record dates — are limited. Still, when the chance comes, he never fails to deliver the goods, as with *Gettin' Together* and both takes of *If You See Me Comin'* — all from the classic (7) — *Just Another Woman* (11), *Blues For Tommy Ladnier* (8), *Bump It* (5), and *Wild Man Blues* (6), last-named finding Bunn in an especially happy-sounding mood, his articulation superb.

Bunn always sounded in fine fettle with both the Washboard Seranaders (1) and the Spirits of Rhythm (4). And his involvement with blues record dates shows just how naturally *en rapport* he was in this area, whether offering sterling accompaniments to singers like Rosetta Crawford, Trixie Smith — both (10) — or Big Joe Turner (13). With Turner he takes a very important role throughout as rhythm guitarist, lifting the rest of the band with his propulsive playing. And his solo contributions — such as during *Playboy Blues, Mad Blues* — are perfect for the occasion.

Teddy Bunn never did get too many chances to record under his own name, and it is a shame that two sides he cut for BLUE NOTE in 1940 (*Blues Without Words, Guitar In High*, both issued on BLUE NOTE 504, and containing archetypal solo work) remain unreissued.

SELECTED DISCOGRAPHY

1 **Washboard Rhythm Kings/Serenaders 1930-1933** RCA VICTOR
2 **Duke Ellington & His Orchestra (1928-1929), Vol 2** MCA
3 **The Works of Duke Ellington, Vol. 4** RCA VICTOR
4 **Swing Street, Vol. 1 (with Spirits In Rhythm)** EPIC
5 **Jimmy Noone, 1937-1941** COLLECTOR'S CLASSICS
6 **Harlem On Saturday Night (with Johnny Dodds)** ACE OF HEARTS
7 **The Panassie Sessions (1938) with Tommy Ladnier, et al** RCA VICTOR
8 **Sidney Bechet Jazz Classics, Vols, 1,2** BLUE NOTE
9 **The Complete Lionel Hampton (1937-1941)** BLUEBIRD
10 **Out Came the Blues (with Trixie Smith, Rosetta Crawford)** MCA
11 **Feelin' High & Happy (with Hot Lips Page)** RCA VICTOR
12 **Great Swing Jam Sessions, Vol. 2** SAGA
13 **Roots of Rock & Roll, Vol. 2 (Big Joe Turner)** SAVOY

Play in the style of Teddy Bunn

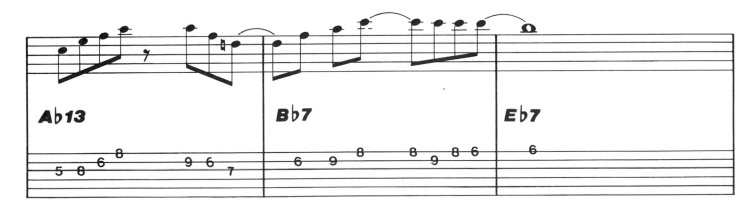

Chris Watson notes: The example of Ted Bunn shows his sense of strong melodic phrasing. Great use of chromatics in bars Three and Four. The B natural has particularly good effect.

Kenny Burrell

Kenneth Earl Burrell: Born Detroit, Michigan 1931. Comes from intensely musical family — mother was a pianist, father played banjo; three brothers all became musicians, two of whom were also guitarists. Under watchful eye of brother Billy, started teaching himself guitar at 12. (Originally, wanted to play saxophone, but couldn't afford to purchase same). Later, was to study classical guitar, but had no real tuition previously. School friends included pianist Tommy Flanagan, bassist Calvin Jackson (brother of Milt Jackson). Musical adviser at Miller High School, Louis Cabrara, became important adviser in young Burrell's musical direction.

Showing strong influences of his then two favourite guitarists, Charlie Christian (q.v.), Oscar Moore (q.v.), played first real professional gigs with Candy Johnson Sextet (1948); then, with Count Belcher (1949), Tommy Barnett (1950). Biggest break — asked by the great Dizzy Gillespie to work with latter's small band (1951). With Gillespie, made record debut, (1). Between 1951-1955, led a succession of first-class small combos, and in latter year received his Bachelor of Music degree from Wayne University, Detroit, as well as staying for six months as member of Oscar Peterson Trio. Moved permanently to NYC, freelanced frequently and led a succession of own small groups. Briefly with Benny Goodman (1957).

During 1960's, established a justifiable reputation as one of the top three others — and topped popularity polls of publications like DOWN BEAT (critics' as well as readers' polls), EBONY, MELODY MAKER, SWING JOURNAL. Made first European trip (1969); same year opened own club: The Guitar. Made several trips to Japan during 1970's, as well as visiting East and West Europe, Australasia, including European tour as member of Newport All Stars (1972). To California (1973), to become active as studio player, as well as continuing to appear at jazz festivals, clubs, concerts and undertaking clinics, seminars, etc. Since when has continued to prove his pre-eminence as one of jazz' great guitar players, both as home and abroad...

In fact, Kenny Burrell is the Complete Jazz Artist. He does not appear to have a fault in his make-up. As a bluesman, he is a consummate performer, never needing to provide histrionics in order to prove his artistry His natural feel for the blues is matched by his real warmth in this genre. Recordings such as those with organist Jimmy Smith (3), (4), (5), and tenorists Coleman Hawkins (33), Stanley Turrentine (10) and Gene Ammons (6), find him more than holding his own as a blues-player. A fact further emphasised in blues recordings of his own like *Everyday I Have the Blues* (18), *Asphalt Canyon Blues* (20), *Wild Man* (16). As a ballad-player, he takes second place to no-one. Beautifully sculpted performances such as *People* (16), *Angel Eyes* (18), (19), *God Bless the Child* and *A Child Is Born* (both 21) are virtually impossible to top. And

when Burrell temporarily switches from electric to Spanish classical guitar for part of (17), he produces stunning interpretations of Alec Wilder's *Moon & Sand*, Gershwin's *Prelude No 2* and, most memorable of all, Harold Arlen's *Last Night When We Were Young*. And for examples of his vibrant bebop-based guitar at its best, Burrell's contributions to such as *Will You Still Be Mine?* (15), *Boo-Hu* (9), *Mambo Twist* (14), and *Tin Tin Deo* (27), are each informed with the kind of running excitement that makes them important, vital statements of real originality.

Burrell's technique has long since made him a legend amongst fellow guitarists. His tone is mellow, rich, distinctive. His articulation is exquisite. His improvisations are always free-flowing, touched with the genuine spontaneity of jazz-improvising at its most lucid — and never lacking in inner fire. Kenny Burrell might not be a true innovator like, say, Django Reinhardt (q.v.), Charlie Christian (q.v.), Tal Farlow (q.v.), or John McLaughlin (q.v.). Yet he is just about the perfect model for any aspiring youngster, an artist whose timeless approach spans all eras of jazz guitar-playing in the most rewarding variety of ways.

SELECTED DISCOGRAPHY

1 DeeGee Days (Dizzy Gillespie) SAVOY
2 Buck'n the Blues (Buck Clayton) VANGUARD
3 The Incredible Jimmy Smith BLUE NOTE
4 Confirmation (Jimmy Smith) BLUE NOTE
5 Organ Grinder Swing (Jimmy Smith) VERVE
6 Juganthology (Gene Ammons) PRESTIGE
7 After Hours (with Thad Jones, Frank Wess, et al) PRESTIGE
8 Original music from the score of "Alfie" (Sonny Rollins) IMPULSE
9 All Day Long & All Night Long PRESTIGE
10 Midnight Blue BLUE NOTE
11 Kenny Burrell Blues BLUE NOTE
12 Freedom BLUE NOTE
13 Swingin' BLUE NOTE
14 Bluesin Around COLUMBIA
15 Cool Cookin' CHECKER
16 Recapitulation CHESS
17 Guitar Forms VERVE
18 Blues — the Common Ground VERVE
19 Guitar VERVE
20 Asphalt Canyon Suite VERVE
21 God bless the Child CTI
22 Newport In New York '72 (with B.B. King) ATLANTIC
23 Handicrafted MUSE
24 At the Village Vanguard MUSE
25 In New York MUSE
26 Moon & Sand CONCORD JAZZ
27 Tin Tin Deo CONCORD JAZZ
28 Night Song VERVE
29 Stormy Monday FANTASY
30 Bluesy Burrell (with Coleman Hawkins, et al) XTRA
31 Kenny Burrell Quintet with John Coltrane PRESTIGE
32 Listen To the Dawn MUSE
33 Quintessence FANTASY

Play in the style of
Kenny Burrell

Chris Watson notes: Here Kenny Burrell uses the 'Blues Scale' to great effect. However, he still spells out the movement of the harmonies. Bars six and seven are a great example of how to build up tension while soloing.

Charlie Christian

Charles Christian: Born Dallas, Texas, 1916. All four brothers were musicians — two (at least) worked professionally (Edward, Clarence). Father, blind musician, played guitar, sang. Christian family moved to Oklahoma City (1921). There, Charlie Christian's first involvement with music was with trumpet; soon, however, at age 12, decided to concentrate exclusively on guitar, although was also to play bass, piano, during 1930's. Played, firstly, in family band, from early teens. Undertook local club work at 15 (where he first met tenorist Lester Young).

Played in Jolly Jugglers band — led by one of his brothers — during early 1930's. During which time also reported to have worked as a tap-dancer, singer, baseball pitcher, prize-fighter. After gigging with Anna Mae Winburn Band, led own unit; then with trumpeter James Simpson in Oklahoma City, and Alphonso Trent (touring). By time he worked with Lester Sheffield (1939), his reputation amongst musicians — visiting as well as locals — was spreading fast.

Seen and heard by John Hammond around the same period and recommended to Benny Goodman. Christian joined Goodman aggregation (August, 1939), making debut following month. Featured mainly with sextat/septet, but occasionally played with Goodman Orchestra. Taken ill on Middle-West tour. Subsequently admitted to Bellevue Hospital, NYC ('41), where tuberculosis diagnosed. Transferred to Seaview Sanitarium,

Staten Island, spending rest of life there. Died March, 1942.

Charlie Christian's position in the pantheon of jazz guitar is of critical importance. It also affects his position amongst the greatest-ever jazz soloists in the history of the music. Of quintessential significance is his overall contribution to the evolution of the amplified instrument. For, despite irrefutable evidence that he was not the first to use amplification during the latter half of the 1930's, his indeed was the premier contribution in ensuring that electric guitar would very soon take over from acoustic as the most emphatic form of expression in this area of instrumental jazz. And Christian's contributions to the evolution of jazz itself are in themselves of historical importance. His unique brand of phrasing is just one aspect of his playing which makes him stand out from jazz guitarists of the Thirties; its horn-like quality parallels the work of tenorist Lester Young — both musicians used unusually long melodic lines, comprising evenly placed notes, phrased in a legato manner. Like Young, Christian concentrated on a freer exposition of the conventional 4/4 time signature, likewise deploying a new approach to the use of basic riffs to produce a kind of rhythmic excitement that was as fresh-sounding as it was exhilarating. And Christian's playing was further enhanced by his subtle use of augmented and diminished chords, plus unusual accents — all of which was to make substantial contributions to the

birth and development of bebop.

As a pioneer of the amplified guitar in jazz, Christian's own sound was extraordinary. Bearing in mind that his amplification at the time of his emergence was, in comparison with later equipment, rather less than truly helpful, he nevertheless coaxed a handsome, distortion-free sound from his instrument. A sound which was an impressive guideline to future guitarists.

Christian's ability to play chorus upon chorus of beautifully flowing jazz remains forever in the memories of those privileged to hear him in live performance, either before or during the 23-months period he spent in the spotlight as a member of the Benny Goodman Sextet/Septet. Indeed, he passed his Goodman audition by improvising 20 glorious choruses on *Rose Room*. Although he was to record prolifically with Goodman, it was with one of Lionel Hampton's all-star pick-up combos that the guitarist made his debut (9). (Christian's 16-bar solo on *Haven't Named It Yet,* at a subsequent Hampton date (9) is as good as any other individual contribution). With Goodman, though, the young Texan received ample opportunities to show his worth. And he responded accordingly, never playing less than well, and more often than not producing definitive jazz-guitar solos.

Amongst a plentiful supply of classic Christian-Goodman solos the following can be ranked with his greatest: *Till Tom Special* with its embryonic bebop phraseology), *AC-DC Current, Wholly Cats, Breakfast Feud* — all (1) — and *I've Found a New Baby, Flying Home, Solo Flight* (a showcase for Charlie, this time backdropped by the full orchestra) — all (2). *Gone With What Wind* (1) fully illustrates yet another important facet of Christian's playing — his pre-eminence as a blues instrumentalist. His blues were never less than magnificent, at all times. Other fine examples of Christian the blues-player are *Boy Meets Goy* (2), and *Blues In B* (1). Both the latter and the absolutely fascinating *Waiting For Benny* (1) offer positive demonstrations of his utter relaxation in performance; *Waiting* — a warm-up performance, *sans* BG — finds him improvising chrous after chorus of superbly cohesive, intensely rhythmic jazz that to-day, over 40 years later, still stuns with its impact.

The opportunity to hear Charlie Christian in company with Lester Young makes for predictably revealing music during both (5) and (3). Of the two, (3) is the more interesting, primarily because the contents originate from a live concert performance. Both men are completely relaxed and at the top in their respective fields. Both *Pagin' the Devil* and *Good Morning Blues* contain music that can be called truly sublime — and Christian and Young provide most of that musical sublimity.

But if there is one series of performances which more than any other really defines the genius of Christian,

then it must be a clutch of items taped by enthusiast Jerry Newman in 1941, during after-hours jamming that took place at Minton's Playhouse and Monroe's Uptown House, both legendary Harlem nightspots (7). This is Charlie Christian, unfettered by time or band restrictions, producing a succession of choruses of magnificent jazz, whose extraordinary quality has rarely, if ever, been surpassed, before and since. His tremendous drive and ceaseless flow of ideas inform each of the performances, but perhaps never more so vividly than during lengthy work-outs on *Swing To Bop* (really *Topsy*) and *Stompin' at the Savoy*. It is further revealing to hear an obviously relaxed, on-form Christian jamming with Thelonious Monk, also at Minton's, on the latter's *Rhythm-a-Ning* (8). Christian recorded only once on acoustic guitar. Which makes the solitary *Profoundly Blue* (10) something special. Especially as it contains a blues statement that ranks with his greatest.

It is impossible to imagine any guitarist who has not been touched by Charlie Christian's brilliance since his meteoric rise to fame in 1939. Certainly, the music he produced during a tragically short period in the top-class of jazz music sounds as irresistible now as it did during his lifetime.

SELECTED DISCOGRAPHY

1 Charlie Chistian with the Benny Goodman Sextet & Orchestra CBS/REALM
2 Solo Flight — Charlie Christian with the Benny Goodman Sextet, Septet & Orch (Vol. II) CBS
3 The Legendary John Hammond's Carnegie Hall Concerts 1938/39: From Spirituals To Swing VOGUE
4 Charlie Christian with Benny Goodman & The Sextet JAZZ ARCHIVES
5 Charlie Christian-Lester Young: Together, 1940 JAZZ ARCHIVES
6 BG, His Stars & His Guests (with Benny Goodman) QUEEN DISC
7 Charley Christian at Minton's SAGA
8 Trumpet Battle at Harlem (with Joe Guy, Hot Lips Page) XANADU
9 The Complete Lionel Hampton (1937-1941) BLUEBIRD
10 Memorable Sessions In Jazz (Edmond Hall) BLUE NOTE
11 Ida Cox/Bertha 'Chippie' Hill (Ida Cox) QUEEN-DISC
12 The Metronome All-Star Bands RCA CAMDEN
13 Benny Carter 1945 + The Metronome All Stars QUEEN-DISC

Play in the style of Charlie Christian

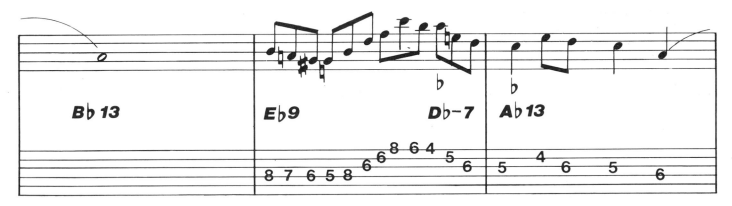

Chris Watson notes: Here Charlie Christian uses complex melodic structures to spell-out the 'changes' best illustrated in bars four and seven. Also he uses triplets to great rhythmic effect. It's easy to see why young Charlie Parker was a great fan of his. A development of Christian's style can be seen in the playing of Joe Pass.

Tal Farlow

Talmadge Holt Farlow: Born Greensboro, North Carolina, 1921. Played guitar from age eight — but only as hobby. Father played guitar, banjo, ukulele, violin; young Talmadge taught himself to play on Farlow Snr's guitar. Did not have any preconceived ideas of becoming a professional musician — wanted to be a sign-painter, something he was to achieve at fairly regular intervals during his life.

Really began to play, with more definite ideas of spending part of his life at least as a performer, in 1943, after hearing Charlie Christian (q.v.) soloing with Benny Goodman on record. His early career accelerated due to opening of US Army-Air Force base at Greensboro, with subsequent big demand for local musicians to play for USO dances. After ending of World War II, played Copacabana nightspot with female pianist Dardanelle, for six months. During which time he became enraptured with the 'new' music being purveyed by such as Charlie Parker, Dizzy Gillespie. In successive years, gigged with vibist Marjorie Hyam's trio (1948), and clarinettist Buddy De Franco (with whom he was to record in '56).

Gained an international reputation during almost four years spent as one-third of Red Norvo Trio (1950-1953). Worked with clarinettist Artie Shaw's last Gramercy Five, (2), between 1953-1954; then, returned for a while to Norvo Trio. Went into self-imposed semi-retirement (1955), emerging occasionally from sign-writing activities to play mostly trio dates at venues like the Composer, NYC. To effect his semi-retirement, moved to Sea Bright, New Jersey, on Atlantic coast. (Had won DOWN BEAT Jazz Critics' Poll as top guitarist previous year). By 1960, was more or less completely inactive as player. And during late-1960's, performed only occasionally — for personal pleasure, usually sitting in at clubs near to his home.

During latter part of 1960's, began to appear more regularly in public, appearing at Newport Jazz Festival between 1968-1970 (latter year as member of Festival entrepreneur George Wein's Newport All Stars — with Red Norvo also in line-up). Still reluctant to make official a full-time comeback, Farlow has continued to appear on a much more regular basis, visiting Europe and Japan, touring the US (often in company of Norvo), and managing to record at fairly frequent intervals — although nowhere as often as his followers would wish...

Of all the guitarists who followed in the wake of Charlie Christian (q.v.), there seems little doubt that, from a technical standpoint at least, Tal Farlow and John McLaughlin (q.v.) remain the most gifted. Over the years, Farlow has become something of a legend in his own lifetime. The kind of astonishing performer about whom even the most blasé, difficult-to-please guitarists continue to wax, both eloquently and at length.

Farlow's awesome skills aren't confined to one area of guitar playing, but one must lay emphasis on his har-

monic sophistication which is second-to-none. His most obvious debt to Christian is manifested in an extraordinary ability to long, flowing solos, superbly constructed at all times, and each invested with the man's own subtle rhythmic powers. And, McLaughlin apart, there is no other jazz guitarist with finer articulation — even when essaying near-ridiculous fast tempos for performances such as *Lover* (6), *Yardbird Suite* (26), *Cherokee* (11), and *Love Letters* (25).

Farlow, who as far back as 1953 played thumb-style guitar, has been something of an innovator on his instrument — and not just because of his overall speed and ingenuity. His use of harmonics (double octaves) — as with *Flamingo* (6), *Isn't It Romantic?* (9), *How Long Has This Been Going On?* (10) — has never been surpassed. And after hearing tenorist Eddie Harris' experiments with the Varitone attachement during the early 1970's, Farlow built his own octave unit for use with his guitar.

When Tal Farlow arrived on the New York jazz scene during the second half of the 1940's, his was more or less a fully-developed talent. His recordings with the Red Norvo Trio show that he had synthesised the music of Lester Young and Charlie Christian, on the one hand, and Charlie Parker and Dizzy Gillespie, on the other, in a completely successful way — but, most importantly, Norvo recordings like *Godchild, Cheek to Cheek, Move, If I Had You, Swedish Pastry* — all (1) — and *Who Cares?, That Old Black Magic* — both (5) — prove he sounded like no-one else but Tal Farlow...

Despite his periods of self-imposed retirement, Farlow's return to the music scene has on each occasion shown that he has not diminished in stature one iota. Nor during the early-1980's has his playing evidenced any kind of disinterest or lack of freshness. Not that he has shown any inclination to incorporate devices from the post-1960's jazz-out-of-rock schools. But, then, he doesn't need to effect any radical changes in his unique make-up. And for jazz guitarists of all eras, that's a situation that can happily last for all time...

SELECTED DISCOGRAPHY

1 The Red Norvo Trio with Tal Farlow & Charles Mingus/The Savoy Sessions SAVOY
2 Artie Shaw & His Gramercy Five COLUMBIA-CLEF
3 Up, Up & Away (Sonny Criss) PRESTIGE
4 Mostly Flute (Sam Most) XANADU
5 Guitar Player (including Red Norvo Trio) PRESTIGE
6 The Tal Farlow Quartet BLUE NOTE
7 The Tal Farlow Album NORGRAN
8 A Recital by Tal Farlow VERVE
9 Tal VERVE
10 This is Tal Farlow VERVE
11 Autumn In New York VERVE
12 The Guitar Artistry of Tal Farlow VERVE
13 Tal Farlow Plays Harold Arlen VERVE
14 Trilogy INNER CITY
15 Fuerst Set XANADU
16 Second Set XANADU
17 The Interpretations of Tal Farlow NORGRAN
18 Cooking the Blues (Buddy DeFranco) VERVE
19 George Wein's Newport All Stars ATLANTIC
20 Trinity CBS/SONY
21 A Sign of the Times CONCORD JAZZ
22 Tal Farlow '78 CONCORD JAZZ
23 On Stage (with Red Norvo, et al) CONCORD JAZZ
24 Chromatic Palette CONCORD JAZZ
25 Cookin' On All Burners CONCORD JAZZ
26 The Swinging Guitar of Tal Farlow VERVE

Play in the style of Tal Farlow

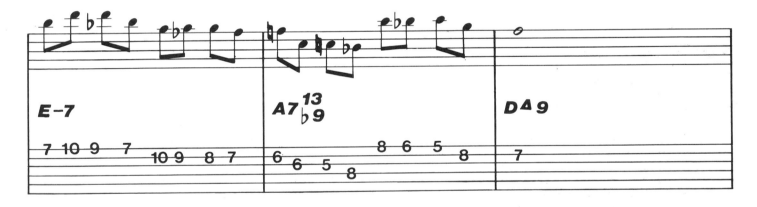

Chris Watson notes: Tal Farlow is one of the most fluent of guitarists. This phrase should be played fast. Notice the use of chromatic harmony linking bars three and four. Also he 'substitues' an E 9 chord for the dominant A7 in bar four.

Freddie Green

Frederick William Green: Born Charleston, South Carolina, 1911. Began playing guitar at 12 years; still in teens, finished his schooling in New York. Began professional gigs during mid-1930's, and it was while appearing at Black Cat Cafe, Greenwich Village, that noted impresario John Hammond heard him and in turn passed on a recommendation to Count Basie. Basie, obviously impressed, asked Green to join his up-and-coming big band. Green, given an offer he obviously could not refuse, said yes, made his first gig with Basie in March 1937, and has been an integral, irreplaceable part of Basie aggregations — mostly large, but sometimes small — ever since.

Irving Ashby (q.v.), one of that select group of rhythm guitar players with out-of-the-ordinary ability, once made the following, telling quote:

'Rhythm guitar is like vanilla extract in a cake. You can't taste it when it's there; but you know when it's left out'.

Ashby was, of course, referring to rhythm-guitar in a general sense, but his remarks might well be applied specifically to the playing of Freddie Green.

Freddie Green... the most famous name of all the rhythm guitarists in jazz. Along with the seemingly indestructible pianist-leader, the immovable force of the Count Basie Orchestra for nearly 50 years. (Even when Basie was, of economic necessity, forced to cut down from big-band size to octet in 1950-1951, Green's presence was

deemed of signal importance). It is safe to assume that, large or small, the Basie band would not have sounded quite the same without its guitarist.

With no disrespect to Claude Williams — Basie's first rhythm guitarist and a good reliable player — reference to recordings by the band before and after Green's arrival (1) show the difference the latter's contributions made to the whole structure of the rhythm section and its impetus to the orchestra itself. Through the following decade-and-a-half, Green's presence was to continue to be a vital component of the band, as one-quarter of possibly the most famous rhythm section in the history of jazz — Green, Basie, bassist Walter Page (who left, finally in '49, after fairly lengthy absence in early-1940's), and drummer Jo Jones.

The omnipresent Green shared in all the Basie band's succession of triumphs from 1937, appearing on acknowledged classic recordings such as *Dark Rapture, Boogie Woogie* both (1); *Ham 'n' Eggs, Tickle Toe,* both (5); *Louisiana, The World Is Mad* both (6). His metronomic guitar also made its presence fet during Basie small-group gems like *Shoe Shine Boy, Oh! Lady Be Good* both (3); and *Dickie's Dream, Lester Leaps In* both (5). With the advent of hi-fi recordings, later stereo, it was possible to really evaluate Green's role within the big band. The post-1950's Basie outfits have been, if anything, even more powerhouse than their predecessors. Yet through even the

band's most ferocious, top-decibels moments, Green's guitar, an acoustic guitar one must never forget is discernible; laying down its four-in-the-bar beat with a clockwork precision that would be impossible to improve upon. Late-1950's early 1960's studio recordings like (8), (10), and most notably (7) — with particular reference to the immortal *Li'l' Darlin'* — really lay emphasis on Green's indestructible talent. A live date like (9) merely amplifies this further. Digital recordings like (12), (13) bring that extraordinary guitar sound more sharply into focus than ever before, and it is these that rhythm-guitar students should home in on at once.

Freddie Green's ominpotence amongst rhythm guitarists is due to his unique, very personal sound, together with his rock-steady beat. He uses a high action (in other words, the heavy-gauge strings on his instrument are further off the finger-board than normal, thus allowing

vibration, resulting in greater volume). Green strikes the strings more powerfully than other rhythm players, using primarily the lower four strings for his chord inversions. Throughout many years, the inimitable tenor-saxophonist Lester Young was to use the services of Freddie Green at numerous recording sessions, including (16), (18), (23). (14) is of particular interest in so far as it features also the electric guitarist Eddie Durham (q.v.). (26) is even more fascinating perhaps as Green's acoustic rhythm guitar is heard in company with another, even more famous, amplified players: Charlie Christian (q.v.)

Freddie Green is the most modest of guitarists where solo playing is concerned; he is seemingly reluctant to take more than eight bars, maybe once in a decade. Which makes (22) something of a unique event — a record date under the great man's own name, plus a Freddie Green solo...

SELECTED DISCOGRAPHY

1 Good Morning Blues (Count Basie) MCA
2 The Great Count Basie & His Orchestra JOKER
3 The Lester Young Story, Vol. 1 (Billie Holiday, Jones-Smith Inc.)) CBS
4 The Lester Young Story, Vol. 2 (Billie Holiday) CBS
5 The Lester Young Story, Vol. 4 (Billie Holiday, Count Basie) CBS
6 The Lester Young Story, Vol. 5 (Billie Holiday, Count Basie) CBS
7 The Atomic Mr. Chairman (Count Basie) VOGUE
8 Count Basie Plays Quincy Jones & Neal Hefti VOGUE
9 Live From Birdland/Breakfast Dance & Barbecue (Count Basie) VOGUE
10 Count Basie Plays Benny Carter/Kansas City Suite VOGUE
11 Count Basie & The Kansas City Seven JASMINE
12 Warm Breeze (Count Basie) PABLO TODAY
13 On The Road (Count Basie PABLO TODAY

14 Kansas City Six & Five (1938) (Lester Young, et al) COMMODORE
15 Cafe Society Swing (1938 & 1940) (Joe Sullivan, Big Joe Turner, et al) SWINGFAN
16 Classic Tenors (Lester Young) STATESIDE
17 The Changing Face of Harlem, Vol. Two (with Illinois Jacquet, et al) SAVOY
18 "Pres" At His Very Best (Lester Young) MERCURY
19 A Buck Clayton Jam Session COLUMBIA
20 The Essential Jo Jones VOGUE
21 Joe Newman, Vol. 2: 'I'm Still Swinging' RCA VICTOR
22 Rhythm Man RCA VICTOR
23 Pres & Teddy (Lester Young, Teddy Wilson) VERVE
24 Revelation (Gerry Mulligan) BLUE NOTED
25 Rhythm Willie (with Herb Ellis CONCORD JAZZ
26 The Legendary John Hammond's Carnegie Hall Concerts 1938/39: From Spirituals to Swing (Vogue)

Play in the style of Freddie Green

Chris Watson notes: There is probably no recording of Freddie Green playing a single line solo. Here is an example of his chord playing. Nobody plays a 'Four in the bar' like Freddie Green. He has spent most of his life as part of the Count Basie rhythm section and there are many examples of his famous 'vamp' that should be studied.

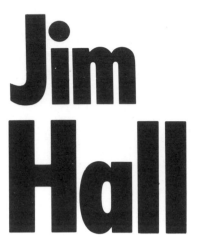

Jim Hall

James Stanley Hall: Born Buffalo, New York State, 1930. Family surroundings ideally musical — mother played piano, grandfather played violin, an uncle played guitar semi-professionally. Latter interested young James in guitar. Professional career started, unofficially, at 13. Charlie Christian (q.v.) first spurred him on to playing jazz on his chosen instrument, especially the Texan's recordings of *Air Mail Special, I've Found a New Baby,* with Goodman. At 16, moved to Cleveland. After obtaining degree from Cleveland Institute of Music, and studying privately with teacher who introduced him to Django Reinhardt's (q.v.) playing, went to Los Angeles for arranging studies with Joe Dolny, with whose rehearsal band he worked.

After rehearsing jazz combo with French hornist John Graas, accepted an offer from drummer Chico Hamilton to join latter's Quintet (1955). Stayed for 1½ years, gaining national and international prominence as guitarists with an original approach. During this time, appeared in movies *Sweet Smell of Success, Jazz On a Summer's Day.* Commenced association with clarinettist-saxist Jimmy Giuffre (1956), including period with popular, folk-influenced jazz trio. During which time toured Europe with Giuffre Trio as part of Jazz At the Philharmonic troupe (1959), and served on faculty at School of Jazz, Lenox, Mass. (1957-1959). Also heard on soundtrack of films *Odds Against Tommorrow* (1959).

Hall's career continued to prosper, musically and artistically, with prestigious collaborations with altoist Lee Konitz (1960-1962), Sonny Rollins (1961-1962). Together with trumpeter Art Farmer, put together widely-praised Quartet (1962-1964), which toured Europe ('64). Had also led own trio (1962-1963), and accompanied Ella Fitzgerald for recordings, European tour (1960). Has continued to lead own small combos from 1966, as well as appearing on numerous TV shows at home and overseas during 1960's/1970's; also played White House for Duke Ellington's 70th birthday party (1969). Won DOWN BEAT-Critics' Poll (1963-1965), then again in 1970's; has been similarly saluted by readers of same publication on several subsequent occasions.

Jim Hall must be considered the Master of Understatement amongst jazz guitarists of all persuasions, from all eras. He is also, without a doubt, one of the most versatile players, eminently capable of bringing his beautifully sculpted solo work into all but the most extreme of musical contexts. As one example of the latter, he proved to be a perfect foil to tenorist Sonny Rollins during 1963, as part of one of jazz' seemingly unlikely collaborations(11). Hall's unique sound — and on more than one occasion he has maintained that his 'must be a natural sound' — is partially explained by the fact that he tunes his instrument a perfect fourth below the normal guitar tuning. Which helps produce the kind of superior, essentially

mellow tone that instantly identifies his playing in any situation. Both harmonically and rhythmically, his performances are beyond reproach; yet for Jim Hall, it is the melodic side of his art about which he continues to challenge himself most of all.

On record as well as in person, Hall is to be found at his all-round best — and, certainly, at his most relaxed — in the more intimate small-group settings; especially, of course, if his colleagues are gifted with the same, or similar, attitude of understatement. Which explains why his on-record collaborations with pianist Bill Evans were particularly successful. (5) contains much subtle interplay between the pair. But nothing to compare with the contents of (4) which, like (5), features just the two. The acutely intuitive interaction that informs cuts like *I Hear a Rhapsody* and *Romaine* (a charming Hall original) nevertheless takes second place to *My Funny Valentine*, a lengthy performance that was ostensibly a warm-up but which, in the event, turns out to be the finest track and something of a true masterpiece.

Elsewhere on record, Hall's artistry is captured at its very best during (30), a guitar-bass-only setting; likewise, (2) his first date under his own name contains delectable examples of Hall's subtle swing, with the exquisite *This Is Always* probably the best of all. (10) is another beautifully structured trio session with not a guitar note wasted or superfluous. The kind of unselfish approach that has always been part of Hall's low-key approach ensured that his contributions to the combos of others never stood out for the wrong reasons... that, and his perpetual good taste. His performances with the Hamilton Quintet (1), the Guiffre Trio (18), and the Farmer-Hall Quartet (16), (17), were important ingredients to the overall excellence of three superior jazz groups of the 1950's and 1960's.

A natural compatability with altoist Paul Desmond makes (9) a constant source of restrained joy. But Hall's undoubted talent for conjoining his own creative brilliance to that of a seemingly incompatible partner, as with (11) and (19), is yet another plus factor in his favour. The manner in which he responds to Rollins during (11), caught at a veritable peak of his not inconsiderable creative powers, is both exhilarating and revealing. Hall's own record dates give the impression at all times of much thought and deliberation. Not that any lacks jazz' essential spontaneity. Not too many comparable musicians could have extrapolated the fundamental beauty from Rodrigo's *Concierto de Aranjuez* (20) as consummately as he. Basically straight-forward record dates like (21), (23), (24), (29), are invested with the kind of variety and subtleties that one rarely finds on the average jazz-guitar album. And the manner in which Hall insists on treating his colleagues as equal partners, not merely accompanists, is another facet of his recordings; perhaps best illustrated by (22), with the guitarist interacting splendidly throughout with bassist Don Thompson and Terry Clarke, as they all sail magnificently through a programme of pop standards like *Angel Eyes,* and *The Way You Look Tonight* and jazz classics' *Round Midnight* and *Scrapple From the Apple.*

Jim Hall: the Master of Understatement. And indeed the Quiet Master of the Jazz Guitar...

SELECTED DISCOGRAPHY

1 Chico Hamilton Quintet PACIFIC JAZZ
2 Jim Hall: Jazz Guitar PACIFIC JAZZ
3 All Night Sessions, Vols. 1,2,3 (Hampton Hawes) CONTEMPORARY
4 Undercurrent (with Bill Evans) UNITED ARTISTS
5 Bill Evans Trio (Motian, Peacock) Duo (Hall) VERVE
6 The Easy Way (Jimmy Giuffre) VERVE
7 Traditionalism Revisited... (Bob Brookmeyer) VOGUE
8 In Person (Jimmy Giuffre) VERVE
9 Paul Desmond ATLANTIC
10 Good Friday Blues (with Red Mitchell, Red Kelly) PACIFIC JAZZ
11 Sonny Rollins, Vols 1 & 2 RCA VICTOR
12 John Lewis Presents Jazz Abstractions ATLANTIC
13 2 Degrees East, 3 Degrees West (with John Lewis, et al) PACIFIC JAZZ
14 "Odds Against Tomorrow" (John Lewis) UNITED ARTISTS
15 Ella In Berlin (Ella Fitzgerald) VERVE
16 Interaction (with Art Farmer) ATLANTIC
17 Live At The Half Note (with Art Farmer) ATLANTIC
18 The Train & The River (Jimmy Giuffre) ATLANTIC
19 Stitt Plays Bird (Sonny Stitt) ATLANTIC
20 Concerto (with Chet Baker et al) CTI
21 It's Nice To Be With You/Jim Hall In Berlin MPS/BASF)
22 Jim Hall Live! A&M/HORIZON
23 Commitment A&M/HORIZON
24 Big Blues (with Art Farmer, et al) CTI
25 Jim Hall & Red Mitchell ARTISTS HOUSE
26 The Interplay Sessions (Bill Evans) MILESTONE
27 Circles CONCORD JAZZ
28 First Edition (with George Shearing) CONCORD JAZZ
29 Studio Trieste (with Chet Baker, Hubert Laws, et al) CTI
30 Alone Together (with Ron Carter) MILESTONE
31 The Lee Konitz Duets MILESTONE

Play in the style of Jim Hall

Chris Watson notes: Jim Hall is a very original guitar player. His 'Horn-like' phraseology is greatly admired and respected. Here he improvises on a basic 'turn-a-round'. Notice his use of space and strong melody.

Lonnie Johnson

Alonzo 'Lonnie' Johnson: Born New Orleans, Louisiana, c. 1889. Brother of pianist James 'Steady Roll' Johnson, with whom Lonnie — who also used violin, piano, and sang — played first gigs. Established useful reputation playing violin, guitar in New Orleans theatres, cafes etc. Sailed to Europe (1917), undertaking revue work in London, theatre tours, including work with Will Marion Cook Orchestra. Returned to New Orleans (1921), to find that 1918-1919 'flu epidemic had taken most of his family. Then, to St. Louis, working with such as Charlie Creath, Fate Marable, Nat Robinson (using mostly piano, violin). For two years, worked in steel foundry, but continued gigging. Entered, and won, talent contest organised by OKEH record company. Thus, began prolific association lasting until 1932. Moved to Cleveland (1932), working by day at tyre factory and local steel mill, playing gigs in evenings. Left Cleveland for Chicago (1937); became resident for almost three years at Three Deuces. In early 1940's, fronted own small combos, but from mid-1940's concentrated on career as solo singer (accompanying himself on electric guitar). Became highly-successful as recording artist during Forties-into-Fifties, especially in R&B field.

Played London concert (1952), before moving to Cincinnati, thence to Philadelphia. Appeared with Duke Ellington (1963); same year toured Europe as part of blues package. Became popular figure from mid-1960's in Toronto, where he appeared regularly. Involved in major

accident. Then, hospitalised for some time following stroke. Participated at Toronto blues concert just prior to suffering heart attack; Johnson died in the Canadian city as a result of the attack...

Lonnie Johnson's is a most important as well as unusual position in any list of Top Twelve greatest jazz guitarists. Basically, he was a bluesman — and a generally superior blues musician, both instrumentally and to a lesser extent vocally — who utilised basic jazz tenets as a player. Which is why, of course, he was able to mix freely and easily between the two allied genres.

During his earlier days, Johnson established a healthy reputation as a guitarist with a style — and most certainly a tone — of his own. Technically, of the 1920's blues-players, only Big Joe Williams and Johnson made use of extra strings. It was this, most certainly, which often gave Johnson such a sumptuous, full-blooded sound. And his use of two or three of the top strings doubled like a 12-string guitar gave him the first really unique sound to be heard in specific jazz circles. Played finger-style, the Johnson sound exudes a natural warmth and a marvellous tonal beauty that contains the essence of the blues. A tonal beauty that is probably due as much to the fact that he played a handsome concert guitar. Stylistically, too, it is worth noting that Johnson probably flat-picked many of his accompaniments.

Johnson's short-lived partnership with Eddie Lang

(q.v.) produced some of the most memorable music in the history of recorded jazz guitar. Usually, it is Johnson who takes the role of 'lead' guitarist, inevitably, perhaps, for classic blues performances like *Bull Frog Moan, Guitar Blues*, both (8), and *Blue Guitars* (7). Johnson's own solo recordings from the same 1920's period, *Playing With the Strings, Stompin' 'Em Along, Blues In G, Away Down the Alley Blues*, all (7), are superlative examples of his artistry and demonstrate his effortless phrasing, the long, langourous lines, and depth of expression.

A supreme individualist at all times, Johnson's performances, even in the most exalted company, never sounded second-best. Lang apart, he was to record exceptional statements together with the Duke Ellington Orchestra, (3), (4); as well as with the Chocolate Dandies (6), and Louis Armstrong. Johnson's solo contribution to *Mahogany Hall Stomp* takes second place only because of a magisterial effort from the trumpeter (1). And King Oliver has strong competition from Johnson, and Lang, during *Jet Black Blues* and *Blue Blood Blues* — both (8).

From the 1940's onwards, Johnson's singing became the predominant feature of his work, and guitar solos of any real length became the exception rather than the rule. But when the mood took him, the great solos of the earlier years were invoked, as individual gems such as *I Don't Hurt Anymore* (14), *Swingin' the Blues* (13), and *Swingin' With Lonnie* (11) prove conclusively. As an ace

bluesman, top-notch jazzman, Lonnie Johnson ranks amongst the first, and important, cross-over musicians around, 50 years before that expression came into common usage. Blues or jazz, or whatever, he remains, historically and musically, a seminal figure.

Mamlish S3807

SELECTED DISCOGRAPHY

1 V.S.O.P. (Very Special Old Phonography) (1927-1928), Vols 5,6 (Louis Armstrong) CBS
2 The Louis Armstrong Legend WORLD RECORDS
3 The Ellington Era (1927-1940) Vol. 1, Part 1 CBS
4 The Ellington Era, Vol 2 :CBS
5 It Feels So Good QUEEN DISC
6 The Chocolate Dandies PARLOPHONE
7 Blue Guitars PARLOPHONE
8 Blue Guitars Vol. 2 PARLOPHONE
9 Stringing the Blues (with Joe Venute, et al) CBS
10 Mr. Johnson's Blues MAMLISH
11 Swinging' with Lonnie (with Otis Spann) STORYVILLE
12 Tomorrow Night KING
13 Lonnie Johnson XTRA
14 Blues By Lonnie Johnson PRESTIGE/BLUESVILLE
15 Idle Hours PRESTIGE/BLUESVILLE
16 Lonnie Johnson RCA/BLUEBIRD
17 Tears Don't Fall No More FOLKWAYS
18 Mr. Trouble FOLKWAYS

Play in the style of Lonnie Johnson

Chris Watson notes: Notice Lonnie Johnson's use of open strings and chords to accompany himself. Also he 'bends' strings in bars Three and Four and creates a 'bluesy' feel throughout the small phrases in bars three and four. Can be played in many contexts to great effect; e.g. try them over a funky E9 type vamp.

Eddie Lang

Salvatore Massaro: Born Philadelphia, Pennsylvania, c. 1904. Father, fretted-instrument maker; sister, also guitar player. Began first, on violin, aged seven years. Studied with two of Philadelphia's leading teachers. Became friends with violinist Joe Venuti while still at school — the careers of both were to be closely united, professionally, for many years afterwards. Played first paid job on violin at a Philadelphia restaurant. Switched to banjo for gig with orchestra of Charlie Kerr. With Venuti in Bert Estlow combo in Atlantic City; Venuti, Lang co-led band for seasons at Silver Slipper club, same city.

Joined Mound City Blue Blowers (1924), visiting London for appearances with the group. Became heavily engaged in freelance work, in recording and radio studios. Worked regularly with Roger Wolfe Kahn Orchestra (1926-1927). Became associated with Don Voorhees Orchestra for series of theatre shows, then re-united with Venuti with own joint group and for work with Paul Whiteman Orchestra (1929-1930), including appearance in film *The King of Jazz*. Back with Kahn Orchestra (1932). For about a year he worked extensively with Bing Crosby, appearing with the singer on radio, records and in movie *The Big Broadcast*. Then, in New York in 1933, and at the peak of his creative powers, Lang died, suddenly, following a tonsillectomy.

Eddie Lang was jazz guitar's first virtuoso performer. A player with a formal background, who had studied with classical teachers, he brought to the jazz world a highly-developed technique that he used — but never over-used — to the maximum effect, in a variety of musical situations. Amongst Lang's many attributes were an instantly identifiable and full tone and an ability to articulate single-string runs or chordal work as cleanly as any of his contemporaries. He possessed an acute sense of pitch and an harmonic awareness that was very much ahead of its time. Rhythmically, he was a constant delight — even though there were occasions, it is true, when he swung in a slightly stiff, even mannered, style. An intelligent, thinking musician, Lang used down-strokes for the most part (Charlie Christian (q.v.) used down strokes exclusively), and he was probably the first acoustic guitarist to use a microphone to some real advantage.

Lang's association with Joe Venuti stretched back to childhood days, when they played duets at home. He was to be heard in the company of the great violinist on a very regular basis, right up until his death. *Stringin' the Blues* (15) celebrating the first time the pair recorded together, alone, in 1926 demonstrates the kind of musical joie de vivre that occurred whenever they got together. *Wild Cat* (12), (15), and *Sunshine* (12) are two further examples of Venuti and Lang duetting alone; they re-recorded *Wild Cat* (10) six months, in '28, with equally productive results. Between 1926-1933, they were to record in excess of 70 titles in their own names. Other memorable cuts co-

featuring the two include *Penn Beach Blues, The Wild Dog,* both (12), (15); *Four String Joe* (12); *The Wild Dog* (a different version), *Really Blue,* both (10); and *Goin' Places,* and *Doin' Things* both (15). Lang also sounded especially inspired in the company of cornettist Bix Beiderbecke. The guitarist participated in Beiderbecke sessions that produced classic items such as *Singin' the Blues, Clarinet Marmalade, I'm Comin' Virginia, For No Reason At All In C, Wringin' & Twistin',* all (3). The two last-named are of particular interest in so far as they feature, Lang apart, Beiderbecke (on piano as well as cornet), and Frankie Trumbauer (playing C-melody) saxophone). Lang's intensely melodic playing during *For No Reason* turns it into a masterful example of his art.

Eddie's Twister (1), Lang's first recorded solo performance, is another superb definition of just how great an individualist he was. As Richard Hadlock (in his *Jazz Masters of the 20's*) described it:

'Here could be found the changing of fingers on the same fret to produce a fresh attack, interval jumps of a tenth to simulate the effect of a jazz piano, parallel ninth chords, flatted fifths, whole tone scalar figures, smears, unusual glissandi, harmonics, harplike effects, consecutive augmented chords, and relaxed hornlike phrasing'.

The unforgettable recordings Lang made with Lonnie Johnson (q.v.) are perhaps his greatest of those which juxtapose his own great talent with someone in the same league — greater even than the collaborations with Venuti. Recording usually under the pseudonym of Blind Willie Dunn, Lang's contributions are wholly supportive, in every way, even though Johnson invariably took on the role as leader. Not quite in the same league as Johnson as a blues player — he was, however, a generally superior improviser — nevertheless Lang expressed himself convincingly in the idiom, as illustrated perfectly during duets of the calibre of *Bull Frog Moan, Guitar Blues,* both (2); and *Have To Change Keys To Play These Blues, Midnight Call Blues,* both (1).

That he could all but match Johnson in terms of heat can be judged further from fiery performances such as *Hot Fingers, Deep Minor Rhythm,* both (1); and *Two Tone Stomp* (2), (15). And Lang's ability to mix with the great black players can be judged by his contributions to record dates featuring Louis Armstrong's *Mahogany Hall Blues Stomp* (1), Bessie Smith's *I'm Wild About That Thing* (18), and *In the Bottle Blues* (15), with Clarence Williams and King Oliver.

Lang's own recordings, often with just piano accompaniment, offer even further insights into his way of thinking. Eddie's *Twister* has been mentioned. But the sheer variety of other performances illustrate that there is much more scope to his playing than any of his contemporaries. These vary from blues, *Church Street Sobbin' Blues* (2), (15); to classical Rachmaninoff's *Prelude (In C Sharp Minor)* (2); to sentimental ballad pieces such as *Rainbow Dreams, A Little Love a Little Kiss,* both (1); and *April Kisses* (2), *Perfect* (2), (15).

SELECTED DISCOGRAPHY

1 Blue Guitars (with Lonnie Johnson, et al) PARLOPHONE
2 Blue Guitars Vol. II (with Lonnie Johnson, et al) PARLOPHONE
3 Bix Beiderbecke: The Studio Groups — 1927 (with Frankie Truumbauer) WORLD RECORDS
4 Bix Beiderbecke: The Studio Groups — Late 1927 (with Frankie Trumbauer) WORLD RECORDS
5 Bix Beiderbecke: The Studio Groups — 1928 (with Frankie Trumbauer) WORLD RECORDS
6 Bix Beiderbecke: The Studio Groups — 1928-30 (with Frankie Trumbauer) WORLD RECORDS
7 Miff Mole's Molers — 1927 — with Sophie Tucker PARLOPHONE
8 Miff Mole's Molers — 1928-30 PARLOPHONE
9 Red Nichols & His Five Pennies: 1926-1928 MCA CORAL
10 The Sounds of New York, Vol. 2 (1927-1933) " Hot Strings" (with Joe Venuti, et al) RCA VICTOR
11 Tommy, Jimmy & Eddie 1928-29 (with Tommy Dorsey, Jimmy Dorsey) PARLOPHONE
12 Venuti-Lang 1927-8 PARLOPHONE
13 The Bix Beiderbecke Legend RCA VICTOR
14 That Toddlin' Town — Chicago (1926-28) (with Red McKenzie, et al) PARLOPHONE
15 Stringing the Blues (with Joe Venuti, et al) CBS
16 Jazz In the Thirties (with Joe Venuti WORLD RECORDS
17 A Jazz Holiday (with Joe Venuti, et al) MCA
18 Any Woman's Blues (Bessie Smith) CBS
19 Crosby Classics (Bing Crosby CBS/REALM
20 Sweet Harmony — Hot Rhythm (Boswell Sisters) VOCALION

Play in the style of Eddie Lang

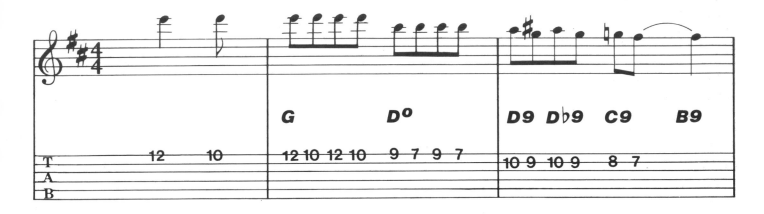

Chris Watson notes: Here is a typical 4 bar 'Tag'. Eddie Lang compliments the movement of the harmonies perfectly by playing a line which is strong enough to stand up as a melody itself. In the third bar the two 'f' naturals are slightly 'bent'. (Less than a semi-tone). This enhances the *bluesy* effect the note has anyway.

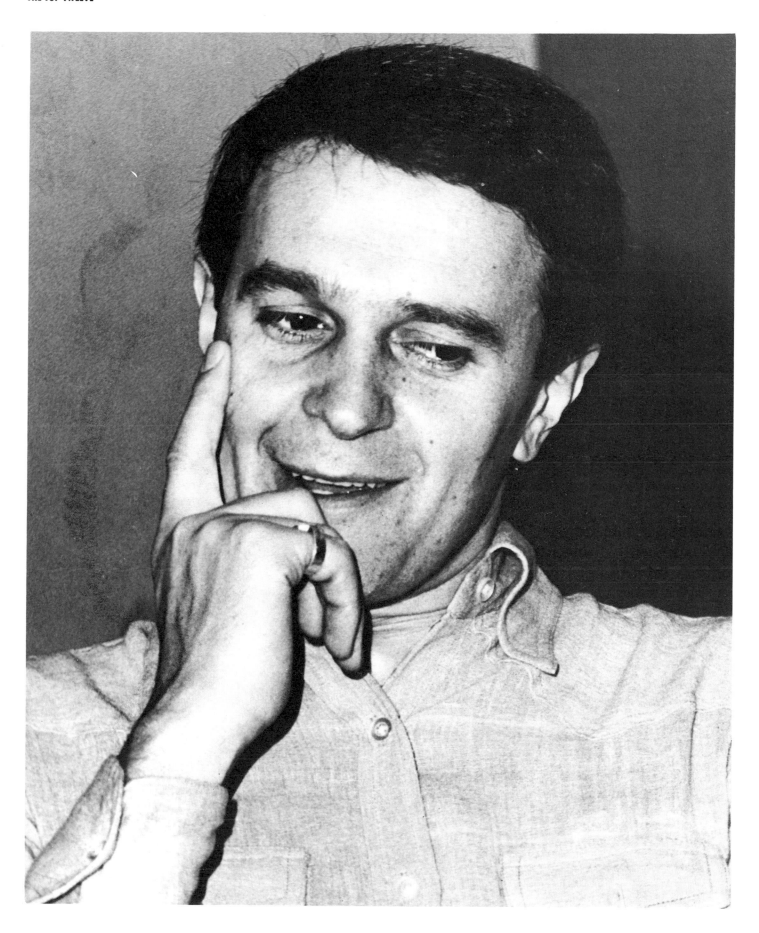

John McLaughlin

John McLaughlin: Born Kirk Sandell, near Doncaster, Yorkshire, 1942. Mother, violinist. Self-taught mostly, except for few piano, violin lessons at seven. First musical experiences, all classical. At 12, one of his brother's guitars became his own personal property. Around which time McLaughlin became aware of bluesmen like Big Bill Broonzy, Muddy Waters, Leadbelly, *et al*. Two years later, became enraptured with the playing of Django Reinhardt (q.v.); very soon, was responding to US jazz guitarists such as Tal Farlow (q.v.), Jim Hall (q.v.), Barney Kessel (q.v.) Fronted own band at school.

During next few years, his musical vocabulary extended further by exposure to recordings by Miles Davis, John Coltrane, as well as with involvement with music of Debussy, Bartok. All of which helped to formulate own eventual style.

Spent six years playing mostly R&B/jazz jobs — first major professional job with the Graham Bond Organisation, which he joined aged 21. Also gigged successfully with other leading British R&B figures like Georgie Fame, Brian Auger, Herbie Goines. During this period, when he was living in London, McLaughlin continued to experiment tirelessly in effort to extend the development of amplified guitar, as well as forge his own highly-personal approach to his playing.

Decided, finally, to leave UK, to try his luck in the States (1968). Biggest break thus far came when top American drummer Tony Williams asked him to join his Lifetime band. With Lifetime, established enviable reputation, resulting in trumpeter Miles Davis inviting him to participate in epoch-making recordings such as (5), (3), (4). Around this time, met his personal guru (Sri Chinmoy). Which changed him completely as a person, and helped further stimulate his musical thinking and increase his restless probings into a myriad of sounds from different cultures — including, not surprisingly, the Far East. Duly inspired, put together his first Mahavishnu Orchestra (1971), a remarkable series of bands that included at various times such as Jean-Luc Ponty, Billy Cobham, Jan Hammer, Rick Laird, *et al*. Name dropped in '75 when McLaughlin became disaffected with Chinmoy. Continued, however, to draw inspiration from Far East, as evidenced by Shakti — although jazz content of this post-Mahavishnu band was minimal (16). (For Shakti, McLaughlin used a custom-built acoustic Gibson that enabled him to play raga-like drones)

At end of 1970's, and up to date, has virtually forsaken amplified guitar for acoustic. A considered decision that has given McLaughlin deep personal fulfilment. It has also shown that far from being in any way less a performer, his artistry continues to mature in an eminently satisfying way.

The re-emergence of John McLaughlin to a premier position amongst jazz guitarists during the frenetic end-

of-1960's period remains probably the most dramatic of any comparable picker, before and since. Not that he was at that time a wide-eyed innocent, with no previous track record. Indeed, his sterling work with the Bond Organisation and other local British outfits had given him a pretty thorough grounding in jazz, blues and R&B. And it was McLaughlin's natural talent, coupled with an ever-increasing desire to make his mark that seemed to some to border on the paranoid, that found him, suddenly, an international star, with a fast spreading reputation that was to achieve rock-superstar proportions in a period of less than five years.

Of course, working alongside musicians whose reputations were formidable didn't exactly retard progress. McLaughlin's decision to leave Britain for the States proved, in the event, a masterful one. His welcome from local US musicians was warm, instantaneous. Typical to the reaction local guitarist is that of Larry Coryell (q.v.), soon to become something of a McLaughlin disciple. Coryell remembers hearing him for the first time, at the old Count Basie Club. 'He'd told my wife, Julie, he was nervous. He took his first solo... I couldn't believe it! I went home and tried to play everything I'd heard. What was it I'd heard? Extending the same unorthodox fingering concept that I had at the time — but really extending it. Expanding it. Stretching even more, and producing incredibly beautiful music, using an unusual series of notes. Which is what I was interested in...'

Since when, McLaughlin has continued to develop into a virtuoso performer of the first rank, a technician of awesome proportions, with a command of his instrument that is second-to-none. He is too a real innovator, the single most dominant influence on jazz guitar from the 1970's.

From the period of his emergence as a world-class player, McLaughlin has continuously given himself a succession of personal challanges in what has sometimes seemed to be an almost demoniac quest for perfection. His playing at ultra-fast tempo is extraordinary — his ideas flow unceasingly, his continuity is virtually matchless, and his articulation is astounding. Just as important, all McLaughlin's most bravura statements are never less than musical. And perhaps most important of all, his music rarely lacks genuine fire and passion. To-day, McLaughlin doesn't seem to be quite the restless explorer of yesteryear. For the time being he seems to have turned his back on amplified music — remember, he was the great electric guitarist of the 1970's — to return to what he calls the *purity* of the acoustic instrument.

Right from his early days, on the British scene, McLaughlin had attained a legendary reputation as a catalytic figure. His late-1960's work with the likes of Gordon Beck (24), and John Surman (26), (8), shows just how accomplished, all-round, he was at that time. His first US collaborations with Tony Williams (1), (2), then Miles Davis, (3), (4), (5), (6), (7), merely reaffirmed what his erstwhile associates knew already: that John McLaughlin was in the forefront of jazz guitarists. Certainly, the period he spent with Lifetime brought out the more aggressive qualities of his playing. The even more instructive on-off period with Davis was of enormous benefit to both. McLaughlin's contributions and overall influence to the seminal (5) were profound...

The manifold influences that had shaped McLaughlin's work of the time — Davis, John Coltrane, Indian music, the blues — emerged under one umbrella with his first Mahavishnu Orchestra. Within this context, his playing soared to fresh heights of creative passion. (10) sent shock-waves around the jazz and rock worlds. The sheer power of the music — emanating primarily from Mahavishnu's leader — turned heads the music world over. (11) disappointed in comparison with its predecessor, but nevertheless contained scorching virtuosic guitar work of the highest calibre. And when, five years later, the Mahavishnu Orchestra ceased to exist, the tireless McLaughlin transferred his passionate endeavours for a while to the all-Indian Shakti (16) — with a loss of jazz content only.

Both the Mahavishnu Orchestra and Shakti were no mere showcases for John McLaughlin, but earnest endeavours to produce superior band music. Outside of any such confines, it is probably easier to evaluate his playing. (9), for instance, gives his acoustic inclinations full reign through a series of well-nigh flawless performances. There are typical flights-of-fancy guitar work during *Song For My Mother* and *Song of the Wind*; a sitar-influenced *Peace Two*; a sensitive short version of Bill Evans' *Blue In Green*; an absolutely breathtaking reworking of Mingus' *Goodbye, Porkpie Hat,* probably the most poignant single item in the McLaughlin discography.

There is more superior acoustic playing throughout (20), with some of McLaughlin's most thoughtful, creative amplified work to be found on (18). Always the catalyst supreme, he sound suitably inspiring — and inspired — in the company of fellow guitarists, as per (21), (22), (28).

SELECTED DISCOGRAPHY

1 **Lifetime** (Tony Williams) POLYDOR
2 **Turn It Over** (Tony Williams) POLYDOR
3 **In A Silent Way** (Miles Davis) CBS
4 **Tribute to Jack Johnson** (Miles Davis) CBS
5 **Bitches Brew** (Miles Davis) CBS
6 **Live/Evil** (Miles Davis) CBS
7 **Big Fun** (Miles Davis) CBS
8 **Extrapolation** (with John Surman, et al) POLYDOR

Play in the style of
John McLaughlin

Chris Watson notes: Here John 'Mac' uses diminished intervals, triplets in fourths moving in minor thirds etc. This has the effect of dissonance.

Wes Montgomery

John Leslie 'Wes' Montgomery: Born Indianapolis, Indiana, 1925. Did not take up guitar seriously until 19, inspired by records featuring Charlie Christian (q.v.). Even at early stage in his career, more or less fully developed his unique style, which involved using his thumb instead of a more conventional finger-style, or even a pick. All of which enabled him to play single-string, chords, and octaves — latter to become a principal trademark of the Montgomery style.

Had been playing barely six months before playing first professional gigs (locally) — repeating, it is said, Christian solos, note for note. Gained reputation in and around Indianapolis while working with brothers bassist Monk, pianist-vibist Buddy (both also destined to become jazz musicians in their own right). Despite enthusiasm of local and visiting jazzmen, Wes Montgomery refused to leave his home town — that is until 1948, when vibist Lionel Hampton persuaded him to pack his guitar, amp and go on the road. Remained with Hampton until 1950, touring, recording, etc. Then, back to Indianapolis, to carry on being devoted family man (with six children), and combining a tremendously demanding schedule of working by day in local radio factory, playing jazz by night — and sometimes by day, too.

Heard by altoist Cannonball Adderley while performing in Indianapolis' Missile Room. Adderley, totally knocked out by Montgomery's playing, raved to Orrin Keepnews, boss of RIVERSIDE RECORDS. Montgomery had recorded in recent past for PACIFIC JAZZ (1), but it was with RIVERSIDE that international acclaim came, finally, to a genuinely modest man . . . this, and his decision to bow to the advice of many, and come to New York. Record-wise, (5) proved to be another clincher, receiving highest rating in practically every respected jazz publication.

During 1960's, Montgomery's became probably *the* name in jazz guitar world. His RIVERSIDE recordings — with own combos, and with Wes presented in company of such as trumpeter Nat Adderley, (8), and George Shearing, Milt Jackson (7) — continued to prove successful, both artistically and commercially. But it was with a move to VERVE RECORDS, that his popularity moved outside the realms of just jazz. Became a huge seller in the LP market, and his interpretation of *Goin' Out of My Head* became a mid-1960's Top Five singles smash on the US pop charts. The record won NARAS Grammy Award following year as Best Instrumental Jazz Performance (Montgomery had been nominated, twice, for similar awards previous year). In addition, readers of DOWN BEAT selected him as premier guitarist between years 1961-1962, 1966-1967; same magazine's Jazz Critics' Poll placed him top during 1960-1963, 1966-1967; and he finished first in PLAYBOY All Stars poll for six consecutive years. Then, came absolute tragedy. At the peak of his powers, his name something of a household world, Wes Montgomery col-

lapsed, died from heart attack in June, 1968. Fittingly, perhaps, his death occurred in Indianapolis, in the company of the family he loved so much...

The sound that Wes Montgomery invented remains as distinctive and as unique as any other produced in the history of jazz guitar... even though so many have tried to equal one or more of its specific elements. Superficial listening to his playing might induce the feeling that, technically, much of its mechanics — disregarding the thumb-picking aspect — sounds fairly commonplace. But, of course, Montgomery possessed immense all-round skills, a fact which The Thumb was to demonstrate in a variety of settings.

Of his decision to use thumb instead of pick, Montgomery offered many explanations. For instance, to DOWN BEAT's Bill Quinn he confided in 1966:

'I started practising with a plectrum. I did this for about 30 days. Then I decided to plug in my amplifier and see what I was doing. The sound was too much even for my next-door neighbours, so I took to the back room in the house and began plucking the strings with the fat part of my thumb. This was much quieter. To this technique, I added the trick of playing a melody in two different registers at the same time, the octave thing; this made the sound even quieter'.

Montgomery's firm decision to favour the thumb instead of the pick continued in its experimental form for several years before he was apparently satisfied with the sound he was getting. That dedication paid off. Listen to virtually any Montgomery record — early or later, small-combo or big-band setting — and if the quality of recording is but merely adequate, one can easily discern the ease with which he imbues each note with a marvellously rounded, uniquely mellow and totally individual quality. Another aspect of his playing that is immediately recognisable is the real spontaneity, not to mention, particularly on ballads and blues, a natural warmth that invests each solo.

Amongst his most memorable recorded ballad solos are such gems as *Polka Dots & Moonbeams* (5), *Ghost of a Chance* (12), *Lover Man*, and *Angel Eyes* — both (3) — and *The Girl Next Door* (19), the last-named conceived as a tribute to Django Reinhardt (q.v.) A magnificent blues-player, Montgomery recorded many impressive solos in this vernacular, including superior examples like *West Coast Blues* (5), *Movin' Along* (6), *James & Wes* (14), (15), *No Blues (15), Willow, Weep For Me (15),* a ballad performance that soon becomes an out-and-out blues statement and two separate recording of *D Natural Blues* (aka *Monterey Blues*), (5), (3) which together, and alone, offer positive proof of his greatness in this field.

It has been said by one or two critics that because of his thumb-instead-of-pick technique he was restricted from really excelling at up-tempo performances. That would be true, of course, if Montgomery had wished to take the path of, say, Tal Farlow (q.v.) Really, though, he never seemed at all bothered by fast tempos. As evidenced in recordings, both live and studio, like *Tune Up, Blue 'n' Boogie, SOS* all (6), *Airegin* (5), *June In January* (3), and an absolutely blistering *Mister Walker* (19). Montgomery always loved the lower strings for extra warmth and richness of sound. *Tune-Up* (6) is interesting in so far as he uses a bass-guitar (not a Fender bass) in order to achieve the sound he wants; the decision was the right one...

Wes Montgomery is one guitarist who should have always been taped in live performance. That extra heat, the immense drive, the humour and depth, and the extra creativity, together always registered strongest during a club or concert, and the sheer power of his playing, especially when using octaves, never comes through quite as potently with his studio efforts. Which makes (9), (15), (19), and half of (6) extra-important amongst the riches of his discography.

While it can be said that the settings he was given for such as (11), (12), (13), (17) didn't in any way stretch his great talent to the maximum, it is scarcely true that his own contributions are as negligible and inferior as some critics would have us believe...

SELECTED DISCOGRAPHY

1 A Portrait of Wes (inlcuding Harold Land, Mastersounds) LIBERTY
2 'Round Midnight RIVERSIDE
3 Groove Brothers (Montgomery Brothers) MILESTONE
4 Wes'Best AMERICA
5 Incredible Jazz Guitar RIVERSIDE
6 Movin' MILESTONE
7 Wes & Friends (with George Shearing, Milt Jackson, et al) MILESTONE
8 Work Songs (Nat Adderley) MILESTONE
8 Live At Jorgies Club VGM
10 Fusion! RIVERSIDE
11 Bumpin' VERVE
12 Movin' Wes VERVE
13 Tequila VERVE
14 Jimmy & Wes/The Dynamic Duo (with Jimmy Smith VERVE
15 The Small Groups Recordings VERVE
16 Eulogy VERVE
17 Going Out of My Head VERVE
18 The Alternative West Montgomery VERVE
19 Solitude SEVEN SEAS
20 California A&M

Play in the style of Wes Montgomery

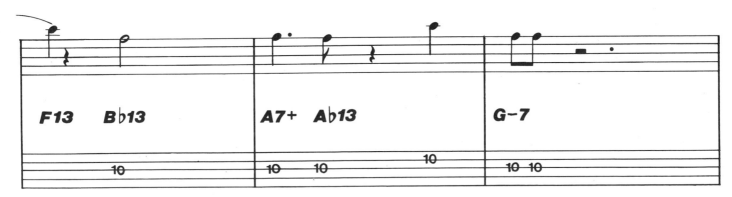

Chris Watson notes: Here Wes uses octaves in the first four bars. In the following five bars the written line is played as the top note of a chord inversion and is a great example of chord soloing.

One characteristic of Wes Montgomery is that he often begins a solo with single line playing, develops that over several chorus into octaves and in turn to chord soloing. This creates a gradual momentum, building to a climax. Here Wes is caught in full flight.

Django Reinhardt

Jean Baptiste 'Django' Reinhardt: Born Liverchies, Belgium, 1910. As a Tzigane gipsy, he and his family — including brother Joseph, also guitarist, who was to work for years with Django when both became involved with jazz full-time — travelled extensively throughout Europe, also visiting North Africa, before settling just outside Paris. First involvement with musical instrument came at 11-12, Reinhardt using banjo-guitar. Soon, he was to acquire working knowledge of guitar, violin, bass.

First public performances took place c. 1923, at various Parisian nightclubs, cafes — inevitably, then, in non-jazz contexts. First recording date, at 15, on banjo, as accompanist to singer called Chabel; no records, however, materialised. Opportunity to join dance orchestra of a vastly-impressed Jack Hylton during 1927-1928 likewise never came to fruition. Injured in accidental fire in Reinhardt's caravan in November, '28, during which he was severely burned. As a result, fourth and fifth fingers of left hand were mutilated. Which meant he could not play violin; and, as guitarist, would be able to use only first two fingers. Despite seemingly insurmountable physical problem, an 18-years-old Reinhardt proceeded to fashion out of apparent disaster a truly formidable technique. One that would make him a legend in his own lifetime — and ensure that forever more that he would be rated in the top three of all-time greatest jazz guitar players. It was a combination of his fierce gipsy pride and real courage,

together with a genuine love for jazz music — he had been introduced to jazz through recordings of such as Louis Armstrong, Duke Ellington, Joe Venuti — that enabled him to become an even greater player than before the terrible accident.

Worked with all kinds of orchestras, bands etc, during early-1930's, as well as accompanying singers like Jean Sablon (3). But it was with the formation of own Quintette du Hot Club de France that the Django Reinhardt Story takes on real significance. Co-led by French violinist Stephane Grappelli, and comprising two rhythm guitars (one, Joseph Reinhardt, his brother), the five-piece band attracted local popularity right from its earliest days. That popularity became internationalised when the combo commenced what was to be a prolific recording lifetime. (QHCF lasted, on and off, until 1939). During which period, Reinhardt's individual brilliance enabled him to work, with ease, alongside visiting American jazz giants such as saxophonists Coleman Hawkins, Benny Carter, trombonist Dicky Wells, violinist Eddie South, trumpeters Rex Stewart, Bill Coleman (2).

During World War II, with Grappelli living in London, Reinhardt worked with various aggregations, occasionally fronting new versions of QHCF, with clarinettist Hubert Rostaing as front-line colleague. Toured US on one-and-only occasion, together with Duke Ellington (1946). Trip, however was not an outstanding success,

Marble Arch MAL 1234

Reinhardt appearing to be not at all happy throughout. Died Fontainebleau, France, in May 1953, following a stroke suffered during River Seine fishing trip...

There have been few, if indeed any, jazz guitarists to equal let alone surpass the sheer virtuosity and natural genius of Django Reinhardt. And make no mistake about it, Reinhardt was both virtuoso and genius. His extraordinary technical accomplishments — bearing in mind, always, his enormous physical handicap — alone are sufficient to elevate him to the pantheon of the top jazz players. His intuitive, totally individual approach to the guitar made him a major pioneer on his instrument, particularly with regard to his experiments with octaves, and, of course, in his having to devise a completely new technique following his crippling accident.

Reinhardt has few rivals with regard to his biting attack and unremitting drive, or indeed in the utterly fearless manner in which he positively leaps into his up-tempo solos. His discography is littered with superlative examples of that ferocious attack, notably *After You've Gone, Limehouse Blues, Nagasaki, Exactly Like You, Shine* all (2); *Twelfth Year* (4). During *Charleston* (2), his use of trills can without exaggeration be described as powerhouse, no wonder Django used to wear out guitars at unnaturally frequent intervals, and his torrid, electrifying performance during *You're Driving Me Crazy* (2) is wildly wonderful, even by his exceptional standards. Chordal or single-string playing alike, only John McLaughlin (q.v.) has ever produced such scorching, sizzling acoustic jazz guitar playing at up-tempos... and there can have been few individual musicians who, by the sheer power of their

own performances, have lifted the collective strength of a jazz combo as Reinhardt with the Quintet of the Hot Club of France.

It is during his exquisitely conceived ballad performances that Django Reinhardt demonstrates a totally different side of his musical personality. During recorded solos like *Solitude, Body & Soul, Nuages* all (2) *Stardust* (6), and *Manoir de mes Reves* (9), his impeccable fretwork is informed by a sensitivity and even poignancy that communicates to the listener at a basic level — the complete antithesis of his roaring solos at fast tempos. Tonally, too, his ballad performances are revealing; the gipsy sound that he never lost is manifestly more obvious on ballads or ballad-type solo excursions. Django's blues, even if rarely profound, have an instantly identifiable and communicative quality. *Big Boy Blues* (2) is, without a doubt, one of his finest blues performances. His solo is not easily comparable to another jazz guitarist's; the blues are Reinhardt's alone.

Reinhardt's reputation enabled him to participate in several record dates during the late-1930's ostensibly featuring distinguished American jazzmen. At all these sessions he sounds not at all inhibited by the presence of such noteworthy soloists as Rex Stewart, Coleman Hawkins, Benny Carter, Dicky Wells, *et al.* His solo opportunities are not plentiful — but as with recordings showcasing the violin artistry of Eddie South (2), Reinhardt made up for any lack of solo contributions by proving again, what an extraordinarily inspiring rhythm guitarist he was. But when Reinhardt does take off, albeit not at any real length, he projects as powerfully as, say,

Ace of Clubs 1158

Play in the style of Django Reinhardt

Chris Watson notes: This passage should be played fast to have its full effect. Typical of Django's style it contains 'grace notes' and 'embellishments', which add excitement and great style. In bar five-six and nine he uses broken arpeggios.

trombonist Wells, especially during *Hangin' Around Boudon, Japanese Sandman,* both (2); and cornettist Stewart and clarinettist Barney Bigard (2). (1) is a fascinating collection of Django Reinhardt recordings, spanning a period in time from 1928 — Django playing banjo with a less-than-jazz-like, accordian-led dance orchestra of the period — until 1946. He performs in a variety of settings, inspiring and otherwise, and rarely does his abounding zest for playing desert him.

By the end of the 1940's, having been impressed mostly by Charlie Christian (q.v.), Django Reinhardt had begun experimenting with amplified guitar. At first, the results were less than wholly satisfactory, but the stub-born streak in the man enabled him to pursue the challenge. For some, his decision to plug in was both heretical and disastrous. As indeed was his growing interest in bebop. (Little bebop-type phrases can be discerned in some of his latterday recordings, like *Swing 48* (20), (11). Reinhardt's involvement with electric guitar was, in the event, not a matter of innovative importance. But, as recordings such as (10), (11), (12), (13), (14), prove it was scarcely the non-event as claimed by some detractors.

Little doubt, though, that Django Reinhardt's greatest years were those between 1934-1940, most times with the QHCF, and usually partnered by his best-known associate, Stephane Grappelli.

SELECTED DISCOGRAPHY

1 Django Reinhardt (Misc.) COLUMBIA
2 The Genius of Django (including Coleman Hawkins, Dick Wells, Bill Coleman, Stephane Grappelli, Eddie South, et al) WORLD RECORDS
3 Jean Sablon/Django Reinhardt PARLOPHONE
4 Rhythm Is Our Business (with Stephane Grappelli) DECCA
5 Django REALM
6 A Swinging Affair DECCA
7 Django Reinhardt (Misc.) DJM
8 En Belgique 1942 POLYDOR
9 Django Reinhardt VOGUE
10 Django Reinhardt Vol. II XTRA
11 Gypsy of Jazz EMBER
12 Django Reinhardt Vol. 1 & 3 RCA VICTOR
13 Django in Rome 1949-50 PARLOPHONE
15 Django Reinhardt et le Quintette du Hot Club du France, Vols. 1,2 BARCLAY
15 Django Story BARCLAY

The Best of the Rest

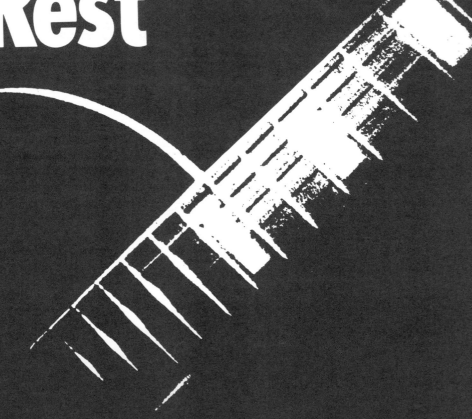

The Best of the Rest

JOHN ABERCROMBIE

John L. Abercrombie: Born Porchester, NYC, 1944. Commenced guitar studies when 14. Received some formal training but, like so many jazz guitarists, mostly self-taught. More comprehensive guitar study during almost five years at Berklee School of Music, Boston (1962-1966), where Abercrombie also learned theory, harmony. Remained in Boston for first professional gig — with organist Johnny 'Hammond' Smith — that lasted a year. Followed by equally interesting jobs with bands, musicians as diverse as Dreams (1969), Chico Hamilton (1970 including first-time trip to Europe), Jeremy Steig ('71). Further invaluable playing experience during 1970's, with Gil Evans, Gato Barbieri, Billy Cobham, Jack DeJohnette. Topped DOWN BEAT Jazz Critics' Poll — Talent Deserving Wider Recognition section — in '75. Since when has worked mostly as leader of own combo. His increasing diversity has enabled his to become a regular, and most welcome, name in connection with a healthy series of recordings.

Since the middle-1960's, John Abercrombie has developed into one of the most adaptable players on the jazz scene. A player of enviable creative powers, who can build solos of genuine excitement and in a completely natural way. It was with Cobham, where Abercrombie's name reached audiences of pop-superstar proportions, that he first evidenced just how exciting a performer he could be. That year with Cobham is documented, interestingly, throughout each of (1), (2) and (3), Abercrombie's performances often taking on hitherto unrealised qualities, inspired almost certainly by the leader's powerhouse drumming.

Amongst his numerous contributions to record dates by others have been those to be found on albums by such as saxophonist Dave Liebman (4), (5); violinist Michael Urbaniak (6); trumpeters Kenny Wheeler (7) and Enrico Rava (8); and fellow guitarists Ralph Towner (q.v.), (9), (10); and Collin Walcott (11). Abercrombie's own recordings, particularly Abercrombie Quartet items such as (12), (13); show that by the 1980's, the now fully-developed New Yorker deserved to be ranked with the finest practitioners of his chosen instrument. His beautifully-conceived duo LP with Towner (10) has added interest insofar as Abercrombie plays, along with the conventional electric and acoustic guitars, both mandolin-guitar and electric 12-string. And his amplified mandolin adds a totally individual touch to Coltrane's *Bessie's Blues* on (14).

SELECTED DISCOGRAPHY

1 Crosswinds (Billy Cobham) ATLANTIC
2 Total Eclipse (Billy Cobham) ATLANTIC
3 Shabazz (Billy Cobham) ATLANTIC
4 Lookout Farm (Dave Liebman) ECM
5 Drum Ode (Dave Liebman) ECM
6 Atma (Michal Urbaniak COLUMBIA
7 Deer Wan (Kenny Wheeler) ECM
8 The Pilgrim and the Stars (Enrico Rava) ECM
9 Sargasso Sea (Ralph Towner) ECM
10 Five Years Later (Ralph Towner) ECM
11 Cloud Dance (Collin Walcott) ECM
12 John Abercrombie Quartet ECM
13 M (John Abercrombie Quartet) ECM
14 Straight Flight JAZZ AMERICAN MARKETING
15 Characters ECM
16 Timeless ECM
17 Untitled ECM
18 Friends OBLIVION
19 Eventyr (Jan Garbarek) ECM
20 Gateway ECM
21 Gateway 2 ECM
22 El Gato (Gato Barbieri) RCA/FLYING DUTCHMAN
23 Un Poco Loco (Bobby Hutcherson) COLUMBIA

BERNARD ADDISON

Bernard S. Addison: Born Annapolis, Maryland, 1905. Played mandolin, violin as a youngster. Switched to banjo before moving to Washington (1920), where he was soon co-leading band with pianist Claude Hopkins. Worked with Oliver Blackwell's Clowns, then to NYC with Sonny Thompson. With Seminole Syncopators ('25), also accompanying singer Virginia Liston. Between middle-and-late-1930's, employed by Ed Small, Claude Hopkins. Swapped banjo for guitar c. 1928, although still continued to use former from time to time. Joined Louis Armstrong (1) at New York's Coconut Grove, then with Bubber Miley's Mileage Makers (2). In Toledo, worked for Milton Senior, Art Tatum, Adelaide Hall. Back to NYC, fronted own combos for seasons at Famous Door and Adrian's Tap Room ('35). Toured with Mills Brothers (1936-1938), including first visit to Europe. During same period, was heard with Mezz Mezzrow's Disciples of Swing; also in tandem with fellow guitarist Teddy Bunn (q.v.) Helped make much joyful music with violinist Stuff Smith's late 1930's jump band, and gave extra spring to the rhythm section of Sidney Bechet (12) for brief period in 1940.

Just prior to, and immediately on release from, US Army service, led own groups. Free-lanced regularly in Canada for several years. Toured with Ink Spots towards end of 1950's. Also took part in Henderson Reunion Band (13), in '57. Worked as accompanist for Juanita Hall, and appeared longside Eubie Blake at the 1960 Newport Jazz Festival (14). During 1960's, continued freelance work,

but gradually his live appearances became less and less frequent. In past 15 years or so, has been active performing, at gigs, and on record, T.V., radio, etc; Bernard Addison continued to earn the respect of his fellow musicians. His unerring rhythmic playing was heard during the 1930's in many kinds of jazz situations. Apart from those mentioned above, Addison also recorded with such top-line names as Fletcher Henderson (3), (4), Henry 'Red' Allen (6), Benny Carter (8), Johnny Dodds (9), and Horace Henderson (5). He remains the finest rhythm guitarist to work with the legendary Jelly Roll Morton (10). Some of his best playing — the modest Addison was an all-too-rare soloist — can be heard in a series of recordings he cut under the leadership of both Adrian Rollini and Freddy Jenkins (7) — and there is actually a little Addison chord-style solo work to be heard... By the time he took part in altoist Pete Brown's final record date (15), he was a name that was beginning to be forgotten.

But for those who heard him, in one or more of his many featured activities, Bernard Addison will remain a thorough-going professional player, who also became a superior guitar tutor as well as immersing himself comprehensively in the study of the classical instrument.

SELECTED DISCOGRAPHY

1 VSOP (Very Special Old Phono-graphy) 1928-1930, Vols. 5,6 (Louis Armstrong) CBS Armstrong) CBS
2 Bubber Miley & His Friends: 1929-1931 RCA VICTOR
3 The Fletcher Henderson Story, Vols. 2,4 CBS
4 Recordings Made Between 1930 & 1941 (Coleman Hawkins) CBS
5 Ridin' In Rhythm (Horace Henderson) WORLD RECORDS
6 Henry Allen & His Orchestra: 1934-1935 COLLECTOR'S CLASSICS
7 Adrian Rollini & His Friends, Vol. 1: "Tap Room Special" RCA VICTOR
8 Swingin' At Maida Vale (Benny Carter) JASMINE
9 Harlem On Saturday Night (Johnny Dodds) ACE OF HEARTS
10 The Big Apple (Mezz Mezzrow) RCA VICTOR
11 Jelly Roll Morton, Vols. 1,7 RCA VICTOR
12 Sidney Bechet, Vol. 2 BLUE NOTE
13 The Big Reunion (Fletcher Henderson All Stars) JAZZTONE
14 Wizard of the Ragtime Piano (Eubie Blake) 20th CENTURY FOX
15 Pete's Last Date (Pete Brown) 77

IRVING ASHBY

Irving C. Ashby: Born Somerville, Massachusetts, 1920. Another guitarist who began with ukulele. Graduated from New England Conservatory, Boston. First important job — working with the first wild-and-wonderful Lionel Hampton Orchestra (1940-1942), (1), (2). Worked in and around Los Angeles, in many jam-session situations, including the classic Gene Norman Presents Just Jazz (5) and Jazz At the Philharmonic (3) stage presentations. Became one-third of Nat Cole Trio (1947-1950) (6); served in a like capacity with Oscar Peterson Trio (7). First trip to Europe with Cole ('50). Career interrupted in 1960's so he could complete 2½ years course on landscape design, following which he freelanced in this non-music area, designing landscaping for apartment buildings. By 1969, was in semi-retirement, comprehensively involved in landscape design, as well as sign-painting. He did, however, take time out to teach guitar and orchestra. But for most of late-1960's/early 1970's, Ashby was inactive as far as gigs and recordings.

A fine, all-round player — as first-rate a rhythm guitarist as a soloist who can play single-string or chorded solos — Ashby's long periods off the scene have robbed the jazz scene of a solid talent.

Still, the odd record date shows little or no diminution in his talent. (1), for instance, finds him supplying firm rhythm guitar in exalted company; (12) is a similar Norman Granz-inspired date that contains a rare event — an Irving Ashby solo (on *Doubling Blues*). A much more uncommon occurrence is (9), an LP under his own name that is his finest individual showcase. (13) is of lesser interest, quantity-wise, but with friend and veteran fellow picker John Collins (q.v.) in complete rapport, it presents two further illustrations of his straight-ahead excellent, of a more recent vintage.

SELECTED DISCOGRAPHY

1 Lionel Hampton I: "Steppin' Out" (1942-1944) MCA
2 The Complete Lionel Hampton (1937-1941) BLUEBIRD
3 Jazz At the Philharmonic 1946, Vol. 2 VERVE
4 The Aladdin Sessions (Lester Young) BLUE NOTE
5 Gene Norman's Just Jazz Concerts (Various) VOGUE
6 Pieces of Cole (Nat King Cole) SWING HOUSE
7 The Voice of Jazz, Vol. 1 (Billie Holiday) VERVE
8 Memoirs ACCENT
9 California Guitar FAMOUS DOOR
10 History of an Artist (Oscar Peterson) PABLO
11 The Bosses (Count Basie, Big Joe Turner) PABLO
12 Basie Jam, (Count Basie, et al) PABLO
13 Guitar Player (with John Collins) MCA CORAL

DEREK BAILEY

Derek Bailey: Born Sheffield, Yorkshire, 1932. Grandson of professional banjoist, and nephew of professional guitarist. Initially, worked in generally boring, unstimulating, non-jazz, areas of popular music. But before leaving Sheffield for London, did lead a group (including drummer Tony Oxley), based at the Grapes, that attracted a small but loyal following. Bailey's career was helped along its way by a mutually productive association with drummer John Stevens' Spontaneous Music Ensemble (1), and the London Jazz Composers' Orchestra. Trio, formed with trombonist Paul Rutherford, bassist Barry Guy (2), another important development. Career further enhanced by frequent collaborations with saxist Evan Parker (3), (5); and perhaps even more expansively, during the 1970's and thereafter, by his involvement with an ever-growing list of similar free-thinking contemporary European musicians — not forgetting his work in company with many visiting US musicians. Principally, the multi-instrumentalist Anthony Braxton (4), (13), who has called

Bailey one of the greatest-ever improvising jazz players.

During the past 20 years, Derek Bailey has become one of the most controversial as well as one of the totally individual guitarists. A performer of obvious technical skills, whose unique approach to extemporisation nevertheless flies directly in the face of anything remotely conventional. Still, there are those who seriously question Bailey's true affiliation with jazz *per se* (some maintain his might well be a kind of extension of late-20th century classical music). Certainly, his 'ideal of free improvisation' is demanding in the extreme — probably best illustrated during unaccompanied performances like (7), (8). And it is true that even during live recordings such as (5) his sometimes atonal, astringent sound, not too often accompanied by much compensatory emotional warmth, has been known to deter all but the deeply committed. His solo work apart, Bailey's involvement with Company (an international pool of free players) continues to provide a nonstop stream of provocative, yet always original music (12).

Whether one thinks of Derek Bailey as a genius or a charlatan, a jazzman or an avant-garde classicist, there is little doubt he has contributed a completely different perspective to jazz guitar-playing. Conventional or otherwise.

SELECTED DISCOGRAPHY

1 So What Do You Think? (Spontaneous Music Ens.) TANGENT
2 Iskra 1903 INCUS
3 The Topography of the Lungs (with Evan Parker) INCUS
4 Duo (with Anthony Braxton)
5 The London Concert (with Evan Parker) INCUS
6 Improvisations CRAMPS
7 Derek Bailey Solo INCUS
8 Lot 74 — Solo Improvisations INCUS
9 Improvisations for Cello & Guitar ECM
10 Drops INCUS
11 Time (with Tony Cole) INCUS
12 Company 1 INCUS
13 Duo 2 (with Anthony Braxton) EMANEM
14 Derek Bailey & Tristan Honsinger INCUS

DAVE BARBOUR

David Michael Barbour: Born New York City, 1912. Before taking up guitar, had played banjo for a while. Worked with fairly nondescript bands at first, but by 1930's was associating with familiar jazz names. Invariably, this involved small combos, like those of Wingy Manone (1934), Red Norvo (1934-1935). During 1930's, also recorded prolifically, in company of other such notables as Louis & Lucille Armstrong, Teddy Wilson (3), Bunny Berigan (1), (2), Mildred Bailey (4), Jack Teagarden

Derek Bailey

(5). Solo-wise, though, usually little or no opportunity for a player whose tasteful, cleanly-picked work never lacked fluency or interest. Also played with studio bands, particularly Lennie Hayton's, and working big bands like those of Glenn Miller, Charlie Barnet, Hal Kemp. Joined Benny Goodman (6) in '42, staying for about a year. During which time met and married Goodman's then singer Peggy Lee (they divorced in '52). When latter commenced solo career, Barbour became her musical director, also playing in accompanying unit. Close at hand, too, on Peggy Lee's recordings for several years — (8), (9), (10) — and between them, the husband-and-wife team composed string of first-class pop songs, including *It's a Good Day, Manana, I Don't Know Enough About You, What More Can a Woman Do?* Had a short film-acting career in 1950.

Dave Barbour, who died in Malibu, California in 1965 — he had suffered stomach problems for years — had been in almost total retirement since mid-1950's. Indeed, apart from a Cuban tour with Woody Herman in 1949, he'd been inactive as a live performer from the early-1950's. A delightful date, headlining the talents of Ben Webster, Barney Bigard, and Benny Carter (10), probably constitutes the very last appearance, on record, of a player whose talents were put into self-imposed retirement much too prematurely . . .

SELECTED DISCOGRAPHY

1 The Great Soloists (Bunny Berigan) BIOGRAPH
2 Bunny Berigan: Decca/Champion Sessions MCA
3 Teddy Wilson & His All-Stars CBS
4 Mildred Bailey: Her Greatest Performances (1929-1946), Vol. 2 CBS
5 Featuring Jack Teagarden MCA
6 Sold Gold Instrumental Hits (Benny Goodman) CBS
7 Jammin' At Sunset (Charlie Ventura) BLACK LION
8 The Fabulous Miss Lee WORLD REC. CLUB
9 You Can Depend On Me (Peggy Lee) GLENDALE
10 The Best of Peggy Lee MCA
11 BBB & Co. (Barney Bigard, Benny Carter, Ben Webster) XTRA

DANNY BARKER

Daniel Barker: Born New Orleans, Louisiana, 1909. Yet another jazz guitarist whose first experience with stringed instruments was with banjo. Received lessons from clarinettist Barney Bigard and drummer Paul Barbarin (Barker's uncle, who taught him how to play drums). Turned to banjo, then guitar, and played first important job with New Orleans trumpeter Lee Collins' band, in late-1920's, with which outfit first came to New York. Subsequently, worked with other name jazz bands, such as Dave Nelson, Albert Nicholas, James P. Johnson, Lucky Millinder, Benny Carter. Spent seven years, touring extensively, with Cab Calloway Orchestra, soloing very little, but always strongly present in rhythm section (3), (4), (5). In post-war years, continued to work with various name musicians — including Sir Charles Thompson record date (17) including also Charlie Parker and Dizzy Gillespie — as well as leading own small units in support of wife, singer Blue Lu Parker. During mid-1950's, Barker, on banjo, heard in company with Uncle Paul Barbarin. In 1960, on guitar, supported pianist Eubie Blake at Newport Jazz Festival. Back on banjo, led own group at 1964 New York's World Fair. Following year, moved back to New Orleans, to take up appointment as Assistant to Curator of Crescent City's own Jazz Museum. Since when has been only intermittently active, both in musical and administrative capacities in city of his birth.

The career of Danny Barker in jazz has been one of extreme versatility, embracing work with musicians of a myriad selection of jazz styles. Apart from those aforementioned, also associated himself with individuals as diverse in approach as King Oliver (2), Adrian Rollini (1), Lionel Hampton (7), Louis Armstrong (9), Chu Berry (10), Billie Holiday (15). And over the years, Barker often supported another distinguished New Orleans citizen: Sidney Bechet (11), (12), (13).

SELECTED DISCOGRAPHY

1 Adrian Rollini & His Friends, Vol. 1: "Tap Room Special" RCA VICTOR
2 King Oliver/Dave Nelson, Vol. 3 (1929/1931) RCA/VICTOR
3 16 Cab Calloway Classics CBS
4 Chu (Chuck Berry, Cab Calloway) EPIC
5 Penguin Swing (Chu Berry, Cab Calloway) JAZZ ARCHIVES
6 Swing Street, Vol. 1 (Billy Kyle) TAX
7 The Complete Lionel Hampton BLUEBIRD
8 Henry Allen & His Orchestra 1933-1934 COLLECTOR'S CLASSICS
9 Louis With Guest Stars MCA
10 The Big Sound of Coleman Hawkins & Chu Berry (Chu Berry) LONDON
11 The Prodigious Bechet-Mezzrow Quintet & Septet FESTIVAL
12 The Genius of Sidney Bechet JAZZOLOGY
13 This Is Jazz, Vols. 1,2 (Sidney Bechet) RARITIES
14 Jam Session At Swingville (Pee Wee Russell, et al) PRESTIGE
15 Billie Holiday, Vol. 1 CBA
16 LaVern Baker Sings Bessie ATLANTIC
17 The Fabulous Apollo Sessions (Sir Charles Thompson) VOGUE

GEORGE BARNES

George Barnes: Born Chicago Heights, Illinois, 1921. Died Concord, California, 1977. Studied guitar with father. Met, hung out with local bluesmen as a youngster, including the great Lonnie Johnson (q.v.), although earliest influences included non-guitarists Louis Armstrong, Jimmie Noone, Benny Goodman. (Barnes got chance to sit in with Noone at 16). Still in his teens, got opportunities to record with blues notabilities Big Bill Broonzy (1), Blind John Davis, Washboard Sam. Toured Midwest with own quartet between 1935-1939, followed by work with NBC staff in Chicago. Worked with Bud Freeman's band (1942); then 4½ years with US Army. Became deeply involved with ABC RADIO Chicago (1946-1951); also became contracted, lucratively, to DECCA RECORDS, as guitarist, writer, arranger. Formed working two-guitar duo with Carl Kress (q.v.) that toured nationally, visited Japan (1965), played White House jazz party ('64), and recorded (4), (5), (6). Partnership concluded only with Kress' death ('65). Barnes and Bucky Pizzarelli (q.v.) presented similar partnership for a short while afterwards.

During 1970's, became involved with more regular jazz playing than previous decade. Provided delightful foil to co-leader's mellow cornet in Ruby Braff-George Barnes Quartet (8), (9), (10), (11). And both gigs and recordings, (12), (13); with legendary Joe Venuti elicited kind of excitement he had hitherto rarely demonstrated. Barnes died, suddenly from heart attack, in 1977.

George Barnes never was anything less than a top-class guitarist whose warm, elegant playing endeared itself readily to his fellow pickers. His somewhat low-key approach more often than not sounded more vital and inspiring in the company of more extrovert jazzmen like Venuti, Braff, and Freeman (15).

Barnes, by nature an immensely likeable personality, was not a significant figure in jazz guitar's evolution. But he was a good man to have around at practically any time. One interesting diversion during a thoroughly professional career was his experiment with a band comprising, basically, a bank of guitars. Again, nothing of cataclysmic significance ensued. But, as both (2) and (3) illustrate, most delightfully, it certainly made for one helluva sound. Especially, of course, for the guitar freaks...

SELECTED DISCOGRAPHY

1 Big Bill's Blues (Big Bill Broonzy) CBS/REALM
2 George Barnes Octet HINDSIGHT
3 Guitars Galore! MERCURY
4 Something Tender (with Carl Kress) UNITED ARTISTS
5 Town Hall Concert (with Carl Kr) UNITED
ARTISTS
6 Two Guitars, Vol. 1 (with Carl Kress) STASH
7 Guitars — Pure & Honest A&R
8 The Best I've Heard (Ruby Braff, Geo Barnes) VOGUE
9 To Fred Astaire, With Love (Ruby Braff, Geo Barnes) RCA VICTOR
10 Ruby Braff-George Barnes Quartet Play Gershwin CONCORD JAZZ
11 Ruby Braff & George Barnes Salute Rodgers & Hart CONCORD JAZZ
12 Gems (with Joe Venuti) CONCORD JAZZ
13 Live At the Concord Summer Festival (with Joe Venuti) CONCORD JAZZ
14 Blues Going Up CONCORD JAZZ
15 Swingin' Tenors (Bud Freeman) AFFINITY
16 Two Guitars & A Horn (with Carl Kress, Bud Freeman) STASH

BILLY BAUER

William Henry Bauer: Born NYC, 1915. Like so many guitarists, started on banjo. Mostly self-taught, first important gig with the Jerry Wald Orchestra (1939); subsequently played with other jazz-tinged dancebands (eg Carl Hoff, Dick Stabile, Abe Lyman). Came to national prominence after joining Woody Herman (1944), (1), remaining for almost three years. Returned to NYC, subsequently working with Benny Goodman, Chubby Jackson, Lennie Tristano. Appeared with houseband on Steve Allen TV Show (1953-1954). Thereafter, mostly freelanced — particularly with regard to radio, TV, transcriptions, recordings. Played Brussels World Fair with Goodman ('58), (14), and well-remembered season at Half Note Club, NYC ('59). Put together own small groups, appearing mostly on Long Island (1961-1963), but spent much of '63 with Ice Capades pit band. Also worked with Ella Fitzgerald.

Since 1970's, however, his live appearances have been few and far between. Apart from running own successful publishing company, has devoted much of his time to teaching.

Billy Bauer remains one of the most gifted performers to emerge from the extraordinarily productive 1940's. A deft finger-stylist whose flawless technique, elegant linear approach, and flowing creativity together makes him something of a jazz guitarist's jazz guitarist. Yet, like some other players spotlighted in JAZZ GUITARIST (eg Johnny Smith, Bucky Pizzarelli, Sal Salvador, George Barnes), he's never quite made it to the list of all-time greats. Basically, it would appear that Bauer's only deficiencies appear to be a lack of real assertiveness in his solos, resulting in little hot-blooded excitement, and a seeming disinterest in blues-playing. Billy Bauer, nonetheless, is a talented man to have on the band. As diverse top jazz talents as Herman, Goodman, Jackson,

Tristano, *et al*, no doubt would concur. Even when his lightly-swinging, unobtrusive presence is needed in a rhythm-guitar-only capacity, as on record dates with the likes of Jack Teagarden/Bobby Hackett (12), Cootie Williams/Rex Stewart (13), or Goodman (14).

But Bauer's reputation was made — and likely will remain so for all time — in company with the remarkable blind Chicago pianist-composer-teacher-philosopher, Lennie Tristano. Indeed, he remains one of Tristano's most gifted disciples. Their association began in 1946, and continued for several years. Together with his filligree solo work, one remembers, with perhaps even more affection, the flowing contrapuntal lines Bauer played with his mentor — (2), (3), (4), (5). And he was a member of the Tristano Sextet that recorded the exhilirating *Intuition* session (6), probably the first recorded example of 'free' jazz playing. Bauer's collaborations with another Tristano alumnus, altoist Lee Konitz, have been invariably mutually stimulating affairs (7), (8), (9), (10). Of special interest on (7) are the Konitz-Bauer duets on *Indian Summer* and, in particular, the exquisite *Duet For Saxophone & Guitar*. A DOWN BEAT (1949-1950) and METRONOME (1949-1953) poll-winner, Bill Bauer's absence from full-time playing for so long is to be regretted.

SELECTED DISCOGRAPHY

1 The Thundering Herds (Woody Herman) CBS
2 The Rarest Trio/Quartet Sessions 1946/1947 (Lennie Tristano)
3 The Lost Session (Lennie Tristano) JAZZ GUILD
4 Live At Birdland 1949 (Lennie Tristano) JAZZ RECORDS
5 First Sessions 1949/50 (Lennie Tristano) PRESTIGE
6 Cross Currents (Lennie Tristano) CAPITOL
7 Ezz-thetic (Lee Konitz) XTRA
8 Lee Konitz Just Swings VERVE
9 Lee Konitz Inside Hi-Fi ATLANTIC
10 Lee Konitz & Warne Marsh ATLANTIC
11 Billy Bauer — Plectrist VERVE
12 Jazz Ultimate (Bobby Hackett/Jack Teagarden) CAPITOL
13 The Big Challenge (Cootie Williams/Rex Stewart) CONCERT HALL
14 Goodman Plays Gershwin (Benny Goodman) CBS

JAY BERLINER

Jay Berliner: Born Brooklyn, New York City, 1940. First turned on to guitar, at five, by listening to country singer-guitarist Denver Darling. Next, parents bought him a tiny Martin 0-18K (which he still has). Took lessons for two years. Studied music in general — attended Brooklyn Conservatory of Music. At seven years, composed four-part suite (*Modern Moods*). Two years later, was accompanying sister on popular NBC radio programme called Horn & Hardart Children's Hour. Knocked out on first hearing Les Paul although Paul went down in his estimation on discovery of so much pre-recorded music! Played gigs at 12 with local accordion player. Studied classical guitar. But entered Music & Art High School as 'cellist, playing in school orchestra on that instrument. Attained degree in music theory, also studying more 'cello, at Eastham School of Music. Played jazz gigs, on guitar, at week-ends.

After Eastman, played in off-Broadway show *Hi Paisano* (which closed after only one performance). Toured with harpist Daphne Hellman's Trio (playing both classical, jazz). Worked, travelled, recorded for three years with Harry Belafonte. With Belafonte, visited Kenya

Mainstream MSL 1005

for country's independence celebrations (1963), played Pres. Johnson's White House inaugural ball ('64). Then, decided to concentrate on studio work. On TV, participated in specials involving Dinah Shore, Harry Belafonte, Zero Mostel; recorded and/or worked in live setting with Frank Sinatra, Peggy Lee, Eydie Gormé, Steve Lawrence, Perry Como.

During 1970's, became involved extensively with jingles, as well as working on movie sound tracks (eg *You Light Up My Life, The Missouri Breaks, Barbarella*). Played on musical backgrounds for many TV serials. Recorded three LPs on classical guitar for Japan, involving classical music, pops.

During the past 20-odd years, Jay Berliner has become one of the most respected, as well as one of the

most busy of all New Yorks' many guitar players. Many guitarists to be found within THE JAZZ GUITARISTS have been noted for their versatility and adaptability. Berliner is no exception. Indeed, there can be few, if any, performers who can turn their hands to as many musical situations as he and display the kind of near perfection that has made him something of a legend in his own lifetime.

Berliner's contributions to recordings, etc., of such first-rate singers as Sinatra, Belafonte, Lawrence and Astrud Gilberto have been at all times an enhancement to whatever the particular project may have been at any given time. When he is given the chance to participate in a jazz event — something which seems to happen far too infrequently, on record at least — he can be relied upon to cater for whatever stylistic preference is on hand. Jazz-wise, his most important record sessions remain, indisputably, (1), (2). Despite his misgivings about his own contributions, and bearing in mind he had no previous working experience of Mingus' bands, he sounds not at all out of place; and indeed his playing therein is excellent, if not quintessentially vital to the overall success of the albums

A lengthy association with CTI RECORDS enabled him to play handsomely supportive roles in dates involving major jazz talents like Milt Jackson (6), Ron Carter (7), Airto (4), and one of his own favourite guitar players George Benson (q.v.), (3). And that astonishing versatility finds him sounding happy and at home in such different musical situations as (10), (11) and (9). It is to be regretted, however, that Jay Berliner has been scandalously neglected with regard to record-making under his own name. While (12) is a fine album, it in no way stretches his obvious talents, and barely hints what might happen if the right kind of situation, involving perhaps other major forces, presents itself...

SELECTED DISCOGRAPHY

1 **The Black Saint & The Sinner Lady (Charles Mingus)** IMPULSE
2 **Mingus, Mingus, Mingus, Mingus** IMPULSE
3 **White Rabbit (George Benson)** CTI
4 **Free (Airto Moreira)** CTI
5 **Prelude (Deodato)** CTI
6 **Sunflower (Milt Jackson)** CTI
7 **Spanish Blue (Ron Carter)** CTI
8 **A Song For You (Ron Carter)** MILESTONE
9 **Le Catedral ye el Toro (Joe Farrell)** WARNER BROS.
10 **Uptown Dance (Stephane Grappelli)** COLUMBIA
11 **Spanish Fever (Fania All Stars)** COLUMBIA
12 **Bananas Are Not Created Equal** MAINSTREAM
13 **Watertown (Frank Sinatra)** REPRISE
14 **Trilogy (Frank Sinatra)** REPRISE
15 **That Girl From Ipanema (Astrud Gilberto)**

IMAGE
16 **Reach Out (Burt Bacharach)** A&M

CHARLIE BYRD

Charles L. Byrd: Suffolk, Virginia, 1925. Commenced guitar studies with father (also guitarist) at 10. Played high school dances. First professional 'name' jobs with clarinettist Sol Yaged's Dixieland outfit (1947); with clarinettist/saxist Joe Marsala, pianist Barbara Carroll (both '49); pianist Freddie Slack (also '49). Became seriously smitten by classical guitar (1950) — even studied for a while with Maestro Andres Segovia ('54); gave classical recitals in Washington, DC, and district not too long afterwards. Gained individual recognition, as jazz guitarist, during long residencies at Washington's Showboat nightspot. At which time, also appeared regularly on Mutual's Bandstand USA. Both composed, played music for Tennessee Williams *The Purification.* Worked with Woody Herman (1959), both in small-group setting (5), and as member of Anglo-American Herd that toured UK.

Milestone 47005

During 1960's made Showboat home base, although he never stopped touring throughout US and overseas. Took a combo on State Department-sponsored tour of South America ('61), discovering in the process the subtle delights of the jazz samba. Which, thereafter, became an integral part of the Byrd repertoire. Most especially after huge success of (6), cut in '62, Byrd sharing the spotlight with tenorist Stan Getz. Later during same decade, toured Europe; appeared on several widely-syndicated US TV

Charlie Byrd

shows, and gave a personal recital for Lyndon Johnson ('65). Steady stream of LPs as variously represented by such as (3), (4), (7), (9), (19) continued to flow.

During 1970's, continued to demonstrate his musical ambivalence, both as a solo performer and, together with Barney Kessel (q.v.), Herb Ellis (q.v.), as one-third of self-styled Great Guitars. Providing the acoustic approach to the trio's combined and individual fare, as per (16), (17), (18). Charlie Byrd is, simply, one of the most exceptionally gifted performers to grace the jazz-guitar scene, at any time during its fascinating history. Quite apart from his delightful musical ambivalence, he has brought to the often frenetic jazz world his acoustic Spanish guitar, not to mention his own highly original, *flamenco*-derived finger style. And, of course, Byrd sounds quite unlike anyone else. (If there is any perceivable influence, then his approach is, if anything, more than vaguely reminiscent at times of the great Django Reinhardt (q.v.) — who remains a firm favourite with Byrd).

SELECTED DISCOGRAPHY

1 **Jazz Recital** SAVOY
2 **Blues For Night People** CBS-REALM
3 **Jazz At The Showboat** CBS-REALM
4 **Charlie Byrd At the Village Vanguard**

RIVERSIDE
5 **Woody Herman Sextet** WORLD RECORD CLUB
6 **Jazz Samba (with Stan Getz)** VERVE
7 **Herb Ellis-Charlie Byrd** COLUMBIA
8 **Brazilian Byrd** COLUMBIA
9 **Top Hat** FANTASY
10 **Byrd By the Sea** FANTASY
11 **Crystal Silence** FANTASY
12 **Tambu (with Cal Tjader)** FANTASY
13 **Travellin' Man** COLUMBIA
14 **Onda Nuevea/The New Wave (with Alderman Romero)** CBS
15 **Brazilian South (with Laurindo Almeida)** CONCORD JAZZ PICANTE
16 **Great Guitars, Vols: 1,2** CONCORD JAZZ
17 **Great Guitars At the Winery** CONCORD JAZZ
18 **Great Guitars at Charlie's Georgetown** CONCORD JAZZ
19 **Latin Byrd** ,MILESTONE

ALBERT CASEY

Albert Aloysius Casey: Born Louisville, Kentucky, 1915. Father, drummer. Began on violin, at age eight, then played ukulele. Moved to New York City (1930). Studied guitar at DeWitt Clinton High School. Received some tuition from James Smith. First important professional work with Fats Waller (1934); thereafter, on and off, worked

with Waller until 1943. With Teddy Wilson Big Band (1939-1940); Buster Harding Quartet ('40); then, back with Waller. Fronted own trio from '43, playing residencies in leading US jazz cities. Featured at first Metropolitan Opera House concert for Esquire Award Winners (1944); back, the following year as a repeat winner. Worked with such a Clarence Profit ('44), Billy Taylor ('49), followed by extensive freelancing. Regular gigs with King Curtis All Stars for several years, likewise, with ex-Hampton drummer Curly Hamner's Sextet. By end of 1960's, was beginning, in some quarters, to be rather forgotten. By advent of 1970's, had returned to more or less full-time playing, touring — both home and abroad — with his acoustic guitar, as a solo act, and in juxtaposition with such as Jay McShann, (21), Milt Buckner, Bob Wilber.

Albert Casey's ability to adapt, easily and comfortably, to many kinds of jazz situations has enabled him to work with artists like those above as well as others of the calibre of Edmond Hall (11), Roy Eldridge and Flip Phillips (15), Pete Brown (12), and even proto-beboppers such as Fats Navarro (14), and Dizzy Gillespie, Oscar Pettiford, and Serge Chaloff (13). And he was an obvious — and ideal — choice for clarinettist Tony Scott's studio recreation of some of the great sounds to have emanated during the late-1930's through until the 1950's, from 52nd Street (16).

But, of course, it was Casey's long association with Fats Waller for which he is best remembered. He was Waller's principal guitar player in that superb, jumping little 'Rhythm' band, recording prolifically between 1934-1942. His was primarily the job of helping stoke the potent rhythm section that buoyed up innumerable Waller record dates (1), (2); and there were few chances for Casey to show off his combination of single-note and chordal styles. One notable exception was the 1941-recorded *Buck Jumpin'* (2), indisputably Casey's most famous solo of his best-known composition. Casey's longest absence from Waller, 1939-1940 came during a period spent as rhythm guitarist with Teddy Wilson's short-lived big band (9).

Casey's two ESQUIRE poll victories are documented by both (4) and (5).

SELECTED DISCOGRAPHY

1 Fats Waller Memorial, Vol. 1 RCA VICTOR
2 Fats Waller Memorial, Vol. 2 RCA VICTOR
3 All That Jazz: Fats Waller DJM
4 The First Esquire Concert, Vol. 1 SAGA
5 The Second Esquire Concert, Vol. 2 SAGA
6 All That Jazz: Louis Armstrong DJM
7 The Big Apple (Mezz Mezzrow) RCA VICTOR
8 Swing Street, Vol. 1 (Gene Sedric) TAX
9 Teddy Wilson & His Big Band 1939/40 TAX
10 The Greatest of the Small Bands, Vol. 6 (Una Mae Carlisle RCA VICTOR
11 Jimmy Ryan's & The Uptown Cafe Society (Edmond Hall) COMMODORE
12 The Changing Face of Harlem/The Savoy Sessions (Pete Brown) SAVOY
13 Bebop Revisited, Vol. 2 (Dizzy Gillespie, et al) XANADU
14 Bebop Revisited, Vol. 3 (Fats Navarro, et al) XANADU
15 Saturday Night Jazz Session (Roy Eldridge, et al) AMERICA
16 52nd Street Scene (Tony Scott, et al) JASMINE
17 Swing Exercise CAPITOL
18 Buck Jumpin' PRESTIGE
19 Slamboree BLACK & BLUE
20 Jumpin' With Al BLACK & BLUE
21 Best of Friends (with Jay McShann) JSP

PHILIP CATHERINE

Philip Catherine: Born London, 1942, of English mother, Belgian father. Spent much of his early youth growing up in Belgium. As an aspiring young guitarist, was influenced initially by Django Reinhardt (q.v.) and Rene Thomas (q.v.). At 17, was working professionally in company of the Paris-based US organist Lou Bennett. Apart from regular work with Belgian Radio, during 1960's Catherine's career really began to take shape: amongst those with whom his fluent guitar was heard were Fats Sadi and Jack Sels. By the following decade, had been seriously involved with jazz-rock. Worked, with mutual success, alongside violinist Jean-Luc Ponty. Became a student for a year at Boston's famous Berklee School of Music. In 1973, together with US expatriate saxophonist Charlie Mariano, put together band Pork Pie. And by this time, his obvious major guitar influence was John McLaughlin (q.v.), although Larry Coryell (q.v.), with whom Catherine has worked on numerous occasions since then, has also continued to exert a telling effect on his work.

Since the 1960's, Philip Catherine has continued to make eminently satisfactory progress as a guitar soloist whose impeccable musicianship makes him a formidable exponent. Catherine, whose technique can be breathtaking, rarely goes over the top, preferring, wisely, to utilise his obvious technical skills to the advantage of the music he produces. In the company of other, non-guitarist, musicians, he can adapt freely and tastefully to each and every situation. His contributions to a two-violin date co-featuring Stephane Grappelli and Jean-Luc Ponty (4) are never less than helpful, not only in the way his solo playing is motivated in the direction of the individual violinists, but also with his subtle background support.

Catherine's collaborations with Mariano have been

delightfully successful. The pair's Pork Pie aside, the juxtaposition of Mariano and the guitarist (not forgetting keyboardist Jasper van't Hof) during (7) makes for music high on creative spirit. In a totally different way, Catherine's contributions to (5) are perhaps even more a triumph. His 1975 collaboration with Dexter Gordon (first time the legendary tenorist had used guitar for a recording date) results in one of the older man's most relaxed and worthwhile recordings of the decade. In a more electronically emotive way, it is instructive to hear Catherine's two solos as a member of Peter Herbolzheimer's Rhythm Combination & Brass (6).

The Catherine-Coryell duo has produced thus far at least two albums, (3), (4), that should be on every guitarist's (and guitar fan's) shelves. The rapport established by the pair is maintained from opening track to last, And, for Catherine admirers, his use, on (4), of fretless electric as well as acoustic — which appears also on (3) — is a particular delight.

SELECTED DISCOGRAPHY

1 **Guitars** ATLANTIC
2 **September Man** ATLANTIC
3 **Twin House (with Larry Coryell)** ATLANTIC
4 **Splendid (with Larry Coryell)** ATLANTIC
5 **Something Different (with Dexter Gordon)** STEEPLECHASE
6 **Wide Open (Peter Herbolzheimer's Rhythm Combination & Brass)** MPS
7 **Sleep, My Love (with Charlie Mariano, Jasper van't Hof)** CMP

JOHN COLLINS

John Elbert Collins: Born Montgomery, Alabama, 1913. Studied music with his mother, Georgia Gorham (demo pianist for W.C. Handy). Collins toured with Georgia Gorham band (1932-1935). Worked with Art Tatum (1935). Member of the fiery Roy Eldridge band (1936-1939). In New York City, worked between 1940-1942 with Lester Young, Dizzy Gillespie, Fletcher Henderson, Benny Carter. Service with US Army (1942-1946). With Slam Stewart (1946-1948); member of Billy Taylor's Trio (1949-1951), after which he joined Nat King Cole's outfit, remaining until the pianist-singer's death in 1965. Recorded for Lee Young's production company; also with Benny Carter. Stayed six years with another singer-pianist — Bobby Troup (receiving more solo opportunities than with Cole), working mostly in NYC, Los Angeles. Played gigs with Neal Hefti, also singers like Sinatra, Nancy Wilson, Sammy Davis. Led own quartet — featuring pianist Jimmy Jones — during mid-1970's. Chosen to participate in NEA Jazz Oral History Project of the Smithsonian Institute (1975). Since when, has continued to freelance, primarily in and around Los Angeles.

John Collins remains one of the most unjustly underrated guitarists to emerge in the wake of Charlie Christian (q.v.). A most gifted performer with a beautifully understated way of phrasing, complemented at all times by a superior tonal quality. In truth, the low-key, retiring personality of Collins probably is partially responsible for his not being a more fashionable name in jazz-guitar circles during the past half-century. Certainly, the former ESQUIRE New Star award-winner ('47) has lacked neither all-round ability nor impressive versatility. And he has been a favourite plectrist of a host of top-drawer jazzmen. Including Dizzy Gillespie, with whom Collins was associated for several years during the 1940's (6). Who wrote of Collins, in his autobiography (*To Be Or Not To Bop*/W.H. Allen) that he 'practised hours and hours, man, different variations of chords. John Collins is about the most, the deepest, of the guitarists because he knew a thousand ways to play one thing...'

Apart from Gillespie, and singers Troup and Cole (7), (8), other prominent musicians who have been grateful for his dexterity include Benny Carter (9), Art Tatum (1), Kenny Clarke (5) and, in much more recent times, Ray Brown (12). Collins' sole ESQUIRE victory is documented on record (4), in company with such as Coleman Hawins, J.J. Johnson, and Teddy Wilson. And just how fine a rhythm-section man he could be, even in the early days, can be judged from both (2) and (3), the former containing on *Heckler's Hop* that *rara avis:* a delightful John Collins solo. 40 years on, and in company with Irving Ashby (q.v.), the luxury of no less than two JC solos during (11), shows off a distinguised talent, undiminished by the passage of time.

SELECTED DISCOGRAPHY

1 **Swing Combos (1935-1941) (Art Tatum)** SWINGFAN
2 **Roy Eldridge At the Three Deuces, Chicago** JAZZ ARCHIVES
3 **Roy Eldridge At the Arcadia Ballroom — 1939** JAZZ ARCHIVES
4 **Esquire's All American Hot Jazz** RCA VICTOR
5 **The Bebop Era (Kenny Clarke)** RCA VICTOR
6 **Dizzy Gillespie, Vol 1/2 (1946-1949)** RCA VICTOR
7 **The Nat Cole Story** CAPITOL
8 **After Midnight (Nat King Cole)** CAPITOL
9 **Further Definitions (Benny Carter)** IMPULSE
10 **Thirty By Ella** CAPITOL
11 **Guitar Player (with Irving Ashby)** MCA
12 **Brown's Bag (Ray Brown)** CORCORD JAZZ

Eddie Condon

EDDIE CONDON

Albert Edwin Condon: Born Goodland, Indiana, 1904. Died NYC, 1973. Started on ukulele, switched to banjo, ending up on guitar. Local gigs with Bill Engleman's band in Cedar Rapids (1921). Later, worked in Hollis Peavey's Jazz Bandits (1922). Played in Chicago and Syracuse with cornettist Bix Beiderbecke. Gigged with Austin High School Gang, Chicago; also worked with a variety of scarcely-remembered bands before co-leading with Red McKenzie, the McKenzie & Condon Chicagoans, (1). To NYC ('28), fronting own band, and freelancing in recording studios with such as Louis Armstrong (2). Toured with Red Nichols the following year, then worked again with McKenzie and Mound City Blue Blowers (6), in 1930-1931 and 1933. Played piano on South American cruise with George Carhart Band. Freelanced extensively during the 1930's, with time off for hospitalisation for pancreasitis. Worked at Nick's, NYC (1937), start of a long-term association with club (24). In 1942, organised first-ever televised jam session, and began running own jazz concerts at New York's Town Hall, involving practically all the Dixieland (and others) musicians from the Big Apple. Worked with valve-trombonist Brad Gowans at Nick's in 1943, and brought his guitar into Joe Marsala's big band

(they had worked together on numerous previous occasions). After gigging with trombonist Miff Mole, opened own jazz club, NYC (which changed premises in 1958; closing, finally, in 1967).

Played less frequently at Condon's during 1950's. Undertook brief tours, played residencies in US and Canada. First visit to UK (1957) with own band; toured Japan, Australasia (1964). Underwent serious internal operations (1964-1965). Shared guitar duties with Jim Hall (q.v.) in Roy Eldridge-Kai Winding combo (1970).

Condon's autobiography, *We Called It Music* first published in 1948. Also published: Eddie Condon's *Scrapbook of Jazz* (co-authored by Condon, Hank O'Neal); Eddie Condon's *Treasury of Jazz* (Richard Gehman).

Eddie Condon's status as a performer is, simply, one of a non-soloing rhythm guitarist. Never, at any time, an individualist on his instrument, Condon nevertheless was eminently capable of fine, propulsive playing from within the rhythm section — a fact more easily discernible on later recordings such as (21), (22). But in innumerable record dates from the mid-1930's through until the 1950's, his rhythmic presence is felt as much as heard. To which end he worked alongside a familiar, impressively large group of Condonites who played the kind of jazz that was dearest to the often fiery little man's heart, more often than not under Condon's own leadership, including such as (10), (11), (12), (13), (14), (15), (16), (17). For Eddie Condon's major contribution to the evolution of jazz remains, forever, as a catalyst-leader supreme...

CBS S67273

SELECTED DISCOGRAPHY

1 **That Toddlin' Town — Chicago (1926-1928)** (McKenzie & Condon Chicagoans; Miff Mole; Eddie Condon) PARLOPHONE
2 **The Louis Armstrong Legend** WORLD RECORDS
3 **Recordings Made Between 1930 and 1931** (Mound City Blue Blowers) CBS
4 **Billy Banks & His Rhythmakers** CBS-REALM
5 **Big T's Jazz** (Jack Teagarden) ACE OF HEARTS
6 **Jack Teagarden, Vols. 1,2** RCA VICTOR
7 **Home Cooking** (Bud Freeman) TAX
8 **Chicago Styled** (Bud Freeman) SWAGGIE
9 **Chicagoans In New York** (Bud Freeman) DAWN
10 **We Called It Music** ACE OF HEARTS
11 **The Liederkrantz Sessions (1939-1940)** COMMODORE
12 **Jam Sessions At Commodore** ACE OF HEARTS
13 **Condon A La Carte** ACE OF HEARTS
14 **Commodore Condon, Vol 1** LONDON
15 **Eddie Condon** RARITIES
16 **The Eddie Condon Concerts: Town Hall 1944-45** CHIAROSCURO
17 **Eddie Condon & His All Stars** JAZUM 37, 38
18 **Trombone Scene (Misc.)** LONDON
19 **Great Swing Jam Sessions, Vol. 1** SAGA
20 **The Davison-Brunis Sessions, Vols. 1,2,3** LONDON
21 **Eddie Condon: The Golden Days of Jazz** CBS
22 **Chicago & All That Jazz!** VERVE
23 **Eddie Condon's World of Music** CBS
24 **Nick's New York/April, 1944** (Muggsy Spanier) COMMODORE

LARRY CORYELL

Larry Coryell: Born Galveston, Texas, 1943. Moved with family to State of Washington at age of seven. With rock band at 15. Took some private tuition, although mostly self-taught. Worked in and around Seattle before basing himself in NYC, joining Chico Hamilton (1) in 1966, replacing Gabor Szabor (q.v.). Following period with Free Spirits, gained much international exposure as member of Gary Burton Quartet (1967-1968), touring, recording prolifically. Further wider recognition with flautist Herbie Mann (5), before Coryell put togetehr own band: Foreplay (featuring saxist Steve Marcus, '69). Around the same time recorded superior LP (6) which juxtaposed his individual approach to jazz guitar with that of John McLaughlin's (q.v.) Formed Eleventh House, exciting, extrovert band that gained many admirers, both at home and in overseas territories like Japan and Europe (band played four European tours). Since when, Coryell has toured mostly as a single, except for special concerts with fellow guitarists McLaughlin, Paco DeLucia. In 1975, he and Steve Khan (q.v.) played Carnegie Hall guitar duo. And from the late-1970's, has sometimes been seen and heard in tandem with Philip Catherine (q.v.)

Since his initial 'big-time' break with Chico Hamilton, Larry Coryell has pursued an unswerving course in search of a totally individual style. That he has

Larry Coryell

succeeded is due not only to his passionate dedication to his profession, but also to both his extraordinary technical skills and his ability to incorporate into his playing the precise kind of influences he borrows from those with whom he works. And without at any time losing his individualism, the bespectacled Coryell is often to be heard at peak performances in the company of other especially gifted guitarists. His collaborations with McLaughlin — with or without an additional guitarist — are invariably exciting, marred perhaps only by the occasional excesses that can sometimes materialise when two virtuosi are matched. (6) finds both men close to or at their very best, helped immensely by the Chick Corea-Miroslav Vitous-Billy Cobham rhythm section. Of particular satisfaction: the McLaughlin-Coryell unaccompanied duet on Rene Thomas' *Rene's Theme*. Coryell's contributions to the Burton Quartet have sometimes been undervalued. But although there were times when it seemed that the former's often rock-based offerings might destroy those of the leader, disaster never quite happened. The Burton-Coryell rapport is particularly effective during (2),

Arista Novus AN3024

although (3) runs it very close — most remarkably throughout the title tune of the latter, an astonishing duet. Coryell's playing in company with Catherine has been, if anything, even more consummately compatible. There is very little to choose between (15), (16), (17), with both men near to or at optimum form, using both acoustic and electric guitars. Caught in lower profile, Coryell's responses to Ralph Towner (q.v.) nevertheless help make (20) an eminently satisfying studio get-together.

The Eleventh House Band, while producing much body-level excitement — at most times intensely creative too — nonetheless proved to be somewhat erratic in its overall output. For sheer excitement, (12) is hard to top; for all-round excellence, (9) is probably best representative of Coryell and the Band...

To-day, Larry Coryell's stature as one of the top jazz guitarists extent, is probably best summaried by exceptional recorded statements like (15), (16), (19), (20) and probably finest of all, (4), the talented Texan at his very best.

SELECTED DISCOGRAPHY

1 **The Dealer** (Chico Hamilton) IMPULSE
2 **Duster** (Gary Burton) RCA VICTOR
3 **Lines** (Gary Burton RCA VICTOR
4 **Gary Burton Quartet In Concert** RCA VICTOR
5 **Memphis Underground** (Herbie Mann) ATLANTIC
6 **Spaces** (with John McLaughlin) VANGUARD
7 **Introducing the Eleventh House** VANGUARD
8 **Aspects** (The Eleventh House ARISTA
9 **Level One** (The Eleventh House) ARISTA
10 **Planet End** (Including Eleventh House, John McLaughlin) VANGUARD
11 **Fairyland** PHILLIPS
12 **At The Village Gate** VANGUARD
13 **Barefoot Boy** PHILLIPS
14 **Standing Ovation** ARISTA/NOVUS
15 **Back Together Again** (Alphonse Mouzon, Phillip Catherine) ATLANTIC
16 **Twin-House** (with Phillip Catherine) ATLANTIC
17 **Splendid** (with Phillip Catherine) ATLANTIC
18 **Guitar Player** (two items only) MCA
19 **European Improvisations** MOOD
20 **The Restful Mind** (with Ralph Towner) VANGUARD
21 **Bolero** STRING

BILL DEARANGO

William DeArango: Born Cleveland, Ohio, 1921. Attended Ohio State University. Played with local jazz groups (1939-1942), after interest in jazz-guitar had emerged during high school days. Promising career interrupted by US Army call (1942-1944). Following military service, moved to NYC, playing for a year with Ben Webster combo, on 52nd Street. Fronted own band — which at times also featured vibist Terry Gibbs — that played dated in NYC, Chicago. But in 1948, DeArango retired to Cleveland. Outside of a recording date for Mercury Records in 1954, has remained in obscurity.

The self-imposed retirement of Bill DeArango meant a sad loss for lovers of beautifully played, always tasteful, and eminently creative jazz guitar playing. For DeArango was one

of the first players to respond to the harmonic, rythmic, etc, challenges of bebop. But DeArango — an ESQUIRE New Star award winner in 1946 — stemmed directly from Charlie Christian (q.v.); the Texan remained his inspiration-in-chief.

DeArango's superb articulation and all-round dexterity is documented interestingly on an all-too-short list of recordings, mostly emanating from 1945-1946. Most famous of the sessions is the classic Dizzy Gillespie date for Victor in 1946 (5). DeArango's solo chances were small, but as on *Ol' Man Bebop* and *Anthropology* (especially *Take 2*), his contributions are outstanding. Two dates from May 1946 starring Ben Webster contain further impeccable DeArango solos (4), including a fetching Webster-DeArango duet on *Blues Mr. Brim,* and some lovely double-time picking on *Spang*. Another fine tenorman, Ike Quebec, brings fresh inspiration from the young guitarist (3) at a 1945 session for Savoy. DeArango's one-and-only LP date (from March, 1954) — when he was already in semi-retirement — shows his skills had diminished little since his 52nd Street days. Supported sensitively by a fine rhythm section (pianist John Williams, bassist Teddy Kotick, drummer Art Mardigan), DeArango's single-string playing throughout (6) — particularly on *Alone Together, All God's Chillun Got Rhythm,* and *Dancing On the Ceiling* — is so good that his decision to call it a day, as a full-time pro, is brought even more poignantly into focus.

SELECTED DISCOGRAPHY

1 Swing Classics, Vol. II 1944/45 (Slam Stewart) POLYDOR
2 Six Faces of Jazz (Red Norvo) EMBER
3 The Tenor Sax Album IKE QUEBEC
4 The Big Three (Ben Webster) BOB THIELE MUSIC
5 Dizzy Gillespie, Vol. 1/2 (1946-1949) RCA VICTOR
6 Bill DeArango Quartet EMARCY

AL DiMEOLA

Alan Di Meola: Born Jersey City, New Jersey, 1954. Raised in neighbouring Bergenfield. Started on drums at age five, turning attention to guitar three years later. By his early-teens, had already played in various school bands, using both steel and electric guitars. In those days, played nothing but rock 'n' roll, inspired by the music of the Ventures and such. But Di Meola's first guitar tutor in Bergenfield — a jazz-based player called Robert Aslanian — also showed him jazz guitar techniques, and even a little

Al DiMeola

classical. Which helped map out the route for his eventual playing style and involvement with jazz. Originally, his guitar favourites in jazz were Kenny Burrell (q.v.), Tal Farlow (q.v.). Then, in 1970, heard Larry Coryell (q.v.), on record and in person. Subsequently, met Coryell and the pair became friends. After high school, enrolled at Berklee School of Music, Boston, leaving for a few months at one period to gig with Barry Miles Quintet. Studied guitar, arranging, etc, at Berklee. In 1974, Chick Corea offered Di Meola job with Return To Forever — without even auditioning him — with whom he subsequently toured and recorded. Three years later, was placed third in DOWN BEAT Annual Readers' Poll, behind only Joe Pass (q.v.), George Benson (q.v.) At same time, GUITAR PLAYER magazine selected Di Meola as Best Guitarist, and then current recording (9) as Best LP of the Year (album sold in excess of 700,000 copies). By which time, Di Meola's reputation had reached top-rock proportions — indeed, that reputation was primarily in rock field.

Since when the quiet, bespectacled performer has maintained impressive all-round popularity, enhanced further by prestigious triple-threat concerts with John McLaughlin (q.v.), Paco DeLucia.

With his undoubted all-round skills, there is little or nothing at which to complain about Al DiMeola as a guitarist. The only question mark, for some, is whether or

not he is a convincing performer within a conventional jazz format. And there have been times in the past when he has tended to substitute sheer technique for more basic jazz requirements. Still, there is no doubt about his ability to play. During his tenure with Return To Forever, he displayed commendable restraint, and his playing with that band — especially with regard to (1), (2) — is uniformly fine. Working with a musician as extrovert as Stomu Yamashta (5), (6), (7), brought forth an understandably extra emotional response from Di Meola. Working in conjunction with McLaughlin and DeLucia (15), (16), has elicited a combination of his finest fretting and his occasional excesses.

Di Meola's own recorded work comprises, in the main, a series of beautifully-recorded, finely-conceived albums — like (9), (11), (12), (14), and particularly (13), a really first-rate concert performance. There have been times, however, when his studio recordings have promised more than they actually produced. Hopefully, his satisfying playing on his most recent albums, (13), (14), is concrete evidence that a much-needed maturity has arrived. . . .

SELECTED DISCOGRAPHY

1 **Where Have I Known You Before? (Return To Forever)** POLYDOR
2 **Ny Mystery (Return To Forever)** POLYDOR
3 **Romantic Warrior (Return To Forever)** CBS
4 **Touchstone (with Chick Corea)** WARNER BROS
5 **Go (Stomu Yamashta's Go)** ARISTA
6 **Go Live From Paris (Stomu Yamashta's Go)** ISLAND
7 **Go Too (Stomu Yamashta's Go)** ARISTA
8 **Land of the Midnight Sun** CBS
9 **Elegant Gypsy** CBS
10 **Casino** CBS
11 **Splendid Hotel** CBS
12 **Electric Rendezvous** CBS
13 **Tour De Force "Live"** CBS
14 **Scenario** CBS
15 **Friday Night In San Francisco (with John McLaughlin, Paco DeLucia)** CBS
16 **Passion, Grace & Fire (with John McLaughlin, Paco DeLucia)** CBS

EDDIE DURHAM

Edward Durham: Born San Marcos, Texas, 1906. Comes from intensely musical family. Father played country fiddle. Eddie — who flirted with violin, clarinet, before deciding on guitar, trombone — played with Durham Brothers Band — comprising also two brothers, two cousins. Eldest brother Joseph taught him rudiments of musicianship. Started on four-string guitar. Studied at US School of Music, with brothers, including theory, composition, etc. First professional work with Doug. Moyne's vaudeville tent shows. Then, played with variety of leading Middle West bands (including 101 Ranch Circus Band, Edgar Battle, Jesse Stone, Terrence Holder, Walter Page), working as trombonist, guitarist, writer.

Joined Bennie Moten's celebrated orchestra (1929-1933), where the Eddie Durham solo guitar first heard on record, probably at its best on *I Wanna Be Around My Baby All the Time* (1). Subsequently, associated with Cab Calloway, Andy Kirk, Willie Bryant, before joining legendary Jimmie Lunceford Orchestra. Signed primarily as trombonist-writer, also heard on guitar on recordings like *Bird of Paradise* (2), *Avalon, Hittin' the Bottle* (both 3), *Put On Your Old Grey Bonnet* (4). At this time, became recognised as one of pioneers in jazz of amplified guitar. With Count Basie Orchestra (1937-1938), working in like vein. Featured occasionally on solo electric guitar — as during Basie recording of Durham's own *Time Out*. Thereafter, became involved principally as composer-arranged for name big bands like Glenn Miller, Artie Shaw, Ina Ray Hutton, Jan Savitt. Put together own big band (1940). Between 1941-1943, toured regularly with all-female International Sweethearts of Rhythm (he also fronted own all-girl unit later). Toured with Cavalcade of Jazz (1947); directed band for singers Wynonie Harris, Larry Darnell (1952-1953). During following two decades, remains active, both as writer, player, frequently leading own small bands, or working solo. Featured with tenorist Buddy Tate for a while, then during mid-1970's, co-led combo with trumpeter Franc Williams, playing mostly trombone.

In more recent years, Eddie Durham has reactivated his six-string acoustic, to the delight of a whole new generation of jazz-guitar freaks. His basically warm, simple style — on acoustic or electric — remains a pleasurable listening experience. Stylistically, he has changed little, if at all. And on electric, one can easily understand how he must have influenced the teenage Charlie Christian (q.v.). His all-too-frequent guitar-featured recordings of recent years, (7), (8), continue to tell much about his background as his actual approach to picking. But his finest on-record legacy remains encapsulated at a classic Lester Young/Kansas City Six date from 1938 (6), especially on titles such as *Countless Blues* and *I Know That You Know*.

SELECTED DISCOGRAPHY

1 **Bennie Moten's Kansas City Orchestra, Vol. 5** RCA VICTOR
2 **Rhythm Is Ous Business (1934-1935) (Jimmie Lunceford)** MCA

3 Harlem Shout (1936-1936) (Jimmie Lunceford) MCA
4 For Dancers Only (1936-1937) (Jimmie Lunceford) MCA
5 The Best of Count Basie 1937-1938 MCA
6 Kansas City Six & Five (1938) (with Lester Young, et al) COMMODORE
7 Eddie Barefield RCA VICTOR
8 Eddie Durham RCA VICTOR

HERB ELLIS

Herb Ellis

Mitchell Herbert Ellis: Born Farmersville, Texas, 1921. Began on banjo, but soon fell in love with sound of guitar. A yearning to become a full-time professional guitarist really took shape during his period at the North Texas State College (where he also met future jazz talents such as Jimmy Giuffre, Gene Roland, Harry Babasin). After studies, first worked with Glen Gray's Casa Loma Orchestra (1944); following year started a three-year stint with Jimmy Dorsey. First gained national prominence as a member of the widely respected Soft Winds instrumental-vocal trio, with whom he recorded, as well as part-composing *Detour Ahead* and *I Told Ya I Love Ya Now Get Out* — two of group's best-remembered feature numbers. Biggest single break came when Ellis took place of Barney Kessel (q.v.) with Oscar Peterson Trio (1953). Toured with Peterson, and Jazz At the Philharmonic — visiting Europe several times — until leaving in '58. Toured, next, with Ella Fitzgerald for four years. During early 1960's, was seen and heard on two noted US TV shows — Steve Allen Show (wiht pianist Donn Trenner), Regis Philbin Show (with vibist Terry Gibbs). Later, worked in same media on other popular TV shows, headlined by Joey Bishop, Della Reese, Merv Griffin. From 1972-1974, deserted studio work to play ever-increasing number of concerts, club dates, college seminars and recordings. For a while worked in two-guitar duo format with Joe Pass (q.v.), later doing same with Barney Kessel. In more recent times, has toured/recorded extensively with Great Guitars (with Charlie Byrd (q.v.), Kessel).

One of the finest guitarists to emerge from the 1940's, Herb Ellis' main strengths continue to be his natural ability with blues and his strong, rhythmic approach, something that is apparent whether he is playing bebop-out-of-Christian single-string lines, or in a firmly percussive chordal style. Certainly, when the Great Guitarists triumvirate is playing tout ensemble, (20), (21), (22), (23), it is invariably Ellis who projects with maximum impact.

Technically, Ellis' is a superior talent — as aural reference to any of a string of Peterson Trio LPs on which he appears amply testifies; especially with regard to some of the whirlwind tempos favoured by the pianist — (2), (3), (8). With Peterson, too, Ellis worked prolifically inside the recording studio, both as part of the Trio's own recorded output, and as a member of what amounted to a houseband for impresario Norman Granz, in support of other top talents, such as Ben Webster (6), Stan Getz (4), (5), Sonny Stitt (7). And Ellis' work with Ella Fitzgerald — including (8), (9) — was never less than wholly supportive.

Herb Ellis' own recordings have tended often to find him in the company of a selection of other guitarists, such as Charlie Byrd (25), Freddie Green (29), Joe Pass (26), (27), (28), Barney Kessel (30), Laurindo Almeida (24), or in company with top non-guitar-playing artists of the calibre of those previously mentioned, together with others like Ray Brown (32), Jimmy Giuffre (10), Stuff Smith (16), *et al.*

Throughout all his musical ventures — on-record or otherwise — Ellis evidences the kind of strong consistency and lasting commitment that has made him something of a legend amongst guitarists. Not in any way an innovator, simply a well-seasoned pro of lasting quality....

SELECTED DISCOGRAPHY

1 Jack Teagarden (with Jack Teagarden, Louis Armstrong, et al) QUEEN-DISC Q-012
2 A Night On the Town (Oscar Peterson) VERVE
3 Oscar Peterson Trio At the Stratford Festival VERVE
4 Stan Getz & The Oscar Peterson Trio VERVE
5 Jazz Giants (with Stan Getz, Gerry Mulligan, et al) VERVE
6 Soulville (Ben Webster, Oscar Peterson)

VERVE

7 Sittin' In (Sonny Stitt, Oscar Peterson) VERVE
8 J.A.T.P. In Tokyo (Ella Fitzgerald, Oscar Peterson, et al) VERVE
9 Clap Hands Here Comes Charlie! (Ella Fitzgerald) VERVE
10 Giuffre Meets Ellis (with Jimmy Giuffre) VERVE
11 Softly, But With That Feeling VERVE
12 Nothing But The Blues (with Stan Getz, Roy Eldridge) VERVE
13 Thank You, Charlie Christian VERVE
14 Ellis In Wonderland COLUMBIA
15 The Midnight Roll EPIC
16 Herb Ellis & Stuff Smith: Together! EPIC
17 Man With a Guitar DOT
18 Hello, Herbie! (with Oscar Peterson) MPS
19 A Pair To Draw (with Ross Tompkins) CONCORD JAZZ
20 Great Guitars, Vols. 1,2 CONCORD JAZZ
21 After You've Gone (Great Guitars) CONCORD JAZZ
22 Great Guitars At Charlie's Georgetown CONCORD JAZZ
23 Great Guitars At The Winery CONCORD JAZZ
24 Bossanova Time (with Laurindo Almeida) COLUMBIA
25 Guitar/Guitar (with Charlie Byrd) COLUMBIA
26 Seven Come Eleven (with Joe Pass) CONCORD JAZZ
27 Jazz Concord (with Joe Pass) CONCORD JAZZ
28 Two For the Road (with Joe Pass) CONCORD JAZZ
29 Rhythm Willie (with Freddie Green) CONCORD JAZZ
30 Poor Butterfly (with Barney Kessel) CONCORD JAZZ
31 Guitar Player (two items only, with Barney Kessel) MCA
32 Soft Show (with Ray Brown) CONCORD JAZZ

CHRISTIAN ESCOUDE

Christian Escoudé: Born Angouleme, France, 1947. Started on guitar at very young age. First professional gigs with provincial dance bands. First jazz experience with Aime Barrelli band in Monte Carlo. Began to make impact on French jazz scene following period spent in company of organist Eddy Louiss, principally at Jazz-Inn club, once sited at rue de Beaujolais Palais Royal. Of gipsy origin, not surprisingly one of Escoudé's premier guitar influences remains Django Reinhardt (q.v.) — although American Jimmy Raney (q.v.) was first player to make a profound impact.

Since the late-1960's, his reputation has continued to soar. Won the Prix Django as French Jazz Musician of the Year (1976), and recorded with American greats John Lewis, Charlie Haden two years later. Fellow guitarists have been singing his praises during past decade or so.

Philip Catherine (q.v.) has called him 'the best guitarist in Europe'. Larry Coryell (q.v.) raves: 'He's fantastic. And he's getting better all the time'. Escoudé and Coryell have worked together in concert on several occasions, including wholly memorable gigs in Austria and Switzerland in 1983. And if proof were required of his ability to hold his own in even the stiffest company, that proof was given during a three-guitar concert involving Escoudé, Coryell, and John McLaughlin (q.v.), which took place in Japan a while back. Nevertheless, Christian Escoudé remains a shadowy figure to North American and British fans. Their only contact with his work has come via his mostly French-originated recordings that have appeared since the mid-1970's. These recordings show his ability to move into different areas of jazz expression, using both electric and acoustic instruments. His playing with Confluence, (3), (5), indicates an awareness of the importance of ensuring that the group element is preserved, and not marred by any excess individualism.

His collaboration with bass maestro Charlie Haden (7) is a total success, for both the individual contributions and as a well-nigh perfect bass-guitar duo. It is of particular interest, too, in so far as it is an all-acoustic session — and all but one cut is associated with Reinhardt in one way or another. The great man is remembered with obvious fondness, yet Escoudé, thankfully, does not resort to any totally unnecessary plagiarism. His acoustic tone is particularly pleasing — as evidenced most notably on *Nuages* and *Bolero*. And the long, sweeping runs he uses during both *Nuages* and John Lewis' equally enduring

All Life AL 001

Django are executed with flawless technique. (8), with Haden replaced by Alby Cullaz, is a similar bass-and-guitar-only date (with some tasteful overdubbing on a few tracks). Apart from an astonishingly vibrant solo on *Airegin*, the real highlight is Escoudé's unaccompanied interpretation of another Reinhardt classic, *Melodie au Crepescule*. Just how naturally he can move away from the Reinhardt-Raney influences can be judged by first-rate original solos like *Quiet Waltz* (10) and *Dolores* (11).

SELECTED DISCOGRAPHY

1 Steve Potts Band UN-DEUX-TROIS
2 Reunion MUSICA
3 Quatre Voyages: Confluence RCA
4 Les Quatres Elements MUSICA
5 Arkham CONFLUENCE
6 Libra (Michel Graillier, Christian Escoudé) MUSICA
7 Gitane (Charlie Haden, Christian Escoudé) ALL LIFE
8 Christian Escoudé & Alby Cullaz RED RECORDS
9 Return RED RECORDS
10 Gipsy's Morning JMS
11 Christian Escoudé Group Featuring Toots Thielemans JMS
12 Not Much Noise (Mike Zwerin) SPOTLITE

GEORGE FREEMAN

George Freeman. Born Chicago. Comes from a jazz family — father a frustrated piano-player; brothers Bruz, drums, Earl Lavon 'Von', tenor-sax, have fine reputations in the jazz world. George — youngest of Freeman brothers — inspired to take up guitar after hearing T-Bone Walker at local Rhumboogie Club. Inside three months he was playing — and with fair degree of efficiency. Brother Von helped in basic music tuition. George joined brothers in family band that gigged in Chicago, then played first out-of-town gig with combo co-led by trumpeter Joe Morris, tenorist Johnny Griffin. Although Freeman wrote a popular number for this outfit, he wasn't oversold on its basically R&B policy. Returned home to continue gigging with Von.

Stayed in Windy City until 1959 when he went on the road with Sil Austin; also toured with singer Jackie Wilson. Back to jazz with two important jobs with jazz organists — Wild Bill Davis, Richard 'Groove' Holmes. By which time he was in NYC — although marriage meant a further move, to California. But the latter State's often sunny climes could not compensate for certain problems for GF — personal and musical.

Back with Holmes, touring, recording for 16 months. Then — back to Chicago. There, formed own organ trio, working for some months in local clubs. Also did fine work in support of visiting jazz heavyweights. After Von Freeman came off road with the Treniers, brothers gigged regularly together, again. Following a Chicago concert, working in support band for Gene Ammons, joined the tenorist's band; also taping a TV *Just Jazz* with Ammons. Ranks his most unforgettable experience — jamming in Chicago with the one-and-only Charlie Parker (1).

George Freeman's is not exactly the most fashionable name in jazz circles. But his part-neglect is unfortunate. For Freeman has a more-than-competent technique, backed by an impressive drive and a natural affiliation for the blues — Freeman rates Parker as his biggest influence in this latter area. His decision — like brother Von — to stay in Chicago for the past 15-odd years lessens his ability to make more friends, musically speaking. He has an enviable penchant to fit into practically any jazz context. He doesn't tend to sound, like some guitar players, overwhelmed in an organ-based situation, as recordings such as (4) demonstrate impressively. He sounds not at all insignificant in the presence of majestic soloists such as Ammons and Sonny Stitt (2). And during his all-too-few personal record dates, he manages to produce variation in both repertoire and performance. The thoroughly pleasing (3) probably remains his best recorded legacy thus far.

SELECTED DISCOGRAPHY

1 One Night In Chicago (Charlie Parker) SAVOY
2 You Talk That Talk! (Gene Ammons, Sonny Stitt) PRESTIGE
3 New Improved Funk PEOPLE
4 Fly Dude (Jimmy McGriff) PEOPLE

BARRY GALBRAITH

Joseph Barry Galbraith: Born Pittsburgh, Pennsylvania, 1919. Yet another self-taught guitarist who became in his lifetime something of a guitarist's guitarist. A player of infinite all-round qualities, whose playing was always high on good taste; fleet, elegant and never lacking in swing. Sadly, perhaps, Galbraith was to spend much of his career inside a variety of studios, helping enhance the efforts of innumerable others — TV, radio, recordings — often much less talented than he. Immediately in demand during first year of professional activity (1941), working with bands of Red Norvo, Teddy Powell, Babe Russin. First significant gig, though came (also in '41) with the style-setting orchestra of Claude Thornhill (1). Stayed with Thornhill until accepted offer to join another big band — this one led by Hal McIntyre ('42). Career was interrupted by service with US Army (1943-1946). It was back with Thornhill, once back in civvy street (1946-1947). Then,

came the first lengthy spell, starting in 1947, which found him working extensively as an anonymous studio sideman first, for NBC, then for CBS. During 1950's/1960's played very few out-of-studio gigs — indeed, it has been said he probably was most recorded session guitar player in New York City. At start of 1970's, became involved in much private teaching, also accepting faculty membership at the City College, CUNY.

It says much for Barry Galbraith's deep interest in jazz that, despite his years of virtual self-incarceration inside the studios, whenever the opportunity presented itself to participate in that genre he acquitted himself splendidly. Not that Galbraith was exactly an over-recorded soloists. But whether working for George Russell (2), Coleman Hawkins, J.J. Johnson and other notables (6), in a more experimental vein, for saxist/clarinettist/writer Hal McKusick (3), or even as rhythm-guitar support to Tal Farlow (8), his personal contributions were never less than superb. And when he did get what can be said to be something of a personal showcase — as with Gil Evans' dedicatory *Barry's Tune* (7), or with an equally rare event a Galbraith record date (9) — his playing contains that innate quality of music-making that is made to last.

Although his was never a fashionable name, at any time of a nonetheless distinguished career, Galbraith's death, from cancer in 1963, was an occasion of real sadness — and not just to his fellow guitarits either . . .

SELECTED DISCOGRAPHY

1 The Memorable Claude Thornhill COLUMBIA
2 The Jazz Workshop (George Russell) RCA
3 East Coast Jazz No. 8 (Hal McKusick) BETHLEHEM
4 Manhattan Jazz Septette (Hal McKusick) CORAL
5 Big Band Boogie (Will Bradley, Johnny Guarnieri RCA VICTOR
6 The Hawk Flies MILESTONE
7 Into the Hot (Gil Evans) IMPULSE
8 The Tal Farlow Album VERVE
9 Guitar & the Wind DECCA

HANK GARLAND

Hank Garland: Born Orangeburg, South Carolina, 1930. The story of Hank Garland, jazz guitarist, is short — and a story of what might have been. For ex-banjoist Garland's appearance on the jazz scene — at the start of the 1960's — seemed to presage the start of a second, perhaps even important career. Garland had already established himself on the Nashville country scene, both as a touring musician who never lacked versatility or technical skills, and a much-in-demand studio musician of enviable dependability. Garland had been playing since late-1940's, when he

starred with Paul Howard Orchestra. About which time he discovered jazz and, deeply committed though he became to country music, quickly discovered that jazz was his first love . . . like many other country-based players. Thus, Garland fulfilled his country obligations by day, playing jazz by night. But tragedy struck. Shortly after cutting his last jazz LP (3) — with the fledgling Gary Burton also present — Garland was involved in serious automobile accident. As a result, his injuries left him disabled, and unable to play guitar again. A most promising new career, in jazz, was thus curtailed.

Just how brilliant a guitarist Garland could be is evidenced by his contributions to the pitifully few jazz recordings he made. There is much to admire in his playing throughout (1), but it is (2) — his one-and-only personal record date — that is the proof-positive statement of his undoubted uniqueness as a jazz player. His unceasing flow of ideas and long, flexible lines illuminate *All the Things You Are,* and his flawless articulation — at high speed — and all-round superior technique get handsome exposure during *Move.* His blues-playing is amply on display during *Riot Chorus* — arguably the most electrifying example of his playing on record, wherein he synthesises finger-popping technical skills with playing that is suffused with genuine uncontrived heat.

SELECTED DISCOGRAPHY

1 Nashville All Stars RCA VICTOR
2 Jazz Winds From a New Direction COLUMBIA
3 Hank Garland HARMONY

ARV GARRISON

Arvin Charles Garrison: Born Toledo, Ohio, 1922. Arv Garrison was one of a small coterie of young, white jazz guitarists to make a minor impact on the emerging bebop phenomenon in middle-to-late 1940's (including Barney Kessel (q.v.), Bill DeArango (q.v.), Mary Osborne (q.v.), Jimmy Raney (q.v.), and others). Sad to relate, however, as with DeArango, Garrison's equally promising career in top-line jazz circles had, by the 1960's, to all intents and purposes, finished. Garrison's grandmother, a professional pianist, encouraged Arvin at a very young age, to be interested in music. To which end, he started playing ukulele at nine years. Switching to guitar while at church social — self-taught, as with ukulele — teenage Garrison played lodge dances at 12, high school dances until 18. Put together own combo, playing gigs at Kenmore Hotel, Albany, NY ('41). Next, joined Don Seat band, in Pittsburgh. Between 1941-1948, led a succession of own trios — a 1946 trio working under title of Vivien Garry Trio; Vivien, bassist-vocalist, had become Mrs. Arv Garrison.

Arv Garrison's brief period of relative fame took place in the mid-1940's, during which time he demonstrated an effortless guitar style in a variety of jazz company. Including the forward-looking orchestra of Earl Spencer, with whom he made his own favourite recorded solo — on *Five Guitars In Flight*. Recorded with the Vivien Garry Quartet (including also pianist-composer George Handy) in 1945 (1), his solo on *Hot Scotch* is particularly delightful. Trumpeter Howard McGhee used Garrison for an October 1946 recording date for DIAL (3), with the his filligree playing at its best on *Up In Dodo's Room* (Take 2), *Dialated Pupils* (Take 5). But Garrison's single most important recording session — also from '46 — was that with Charlie Parker (2), again on DIAL. Even in the company of top-ranking soloists, Parker, Lucky Thompson, Dodo Marmarosa, Miles Davis, his own contributions to various takes of such classic sides as *Yardbird Suite, A Night In Tunisia, Ornithology* are never less than brilliant.

By the 1950's, Arv Garrison had returned to Toledo — this time, as events transpired, for good — where he lived and played regularly for some time at least. His early death, in 1960, was scarcely the subject for much comment: by this time his had become a forgotten jazz name. Garrison's pitifully small, yet uniformly excellent, recorded legacy tends merely to emphasise the loss his early removal from the jazz scene meant.

SELECTED DISCOGRAPHY

1 **Central Avenue Breakdown, Vol. 1 (Viven Garry)** ONYX
2 **The Essential Charlie Parker** B&C
3 **Trumpet At Tempo (Howard McGhee)** SPOTLITE

GRANT GREEN

Grant Green: Born St. Louis, Missouri, 1931. Early study on guitar while in grade school. Began playing with local St. Louis bands from around 1944, working in both jazz and R&B situations. Which, in turn, led to gigs with name jazzmen, Jimmy Forrest and Brother Jack McDuff (Green always sounded good in the organ-tenor-guitar format). Green moved to New York (1960), creating an immediate favourable impression, both with musicians and critics. Perhaps biggest break, though, was contract with BLUE NOTE RECORDS. With BLUE NOTE, recorded numerous LPs under own name, amongst best of which remain the first (1), plus (2), (3), (4), (5), (10), (13), (14), (15). And his commendable adaptability enabled him to sit in on a variety of other BLUE NOTE sessions, with particularly rewarding results, for Green and the others, on albums like those headlined by such as tenorists Stanley Turrentine (19), Hank Mobley (20), Ike Quebec (21), Harold Vick

Grant Green

(22), altoist Lou Donaldson (23), (24), pianist Horace Parlan (26). Green's excellence alongside jazz organists is likewise amply evidenced on other BLUE NOTE recordings, such as those with John Patton (27), Brother Jack McDuff (3), Don Wilkerson (28). In 1962, won DOWN BEAT Jazz Critics' Poll (Talent Deserving Wider Recognition).

Continued to lead own groups in and around NYC, but was off the jazz scene for most of 1967-1969 due to major personal problem. Performed music for soundtrack of movie *The Final Comedown*. By 1974, was living, working in Detroit, but it was back in New York, in 1979, that he died.

Grant Green's guitar playing contained a warmth and deep appreciation for the blues, both aspects never being absent, no matter what the musical context. His was a basically straight-ahead approach to jazz guitar — no frills, no superfluous embroidery. Tonally, he produced a gorgeously smooth and essentially warm sound, and his jazz phraseology was both mellifluous and unabrasive. It could be said that Green tended to be over-recorded during his most hectic days of the 1960's, and it is true that first time round some of his albums tended to be dismissed by certain of the critics who had once heralded his appearance on the New York scene with hosannahs. But listened to

retrospectively, by far the major part of his recorded work bears testimony to a particular talent whose premature death, at 47, robbed jazz guitar of a really first-rate performer.

Grant Green

SELECTED DISCOGRAPHY

1 Grant's First Stand BLUE NOTE
2 Green Street BLUE NOTE
3 Grandstand BLUE NOTE
4 Sunday Mornin' BLUE NOTE
5 The Latin Bit BLUE NOTE
6 Feelin' The Spirit BLUE NOTE
7 Am I Blue BLUE NOTE
8 Idle Moments BLUE NOTE
9 Talkin' About BLUE NOTE
10 Grant Green Quartet (with Hank Mobley, et al) BLUE NOTE
11 Street of Dreams BLUE NOTE
12 Goin' West BLUE NOTE
13 Live At the Lighthouse BLUE NOTE
14 Shades of Green BLUE NOTE
15 Alive BLUE NOTE
16 Solid BLUE NOTE
17 Nigeria BLUE NOTE
18 Green Blues MUSE
19 Up At Minton's, Vols. 1,2 (Stanley Turrentine) BLUE NOTE
20 Work Out (Hank Mobley) BLUE NOTE
21 Blue & Sentimental (Ike Quebec) BLUE NOTE
22 Steppin' Out (Harold Vick) BLUE NOTE
23 Natural Soul (Lou Donaldson) BLUE NOTE
24 Good Gracious! (Lou Donaldson) BLUE NOTE
25 Two Souls In One (Lou Donaldson) BLUE NOTE
26 Up & Down (Horace Parlan) BLUE NOTE
27 The Way I Feel (John Patton) BLUE NOTE
28 Shoutin' (Don Wilkerson) BLUE NOTE
29 Cantaloupe Woman VERVE
30 Iron City COBBLESTONE

TINY GRIMES

Lloyd 'Tiny' Grimes: Born Newport News, Virginia, 1916. Played drums in Huntington High School band, plus some local gigs, before working as pianist, dancer in Washington, DC 1935, situation continuing until '39, including residency at New York's Rhythm Club in '38). After which, started working on guitar. Eight months later, was featuring his amplified instrument as part of The Cats & A Fiddle, leaving in '41 to work in California. Where he joined the Art Tatum Trio, staying until '44. Then, led own trio at the Tondelayo Club, NYC. Put together his own Rocking Highlanders, working in New York, Cleveland, etc., during late-1940's. Spent long periods touring with other combos during 1950's — still playing four-string guitar — including lengthy Philadelphia residencies. Played memorable season at Village Gate, NYC ('62). Inactive through illness, but returned to regular gigging (late-1966). Toured France, with organist Milt Buckner (1968), and again, two years later (with pianist Jay McShann). Played successful seasons during the 1970's at New York joints like the Cookery and the West End Cafe. Played dates with the Countsmen, and also with pianist Earl Hines (1972). Since when, has continued to tour as solo act — including further trips to Europe — and to lead own small combos in the US.

Tiny Grimes, as the late jazz critic Hugues Panassie would no doubt agree, sometimes tends to be overlooked and neglected when assessing the better jazz guitarists through the years. True, he is no fast-fingered magician with awe-inspiring harmonic sense. But in his own very basic way, Grimes is a great player. Certainly, he could teach many of the players with far superior techniques a lot about basic, raw swing and drive. And as a blues-player he has very few peers.

After several years of dues-paying, it was Grime's association with extraordinary Art Tatum which finally brought Grimes to widespread prominence. He proved to be the perfect foil to Tatum's piano pyrotechnics, yet as the records they made together illustrate interestingly, including (1), (2), (3) he never seemed too bothered with the kind of whirlwind tempos the great man often chose. After leaving the Tatum Trio, Grimes became a familiar figure on the New York scene. It was Grimes who asked Charlie Parker to play at a 1945 record date, (6), that

demonstrated the fundamental difference between bebop and Grimes' mainstream style. Grimes' approach to jazz was ideal for a Billie Holiday session, (7), with no stylistic differences present.

As the years rolled by, Grimes' was not always a prolific recording name. But when he did record — as with a trio of hard-swinging, timeless Prestige-Swingville albums: (9), (10), (11) — the music was charged with red-hot excitement and the sheer joy of playing. With Grimes' plangent guitar adding its own bite to first-rate contributions by luminaries like Coleman Hawkins (9), J.C. Higginbotham and Eddie 'Lockjaw' Davis (8), and Ray Bryant (8), (10). Grimes' best playing on these LPs probably is during *Callin' the Blues* and *Blue Tiny* (8), and the splendid *Tiny Bean* (9). Of more recent vintage, (13) remains his finest recorded work.

SELECTED DISCOGRAPHY

1 **Art Tatum Masterpieces** MCA
2 **Art Tatum: The V-Discs** BLACK LION
3 **Masters of Jazz, Vol. 3: Art Tatum** CAPITOL
4 **Jazz 44 (Cozy Cole)** BLACK & BLUE
5 **Swing Classics, Vol. 1 (1944/45) (Cozy Cole)** POLYDOR
6 **Charlie Parker/The Complete Savoy Sessions** SAVOY
7 **Billie Holiday: 1943-1951-1954** CAPITOL
8 **Callin' the Blues** PRESTIGE/SWINGVILLE
9 **Blue Groove** PRESTIGE/SWINGVILLE
10 **Tiny In Swingville** PRESTIGE/SWINGVILLE
11 **Jam Sessioon At Swingville (Coleman Hawkins, J.C. Higginbotham, et al)** PRESTIGE/SWINGVILLE
12 **An Evening With Earl Hines** VOGUE
13 **Profoundly Blue** MUSE/BLACK & BLUE

JERRY HAHN

Jerry Donald Hahn: Born Alma, Nebraska, 1940. Son of a guitarist, studied at Wichita University, Kansas, where he also played first jobs. Moved on to San Francisco, acquiring work in hotels, studios. First major exposure — as member of exciting, freewheeling John Handy Quartet (1964) that stole most of rave notices at 1965 Monterey Jazz Festival. Stayed with altoist until 1967. Toured with 5th Dimension vocal quartet (1968). Recorded, toured (including US, Japan, Europe), appeared at Carnegie Hall with Gary Burton Quartet (1968-1969). Formed own Jerry Hahn Brotherhood ('70), making innumerable Stateside appearances, visiting Bahamas, and cutting one LP. Toured further with another own quartet (1972-1975). With effect from 1972, became full-time professor at Wichita State University; also became clinician for C.G. Cohn, the instrument manufacturers. And between 1974-1975, wrote regular, well-informed monthly column for GUITAR PLAYER magazine.

Jerry Hahn remains a fine, all-round-accomplished guitarist, with admirable technique — but someone who hasn't really fulfilled his early potential with Handy and Burton. Hahn's period with the former is documented best of all by (1), his playing style more or less fully-developed. That he continued to grow can be heard by recourse to (3), (4), and particularly (2), latter containing one of his best recorded solos on *Wichita Breakdown*, a collaboration between Hahn and his then employer.

There is much good music on practically all Hahn's recordings, without any one ever likely to be considered amongst the all-time great jazz-guitar albums. Best of these is (6), a quintet date, that contains his most consistent series of performances, but both (5) and (8) have their moments.

SELECTED DISCOGRAPHY

1 **John Handy: Recorded Live At the Monterey Jazz Festival** CBS
2 **Country Roads & Other Places (Gary Burton)** RCA VICTOR
3 **Throb (Gary Burton)** ATLANTIC
4 **Good Vibes (Gary Burton)** ATLANTIC
5 **Brotherland** COLUMBIA
6 **Jerry Hahn Quintet** ARHOOLIE
7 **Are-Be-In** CHANGES
8 **Moses** FANTASY

ALLAN HOLDSWORTH

Allan Holdsworth: Born Bradford, Yorkshire, 1948. Did not become interested in guitar-playing until 17. First instrument, second-hand acoustic model; acquired first electric guitar at 19. Worked first pro gig with Glen South dance band in Sunderland, but mostly employed as factory hand. Gigged in Sunderland for about three years, and also fronted first own rock combo. With South band in Manchester for six months. First jazz involvement — still playing rock-style guitar — with Graham Collier Band at Musicians' Union clinic.

Moved to London (1972). Played with drummer Jon Hiseman's Tempest (1) — for year, then London pub gigs. Made first jazz broadcasts with pianist Pat Smythe, also appearing with Smythe at Ronnie Scott Club. Joined Soft Machine (1974), remaining for two years; recording (2) — and touring US, UK, Europe. Gained further international exposure as member of drummer Tony Williams New Lifetime, working primarily in the States. Then, played with another top British rock band, Gong (1977). Became member of drummer Bill Bruford's co-operative rock-jazz outfit (8), in '78, revisiting US. Put together own IOU band before deciding, in 1982, to move permanently to the States. Has established reputation as one of US' top jazz-

rock players, his Stateside reputation is far greater than in his home country.

Allan Holdsworth is a notable exception — a respected rock guitarist who established himself firmly in that area, before emerging as a potent contributor to jazz. His rock-jazz ambivalence is apparent during his recordings with Tempest (1), Soft Machine (2), and Gong (6). But his real development as a jazzman came with his soaring solo work with Lifetime (3), (4). His playing throughout an LP by violinist Jean-Luc Ponty (7) is equally fine.

Just how far Holdsworth had developed can be judged by (9), which places his keening guitar in the company of pianist Gordon Beck. A further date with Beck (10), produced almost equally satisfactory results. (11), his first solo LP, doesn't really do justice to his talents, but (12), with all the material written by Holdsworth, demonstrates that he looks likely to become one of the significant jazz-guitar figures of the 1980's.

Warner Bros 7599-23959-1

SELECTED DISCOGRAPHY

1 Tempest (Tempest) BRONZE
2 Bundles (Soft Machine) HARVEST
3 Believe It (Tony William's Lifetime) CBS
4 Million Dollar Legs (Tony William's Lifetime) CBS
5 Belladonna (Ian Carr's Nucleus) VERTTIGO
6 Gazeuse! GONG
7 Enigmatic Ocean (Jean-Luc Ponty) ATLANTIC
8 Feels So Good (Bill Bruford) POLYDOR
9 The Things You See (with Gordon Beck) JMS
10 Sunbird (Gordon Beck) JMS
11 Velvet Darkness CTI
12 Road Games WARNER BROS
13 Metal Fatigue WARNER BROS
14 Allan Holdsworth, I.O.U. (Allan Holdsworth)

BARNEY KESSEL

Barney Kessel: Born Muskogee, Oklahoma, 1923. Mostly self-taught, beginning on guitar from age 12. Music-mad young Kessel sold newspapers in order to buy his first instrument.

By 14, was only white musician in otherwise all-black Muskogee band. First great thrill — meeting, playing with Charlie Christian (q.v), the man who was to become, almost at once and thereafter, his principal influence. Left Oklahoma and Mid West to seek jazz chances in California, soon became a familiar, boyish figure on the Los Angeles jazz scene. By 1943, was good enough to take guitar chair in Chico Marx Orchestra (directed by Ben Pollack) touring for about a year. Then, back to LA, for more local gigging and jamming. Participated in classic, award-winning jazz movie *Jammin' the Blues* — single honour for a comparative unknown youngster. Worked with big bands of Charlie Barnet (1945), Hal McIntyre (1945), Artie Shaw (1946). Recorded with Charlie Parker (1947), then undertook much West Coast freelance work, especially in radio. Spent some time with Oscar Peterson Trio (1952-1953), touring with Jazz At the Philharmonic. Appointed musical director for Bob Crosby TV Show (1954), and spent just over year as A&R chief (pop music) for VERVE RECORDS. Visited Venezuela ('57), playing with various local bands. Spent even more time freelancing, on radio, TV, recording dates, in latter part of 1950's. During early-1960's, took some time off from his continuing freelance activities to undertake nightclub work. Continued to appear on major TV shows, such as *Hollywood Palace, Man from UNCLE,* etc.

Emerged from studios for more live performances, including European tour, as part of Guitar Workshop (*avec* Jim Hall, George Benson, Larry Coryell, Elmer Snowden). Moved to London (1969), living, working there and in Europe for 14 months. Returned to LA (late-'70), to resume studio work, and playing gigs with own groups. At this stage, even flirted with certain rock devices for guitar. Spent much of 1970's touring the US — and revisiting Europe, where his work schedule included recording, TV, radio, seminars as well as gigs. Played for rated US TV shows *The Odd Couple, Love American Style*, and also played soundtracks for four Elvis Presley movies. Visited South Africa (1976), also touring with Great Guitars presentation (which also played Kennedy Centre, Carnegie Hall, '74-75).

A prolific award-winner during a distinguished career, Kessel received ESQUIRE Silver Award (1947); won DOWN BEAT'S Readers Poll (1956-1959) and Jazz Critics' Poll (1953-1959); the METRONOME Readers' Poll (1958-1960); and the PLAYBOY Readers Poll (1957-1960).

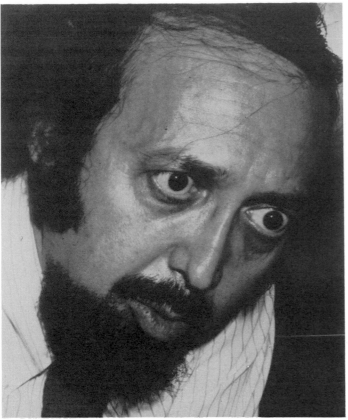

Barney Kessel

Right from the outset of his career proper, Barney Kessel showed an astonishing versatility, fitting in with practically any kind of jazz situation. A superior, natural blues-player, Kessel's tonal quality, like Herb Ellis' (q.v.), redolent of his background. A Christian disciple, right from his earliest records — like (1), (2), (3), (4) — he nevertheless quickly picked up on bebop's artifices, recording with Charlie Parker and Howard McGhee in '47 (30), and jamming with such as Dexter Gordon, Wardell Gray, (3), (5). His sensitivity, good taste has enabled him to supply superb accompaniments for the best singers — (9), (10), with particular reference to (9), that contains two Fitzgerald Kessel duets (*In a Sentimental Mood; Solitude*) that are exquisitely conceived. Kessel's recordings during the 1950's for the CONTEMPORARY label — most notably (12), (13), (16) — involved with a variety of musicians whose admirably catholic approach to jazz has been a Kessel trademark. Likewise, the Poll Winners albums — (14), (15), with bassist Ray Brown, drummer Shelly Manne — produced much delightful, timeless, unpretentious music.

Kessel has retained a consistency in his work since then, although rarely have his records equalled or even surpassed the Contemporaries. Apart from leading own trios, Kessel has worked with mostly modern-mainstream jazzmen, (11), (17), including fellow guitarists like Herb Ellis (23). Although it is true that too often his work as part of Great Guitarists, (26), (27), (28), has tended to lack his

customary sparkle. Of more recent times, (29) is far more successful, hinting perhaps that a solo career (mostly) remains an intriguing — and worthwhile — prospect for someone who has contributed handsomely to jazz-guitar evolution during four decades.

SELECTED DISCOGRAPHY

1 Jammin' With Lester (including Jammin' the Blues) JAZZ ARCHIVES
2 Artie Shaw & His Gramercy Five RCA VICTOR
3 The Hunt (including Dexter Gordon, Wardell Gray, et al) SAVOY
4 Gene Norman Presents Just Jazz (including Lionel Hampton) CORAL
5 Just Bop (Just Bop All Stars) QUEEN-DISC
6 Memorable Concerts (Lionel Hampton) VOGUE
7 JATP Carnegie Hall Concert, 1952 (No. 2) (Oscar Peterson) VERVE
8 The Voice of Jazz, Vols. 6,8 (Billie Holiday) VERVE
9 Ella Fitzgerald Sings the Duke Ellington Songbook Vols. 1,2. VERVE
10 Two Sounds of Sarah Vaughan VOGUE
11 Walkin' With Sweets (Harry Edison, Ben Webster) VERVE
12 To Swing Or Not To Swing CONTEMPORARY
13 Barney Kessel Plays Some Like It Hot CONTEMPORARY
14 Barney Kessel: The Poll Winners CONTEMPORARY
15 Exploring The Scene/Poll Winners CONTEMPORARY
16 Let's Cook CONTEMPORARY
17 Swing That Music (Red Norvo, Ruby Braff, et al) AFFINITY
18 Swinging Easy BLACK LION
19 Blue Soul BLACK LION
20 Just Friends SONET
21 Barney Plays Kessel CONCORD JAZZ
22 Soaring CONCORD JAZZ
23 Poor Butterfly (with Herb Ellis) CONCORD JAZZ
24 Summertime In Montreux BLACK LION
25 Jellybeans CONCORD JAZZ
26 Great Guitars, Vols. 1,2 CONCORD JAZZ
27 Great Guitars At the Winery CONCORD JAZZ
28 Great Guitars At Charlie's Georgetown CONCORD JAZZ
29 Solo CONCORD JAZZ
30 The Essential Charlie Parker B&C

STEVE KAHN

Stephen Khan: Born Los Angeles, 1947. Son of well-known standard pop songwriter Sammy Cahn. Started as drummer with surfing group, the Chantays (1962-1963); guitar came soon afterwards. Switched from psychology major to music major to UCLA, graduating in 1969. To

New York (1970), together with a Gibson Super 400 jazz guitar and David Russell Young acoustic — didn't own solid-body guitar at that time. Became deeply involved with studio work, thanks to enviable reading ability and all-round versatility. Cut LP with Larry Coryell (q.v.), (2), that helped spread a growing reputation as jazz player in and around NYC. That reputation grew after working with Brecker Brothers, (4), (5), and recording with such as Steely Dan (7), Billy Joel (8), Bob James (9).

Steve Khan is one of the most promising jazz guitarists to emerge from the early-1970's. An excellent picker ('I do things with my fingers, but I am primarily a plectrum player', he says), with a superior technique, he can also raise genuine exciting without needing to resort to flashy histrionics. Only during the 1980's is he beginning to find his own voice — he seems to have multifarious influences, including Coryell, John McLaughlin (q.v.), Wes Montgomery (q.v.), John Scofield (q.v.)

Khan's association with Larry Coryell has been a mutually profitable one. The first recording collaboration (2) produced much fine music; if anything, both (1), (3) are even better. His ability to sound at home in a basically jazz-funk bag is illustrated beautifully during both (4), (5), and he sounds good even in heavy jazz company during both volumes of (16). His own recordings together make an interesting documentation of his developing talent. His CBS albums, (10),(11),(12), are all beautifully put together, with Khan showing interesting development as a composer during all three, as well as a real talent in his choice of sidemen. Of particular note is (13), a fine, sensitive, solo-acoustic tribute to Thelonious Monk.

Khan's coming-of-age during the early part of the 1980's is due as much to his obvious satisfaction with his 1981-formed Eyewitness band. Again, his choice of the right kind of colleagues shows real perception on his part. The live (14) is a marvellous example of the Eyewitness quartet operating at high-energy level — and without extravagances — but (15), recorded in '81, is probably the finest example of Khan & Co. thus far. Quite apart from showcasing the leader's constantly-developing guitar-playing, it lays emphasis on the kind of free-sounding interaction that will surely make Eyewitness one of the top guitar-led combos of the decade...

SELECTED DISCOGRAPHY

1 **Two For The Road** (with Larry Coryell) ARISTA
2 **Level One** (with Larry Coryell) ARISTA
3 **Aspects** (with Larry Coryell) ARISTA
4 **Back to Back** (with Brecker Brothers) ARISTA
5 **Don't Stop the Music** (with the Brecker Brothers) ARISTA
6 **Taking Off** (with David Sanborn) WARNER BROS
7 **Gaucho** (with Steely Dan) MCA
8 **The Stranger** (with Billy Joel) CBS
9 **The Genie** (with Bob James) CBS
10 **Tightrope** CBS
11 **The Blue Man** CBS
12 **Arrows** CBS
13 **Evidence** ARISTA/NOVUS
14 **Modern Times** TRIO
15 **Eyewitness** ANTILLES
16 **Montreux Summit, Vols. 1,2** (CBS Jazz All Stars) CBS

EARL KLUGH

Earl Klugh: Born Detroit, Michigan, 1953. First instrument — piano. First guitar age 10. Musically, initial interest was with folk. At 13, heard Chet Atkins and was suitably impressed. Then, was turned on to George Van Eps' seven-string guitar playing. After which he tried to play the same with his own six-string guitar, by moving up a key. Taught music in music store in Detroit. Heard by multi-reedman Yusef Lateef, at 16, playing nylon-string guitar. Lateef, impressed, invited him to play on his *Suite 16* album. Following year met George Benson (q.v.) Latter fascinated by Klugh's classical guitar, encouraged him to work out some duets. Which led, in '73, to Klugh touring with Benson's quarter (Klugh also recorded with Benson).

Further important exposure for his developing talent came with national tour as member of Return To Forever, playing electric guitar. Following which he was to work with singer Flora Purim, and George Shearing. In 1978, appeared together with Benson, Atkins on PBS/TV's *Guitar Summit.* Collaborated with flautist Hubert Laws on film soundtrack music for *How To Beat the High Cost of Living* ('81). Also featured performer throughout John Cassavetes — Billy Dee movie *Marvin & Taig.*

Earl Klugh — who plays a Gibson Chet Atkins guitar, solid body, with nylon strings — has developed interestingly during the past decade into a sensitive, articulate performer, who manages to sound at home both in mainstream jazz and fusion music. His earlier experiences with such as Lateef (1) and Benson (2) has helped, of course; same with his latterday work on record with Bob James (12), (13). But his own numerous recordings chart his progress best of all. The eponymous (3) is as fine an all-round introduction to his talents as any LP. But there is much to admire elsewhere. (9) shows his tender, sensitive side to perfection, and (5) is an admirable example of his finger-style.

In no way is Earl Klugh an innovator on his instrument, but he is likely to show further development during the 1980's and thereafter. It is encouraging too, that he retains a genuine, lasting interest in both acoustic as well as electric guitar.

SELECTED DISCOGRAPHY

1 Suite 16 (Yusef Lateef) ATLANTIC
2 White Rabbit (George Benson) CTI
3 Earl Klugh BLUE NOTE
4 Living Inside Your Love BLUE NOTE
5 Finger Paintings BLUE NOTE
6 Dream Come True UNITED ARTISTS
7 Magic In Your Eyes UNITED ARTISTS
8 Heartstring UNITED ARTISTS
9 Late Night Guitar LIBERTY
10 Crazy For You LIBERTY
11 Low Ride CAPITOL
12 Two of a Kind (Bob James) CAPITOL
13 One on One (Bob James) COLUMBIA
14 How To Beat the High Cost of Living (Hubert Laws) COLUMBIA

CARL KRESS

Carl Kress: Born Newark, New Jersey, 1907. First instrument — piano. Turned to banjo, finally guitar. Gigged with many bands in and around New York, working regularly with Eddie Elkins band. Mainly employed in recording/radio studios during late 1920's, with contracts with many orchestra leaders, including Ray Sinatra, Al Goodman et al. Worked regularly with Dorsey brothers, Frankie Trumbauer, Red Nichols, Paul Whiteman. Made innumerable recordings with these and many others, including guitar duets with Eddie Lang, Dick McDonough, George Barnes. Played with clarinettist Clarence Hutchenrider's Trio (1960). Was a partner in original Onyx Club on 52nd Street. Suffered heart attack while appearing in Reno, Nevada, while appearing with George Barnes, and died almost immediately.

Since around the mid-1920's, the name Carl Kress has been synonymous with jazz guitar playing at its most sophisticated and tasteful. Very much a guitarist's guitarist, Kress is acknowledged as a pioneer of the chord-style — indeed, a master of that genre, and one who has inspired scores of others who have sought, in vain, to emulate his brilliance. Very much a quintessential part of his importance is Kress' unique sound — a sound that is like none other. A sound that he obtains thanks to his unorthodox tuning — instead of the customary E,A,D,G,B,C, Kress tuned his guitar B-flat, F,C,G,A,D.

During the late-1920's, Carl Kress' name was frequently to be bracketed with most of the leading white jazz players, particularly those associated with the New York scene. Whereas many of his contemporaries toured frequently with a variety of jazz or dance bands, Kress' involvement tended to be with record and radio studios (although he was featured for a while with the Paul

Whiteman Orchestra). To which ended his elegant, yet always intensely rhythmic, guitar work graced sessions with bands fronted by such early-jazz figures as saxist Frankie Trumbauer (featuring also Bix Beiderbecke) (4), trombonist Miff Mole (2), trumpeter Red Nichols (1), (5). Regrettably, though, unlike Eddie Lang (q.v.), Kress received few solo opportunities, one notable exception being *S'Wonderful* (6), a delicious example of his by now fully-matured style (in 1936).

Kress' playing never was lacking in humour *Walking Behind Miss Lucy* (a duet with Tony Mottola), *Blonde On the Loose, The Goose From Gander* — all (12), give proof-positive demonstrations of this aspect. And his ability to blend his talent with another guitarist has also made him something of a legend. His 1930's duets with Dick McDonough (q.v.), (9), are beyond reproach; later collaborations with George Barnes (q.v.), (10), and best of all (7), are even more exquisite.

SELECTED DISCOGRAPHY

1 Jazz Holiday (Red Nichols) MCA
2 Miff Mole's Molers 1928-30 PARLOPHONE
3 Bix Beiderbecke: The Studio Groups — 1928 (Frankie Trumbauer) WORLD RECORDS
4 Bix Beiderbecke: The Studio Groups — 1928 (Frankie Trumbauer) WORLD RECORDS
5 Red Nichols & His Five Pennies (1926-1928) MCA CORAL
6 50 Years of Jazz Guitar (Frankie Trumbauer — one number only) COLUMBIA
7 Town Hall Concerts (with George Barnes) UNITED ARTISTS
8 Pioneers of Jazz Guitar YAZOO
9 Guitar Genius In the 1930s (with Dick McDonough) JAZZ ARCHIVES
10 Two Guitars, Vol. 1 (with George Barnes) STASH
11 Something Tender (with Bud Freeman) UNITED ARTISTS
12 Carl Kress: Guitar Stylists CAPITOL
13 Ten Guitar Solots MUSIC MINUS ONE
14 Two Guitars & A Horn (with George Barnes, Bud Freeman) STASH

VOLKER KRIEGEL

Volker Kriegel: Born Frankfurt, Main, West Germany, 1944. Attended high school, where his interest in music really started — although he didn't study subject. In fact, went on to university, taking social sciences. Kriegel maintains he never wanted to become a professional musician, but during high school days played guitar regularly, in a strictly amateur capacity. Gradually slipped into music, he says: 'It was a matter of the number of engagements.

There were so many that I thought that was where I should be...' Helped vibist Dave Pike put together very successful Dave Pike Set (1968), touring four years — throughout Europe, visiting North and South America, Mexico. Then, teamed up with bassist Eberhard Weber to form Spectrum, venture that lasted three years. After which, formed own Mild Maniac Orchestra, featuring also three very young rock-based musicians. Played Newport Jazz Festival (1971), and has played most if not all European jazz festivals during past 15 years.

A self-taught guitar player, Volker Kriegel has continued to develop — unspectacularly, but impressively nevertheless. During the past decade, he has seemingly drawn as much inspiration from the rock field as from jazz *per se* — engendered, no doubt, from his experiences with Mild Maniac Orchestra. His plangent guitar has also added excitement and colour to fellow West German Klaus Doldinger's Jubilee (2), never more emphatically than during (3), where his playing really challenges the leader's own contributions for solo honours. As a member of Peter Herbolzheimer's Jazz Gala Big Band Orchestra (4), Kriegel's solo on the former's *Gentle Mood* demonstrates a restrained, more sensitive side to his work that isn't too often heard.

Summarising his attitude to jazz guitar playing, one of Europe's finest performers explained several years ago: 'My background is actually the classic jazz guitar tradition of Jim Hall, Barney Kessel and Wes Montgomery... I'm not a bebop player, because when I started to make music it was more the time of the Beatles than Charlie Parker's time. I have a deep love for those old jazz styles, but I never wanted to play them'.

As his fine all-round playing on (1) illustrates, most handsomely, Volker Kriegel doesn't need to copy or borrow from anyone. He has long since found his own voice...

SELECTED DISCOGRAPHY

1 Topical Harvest MPS
2 Doldinger Jubilee ATLANTIC
3 Doldinger Jubilee Concert ATLANTIC
4 Jazz Gala (Peter Herbolzheimer) ATLANTIC

MUNDELL LOWE

Mundell Lowe: Born Laurel, Missouri, 1922. Studied with father, a music teacher. Moved, with family to New Orleans at 13. Played first musical jobs there, with Abbie Brunis, Sid Devilla, plus various Bourbon Street jazz combos. To Nashville (1939). Played six months with Pee Wee King on Grand Ole Op'ry radio show. Toured Louisiana, Florida. Worked briefly with Jan Savitt Orchestra before joining US Army (1943). First post-Service gig — with bandleader Ray McKinley (1945-1947). Spent two years with Dave Martin, few months with pianist Ellis Larkins, four weeks with Red Norvo Trio at New York's Bebop City (1949). After which also appeared in pit bands for Broadway musicals — including appearance as actor-guitarist in *Bye Bye Birdie*. Joined NBC staff (1950). Also worked with Sauter-Finegan Orchestra, pianist Billy Taylor, and own quartet. Left NBC (1958) to write for own LP dates.

Undertook commission to write jazz scores for series of documentary films, as well as charts for NBC orchestra, including *Castro's Year of Power* (1960), *The Marriage Racket* (1962), *The Poor People of Mexico* (1962), last-named an award-winner. Lowe's writing capabilities also encompassed jingles, TV commercials. Moved to California (1965), where he occasionally worked with Peggy Lee, and others. But it was writing which, again, took most of his time at this period, including regular gigs for ABC/TV series *Love On a Rooftop, I Dream of Jeannie, The Iron Horse, Wild, Wild West, Hawaii Five-O*.

Appointed musical supervisor for education TV station KCET (1969). Composed comprehensively for Hollywood Telvision Theatre productions. Co-produced *Jazz In the Round* (PBS network), also conducting house band. After leaving KCET (1972), became arranger-producer for several LP dates. At this time, also began to play more guitar at gigs in and around Los Angeles, as well as teaching and undertaking clinics.

For the guitar connoisseurs, Mundell Lowe's more regular jazz appearances during the early 1970's (including consecutive appearances at the Monterey Jazz Festival) were special delights. For his admirers must have begun to despair that, because of his comprehensive involvement with studio work and composing and arranging, his well-nigh faultless, loose-swinging guitar-playing would hardly ever be heard in live performances again.

Never at any time during a distinguished career in any way an innovator or a leader on his instrument. Hardly an out-and-out, rip-roaring exciting player, his solos invariably contain warmth and rich tonal quality.

Exceptional versatility is another Mundell Lowe trademark. Which means he can slot in, with ease, in all kinds of musical situations, as evidenced by recording under his own name such as (4), (5), (6), (7), as well as those in the employ of Georgie Auld (10), Richie Kamuca (13), Ruby Braff (12). His sensitivity as accompanist is manifested superbly in album dates with top-line singers like Sarah Vaughan (15) and Carmen McRae (16).

SELECTED DISCOGRAPHY

1 The Essential Charlie Parker B&C RECORDS
2 Concert Jazz (Eddie Safranski) BRUNSWICK
3 New Music of Alec Wilder RIVERSIDE
4 The Mundell Lowe Quintet HIS MASTER'S VOICE
5 Mundell Lowe Quartet RIVERSIDE
6 Porgy & Bess RCA VICTOR
7 A Grand Night For Swinging RIVERSIDE
8 Blues For Tomorrow (one track) RIVERSIDE
9 Satan In High Heels (Charlie Parker)
10 Jazztime U.S.A.: The Best of Bob Thiele's Classic Jam Session of the 1950s (George Auld's All Stars; Stash Lawler) MCA
11 Guitar Moods RIVERSIDE
12 The Mighty Braff (Ruby Braff) AFFINITY
13 Richie (Richie Kamuca) CONCORD JAZZ
14 52nd Street Scene (Tony Scott, et al) JASMINE
15 The Intimate Sarah Vaughan ROULETTE
16 Bittersweet (Carmen McRae) FOCUS

DICK McDONOUGH

Richard McDonough: Born New York City, 1904. Yet another guitarist originally banjoist. By the time he had reached twenties, was accomplished player on both instruments. From early-1920's, right through 1930's, became a much-in-demand performer, both as strictly rhythm player and as soloist who could handle both single-line or chordal styles with absolute ease. Influenced comprehensively by Eddie Lang (q.v.) — his Number One idol on guitar at all times — McDonough played in both jazz and dance band groups, large and small, appearing on literally hundreds of record sides. First recording, with danceband-leader Don Voorhess. Another strong guitar influence was Carl Kress (q.v.), with whom he had a notable partnership during 1930's. Pair's recordings — such as (7) remain much sought-after to this day. As a fine reader and a readily adaptable player, McDonough was, perhaps, pre-destined to involve himself in studio work. In such capacity, he worked extensively at NBC Studios, NYC. Which was where he collapsed, while working, in May, 1938, and was taken to hospital. Where, after an emergency operation, he died — much too prematurely — very shortly afterwards.

Dick McDonough, who also fronted his own bands, inside both recording and radio studios, remains a much-admired contributor to jazz guitar, especially by those who knew and heard him in live performance. His impeccable technique remains the envy of most fellow guitarists. During his career, McDonough worked with diverse leaders such as Red Nichols (1), Adrian Rollini (4), Sam Lanin, Benny Goodman (4), (5), Joe Venuti (4), the Dorsey Brothers (6), and Miff Mole (2), (3). With Mole (2), he accompanied singer Sophie Tucker; and in 1927, on Mole recordings such as *Darktown Strutters' Ball, Feelin' No Pain, My Gal Sal,* and *The New Twister* (all 2), played banjo alongside his hero Eddie Lang's guitar.

The delightful Kress-McDonough partnership (8) is full of delightful surprises and much superior guitar playing by both. McDonough's recordings as leader of his own orchestra — during the period when it is said he sometimes earned $1,000 a week as a freelance musician — weren't too plentiful or, frankly, of great importance. But the music was good, and the leader apart, there were often top sidemen like Bunny Berigan (10).

Perhaps McDonough's most exciting single performance on record came, appropriately, in an RCA VICTOR organised studio jam session (11), with the guitarist supporting top names like Berigan, Waller, and Tommy Dorsey. But for a definitive example of Dick McDonough's artistry — exemplifying all that was so good about his playing — one needs look no further than a sparkling solo interpretation of *Honeysuckle Rose* (9).

SELECTED DISCOGRAPHY

1 Red Nichols & His Five Pennies (1926-1928) MCA CORAL
2 Miff Mole's Molers — 1927 (with Sophie Tucker) PARLOPHONE
3 Miff Mole's Molers 1928-30 PARLOPHONE
4 Jazz In The Thirties (Joe Venuti; Adrian Rollini; Benny Goodman) WORLD RECORDS
5 Recordings Made Between 1930 & 1941 (Benny Goodman) CBS
6 Bring Back the Good Times (Dorsey Brothers) MCA CORAL
7 Pioneers of Jazz Guitar YAZOO
8 Dick McDonough & Carl Kress JAZZ ARCHIVES
9 50 Years of Jazz Guitar (one item only) COLUMBIA
10 The Great Soloists: Bunny Berigan 1932-1938 BIOGRAPH
11 Jam Session READER'S DIGEST RDS 6181
12 Mildred Bailey: Her Greatest Performances (1929-1946), Vols. 1,2. CBS

PAT MARTINO

Pat Azzara: Born Philadelphia, Pennsylvania, 1944. His singer-father-guitarist encouraged son's interest in music in general and guitar in particular at very tender age. A cousin — also a guitar player — gave him some early tuition. Enthusiasm waxed through listening to father's extensive collection of jazz records, including many by Django Reinhardt (q.v.), Eddie Lang (q.v.), *et al.* Further help given by another local guitarist, Dennis Sandole, who also added tutorial expertise. Started gigging professional-

ly at teen-ager — and after only four years' instruction — operating in both jazz and R&B contexts. In fact, spent first nine years of career on the road, with such as Lloyd Price, Willis Jackson (1), (2), Red Holloway; also much work with jazz organists of the calibre of Brother Jack McDuff (3), Richard 'Groove' Holmes (4), Jimmy McGriff. Also four months in saxist Sonny Stitt's combo. After spending so long on the road, returned to Philadelphia (1966), staying for six years, last two devoted mainly to learning more about music and his instrument. Also worked eight months with altoist John Handy (5), demonstrating his flexibility, also just how much that long period of touring had developed his style and all-round ability. Began to teach privately at end of 1960's, and also to show some real development as composer of merit. His emergency coincided with recognition as first-place guitarist (in Talent Deserving Wider Recognisiton category) in 1969 DOWN BEAT Jazz Critics' Poll. Martino tied for first place in same category, with Tiny Grimes (q.v.), in 1972.

Apart from his obvious technical facility, and ability to project both as an exciting and a quietly sensitive performer, it is Pat Martino's individual sound that lifts him from the plethora of good-but-unexceptional guitarists on the jazz scene. Through the years, he has continued to show an impressive improvement rate. Not, for a moment, to suggest that his own earliest recordings — including (9), (10), (11), (12) — are in any way ordinary. Same with those, like (5), (6), (7) and (8), where his excellent guitar lines enhance record dates headed by other notable jazzmen. It is just that during the past decade, Martino seems to have found the voice his hard work and dedication to guitar-playing had been moving towards. Four LPs he made for MUSE — (13), (14), (15), (16) — offer conclusive proof of his pre-eminence, and, more recently, his contributions to a solid Stanley Clarke record date (20), show absolutely no diminution of his talents.

SELECTED DISCOGRAPHY

1 Grease & Gravy (Willis Jackson) PRESTIGE
2 More Gravy (Willis Jackson) PRESTIGE
3 Walk On By (Brother Jack McDuff) PRESTIGE
4 Get Up & Get It (Richard 'Groove' Holmes) PRESTIGE
5 New View! (John Handy) CBS
6 Sky Shadows (Eric Kloss) PRESTIGE
7 From This Moment On (Charlie McPherson) PRESTIGE
8 Horizons (Charlie McPherson) PRESTIGE
9 El Hombre PRESTIGE
10 Strings! PRESTIGE
11 East PRESTIGE
12 Baiyina PRESTIGE
13 Live MUSE
14 Consciousness MUSE
15 Exit MUSE
16 We'll Be Together Again MUSE
17 The Visit COBBLESTONE
18 Starbright WARNER BROS
19 Joyous Lake WARNER BROS
20 Children of Forever (Stanley Clarke) POLYDOR

CARMEN MASTREN

Carmen Nicholas Mastren: Born Cohoes, New York, 1913. Four brothers — Al, John, Frank, Eddie — also musicians. Before guitar, played banjo and violin. Switched, finally, to guitar in 1931, working regularly in Mastren family band several years. First important professional gig: with trumpeter Wingy Manone (1935) (1). But obtained much wider exposure for his talents in 1936, when he joined the Tommy Dorsey Orchestra. Remaining with Dorsey until 1940, Mastren's became a familiar face with the band. Solo opportunities were rare, but his clean, unmistakable unamplified sound was a decided asset to the rhythm section, sounding particularly fine on recordings such as *After You've Gone* (4). Joined Joe Marsala's combo (1940-1941) — (11) — then worked briefly with Ernie Holst Orchestra. Became NBC staffman. Later, played with Raymond Scott, Bob Chester. To Europe with Glenn Miller's AAF Band, returning to US in 1945. Resumed studio work in 1946. Combined performing with spell of arranging-conducting (including Morton Downey on Coca-Cola radio series — had done some arranging in Dorsey days). Worked with Skitch Henderson and other notable leaders, in further NBC work (1953). Remained with NBC through 1960's. Worked on bands for *Today*, *Tonight* and *Say When* TV shows (wrote, played most of music on latter). Produced innumerable jingles (1970-1973), before concentrating on freelance playing. Appeared in Broadway musical production *Over Here*, together with Andrews Sisters (1974). Performed with New York Jazz Repertory Company, playing music of Jelly Roll Morton, Louis Armstrong, using banjo as well as guitar (10).

Carmen Mastren — who composed-played banjo music for the film *The Wild Party* — never quite made the big-time as a jazz guitarist. He was a gifted player, nevertheless, whose skills were obvious for all to hear and appreciate. Capable of single-line and chordal work — especially effective in the latter metier — of superior quality, he fitted unobtrusively and well into a variety of jazz situations. Interesting to hear Mastren working in tandem with fellow guitarist Eddie Condon (q.v.) (5), and as a member of Glenn Miller's Uptown Hall Gang (8), a splinter group from the AAF Band. A winner of the METRONOME Readers' Poll on two consecutive occasions (1939-1940) — (6) — Mastren was a popular musician with fellow per-

formers as well as fans.

Perhaps his finest playing on record — both with the marvellous spring-heeled support he gives as a strictly rhythm-section contributor and as occasional chordal soloist — originates from a classic Bechet-Spanier Quartet date from 1940. A fitting testimony to a supremely gifted picker, who died — mourned by his fellow guitarists — in 1983...

SELECTED DISCOGRAPHY

1 The Great Soloists: Featuring Jack Teagarden BIOGRAPH
2 Adrian Rollini & His Friends, Vol 1: "Tap Room Special" RCA VICTOR
3 Tommy Dorsey & His Orchestra RCA VICTOR
4 Tommy Dorsey, Vol. II RCA VICTOR
5 Decca/Champion Sessions (Bunny Berigan) MCA
6 The Metronome All-Stars Band RCA CAMDEN
7 In Memoriam (Sidney Bechet, Muggsy Spanier) RIVERSIDE
8 Glenn Miller's Uptown Hall Gang ESQUIRE
9 Banjorama MERCURY
10 Satchmo Remembered (New York Jazz Repertory Company) ATLANTIC
11 Great Swing Jam Sessions, Vol. 2 (with Joe Marsala, et al) SAGA

PAT METHENY

Patrick Metheny: Born Lee Summit, Missouri, 1954. Started on guitar 14, influenced jointly by Wes Montgomery (q.v.), Miles Davis. Played in various jazz groups in Kansas City high school. Won scholarship offered by DOWN BEAT magazine to a stage band camp. Met fellow guitarist Attila Zoller (q.v.), who urged him to take in the New York City jazz scene — which, once and for all, decided him on becoming a full-time professional jazzman. Attended University of Miami where he taught guitar for a year. First met Gary Burton — an especially helpful and influential jazz personality in Metheny's career — Withita, Kansas. Burton, most impressed with the young guitarist's potential, helped him gain teaching post at the Berklee College of Music, Boston, as well as introducing him to ECM RECORDS boss Manfred Eicher. Metheny's long-time association with ECM has been of signal importance in his continued growth as a player and in his widespread acceptance as a musical personality whose popularity during the past five years has permeated way outside any remotely conventional jazz arena. Since that time, has taught in both NYC and Boston. Amongst jazz guitarists of the past 25-odd years, it could be said that Pat Metheny has been more interested than most in the actual sound (or rather sounds) that can be coaxed from his instrument — utilising amplifiers, speakers, digital synthesisers, et al. To this end, his detractors will tell you, he has at times tended to neglect the emotional side of music in pursuance of a myriad of sounds of often impressionistic quality. But Metheny's dedication to his own art has never been in doubt.

Metheny's dedication has meant much hard work, both to improve his standard of musicianship — which was impressive at a very young age. Certainly, even as a 19-year-old, Metheny acquitted himself splendidly when touring with vibraharpist Burton, on his first important touring gig. Indeed, Burton is something of an alter ego for Metheny. On record, Metheny matched Burton's unique delicacy with his own brand of sensitivity and creativity. Indeed, some of the former's finest recorded statements are to be found within (1), (3), and particularly (2), with special reference to the title track.

Of Metheny's steady stream of ECM recordings — right from initial Metheny Trio LPs such as (4), (5) — there is an admirable consistency in performance, even although not too many of these can be truly considered to be of innovative importance. Of the more significant recordings, (10) has some astonishing duetting between Metheny and keyboardist Lyle Mays, latter an important collaborator during the past few years, as further evidenced by (11), (12). There is much good music to be found throughout (9), thanks as much to the contributions of star guests Charlie Haden, Michael Brecker, Dewey Redman, Jack DeJohnette. And Metheny's pastel-shade backgrounds and ingenious guitar-sound devices for so much of (13) is a futher enhancement to a superb live Joni Mitchell double-album. (Metheny toured with the singer-composer at the beginning of the 1980's as a member of an all-star unit).

It is interesting to specualate in what directions Pat Metheny will veer during the rest of the present decade.

SELECTED DISCOGRAPHY

1 Ring (Gary Burton ECM
2 Dreams So Real (Gary Burton) ECM
3 Passengers (Gary Burton) ECM
4 Bright Size Life ECM
5 Water Colours ECM
6 The Pat Metheny Group ECM
7 New Chautauqua ECM
8 American Garage ECM
9 80/81 (with Mike Brecker, Dewey Redman, et al) ECM
10 As Falls Wichita, So Falls Wichita Falls ECM
11 Offramp ECM
12 Travels ECM
13 Shadows & Light (Joni Mitchell) ASYLUM

OSCAR MOORE

Oscar Frederic Moore: Born Austin, Texas, 1912. Yet another early starter on his chosen instrument. Made professional debut with brother Johnny Moore (also guitarist) in 1934. First came to national prominence after joining the King Cole Trio (fall of 1937). Was to stay, as a major contributor to Cole Trio's exceptional popularity, both on record and as in-person combo favourite. Trio itself won many polls. Its guitar player attained impressive popularity, winning ESQUIRE Gold Award (1946-1947), Silver Award (1944-1945); METRONOME Readers' Poll (1945-1948); DOWN BEAT Readers' Poll (1945-1948). Also appeared in numerous films/film shorts with Cole Trio. During this 10-year period, also gained deep respect of fellow musicians — especially, of course, guitarists — as a truly gifted performer whose technique was beyond reproach. Left Cole in 1947 to work in brother Johnny's Three Blazers, with which group recorded extensively between 1947-1951 for small labels ALADDIN, MODERN MUSIC, EXCLUSIVE, ATLAS. After which, gradually drifted away from the jazz scene, except for a very rare record date. During 1950's, even worked as bricklayer for a while. Cut series of pop-slanted LPs in 1959, but worked only sporadically during 1960's. After long absence, returned to record a Cole tribute album. After which, practically nothing was heard from this exceptional player....

The gradual demise of Oscar Moore remains one of the saddest jazz-guitar stories of all time. During his halcyon days as an integral member of the Nat Cole Trio, he had very few superiors as a jazz player. His gorgeous technique — everything was picked so cleanly, so noiselessly — was matched by a warm, distinctive tone and a fertile mind. Although he was never to become a protobopper, his harmonic awareness and instrumental dexterity enabled him to keep abreast with the jazz revolution happenings of the early-1940's. (As Leonard Feather observed during his liner-note for (2), his use of a ninth chord with a flatted fifth at the conclusion of the Trio's recording of *That Ain't Right* was indeed 'a daring innovation at that point in time...'). The Trio's numerous recordings are littered with plentiful examples of Moore's delicious single-line amplified solos — not to mention his gentle-but-firm chordal playing behind Cole's vocals and keyboard statments. Thus, the contents of (2), (3), (4), (5), and (6) are of collective real importance in any assessment or analysis of his playing.

His subsequent gradual removal from the music scene is, as previously mentioned, something of a major loss to the evolution of the guitar in jazz. And not all the occasional record dates did him justice. His versatility enabled him to switch to a more-or-less R&B stance with the Three Blazers. The deft touch and good taste, however, never deserted him,. And even on not-totally-satisfactory recordings such as (8), (9), (11), there is much to admire. (12) is much better, but for a personal legacy, the four items to be found within (10) remain best of all. With that superb, idiosyncratic pianist Carl Perkins also in top form, Moore's playing on all four tracks — most notably a marvellously conceived *Oscar's Blues* — is magnificent. This justly celebrated player died in 1981, while visiting Las Vegas.

SELECTED DISCOGRAPHY

1 The Complete Lionel Hampton (eight tracks only) BLUEBIRD
2 From the Very Beginning (Nat King Cole) MCA
3 Too Marvellous For Words (Nat King Cole) MUSIC FOR PLEASURE
4 Nat King Cole & Big Band — Rare Live Performances in Los Angeles 1944 JAZZ ANTHOLOGY
5 Pieces of Cole (Nat King Cole) ONE-UP
6 Trio Days (Nat King Cole) SWING HOUSE
7 Gene Norman's Just Jazz Concerts VOGUE
8 Oscar Moore Quartet LONDON
9 Oscor Moore Quintet TAMPA
10 Swing Guitar (four tracks only) VERVE
11 Oscar Moore Trio VEDETTE
12 Fabulous Guitar (Charlie Parker)

JIM MULLEN

James Mullen: Born Glasgow, Scotland, 1945. Acquired first guitar at 10, although appreciated music from earlier years. First became interested in jazz around 12 years. Switched to bass — temporarily — at 14, but was back with guitar four years later. First (non-pro) gig — church hall dance, at 11. First pro gig — aged 15, playing bass. Continued to play mostly bass during the next few years, including stint with US singer Billy Daniels at Glasgow's White Elephant. Gigged, on bass, with Andy Park's 10-piece, Gil Evans — influenced, Glasgow based big band (1960-1968), playing TV, radio, gigs, soundtrack music.

First important work on guitar (1963), with own band, a vibes-guitar-bass small combo. Which in turn led to a second band which contained two sax players destined to become constituent members of Average White Band. This band — Jim Mullen & Company — lasted three years, playing music written by Mullen and Roger Ball (AWB-to-be).

Left Glasgow for London (1969). Next, worked with Pete Brown Band, for two years. Joined organist Brian Auger (1971), staying with Oblivion Express two years. Worked with Vinegar Joe (six months, in 1973), before becoming member of Kokomo (1973-1975). First met

Jim Mullen

Coda Music for Music Lovers

With Dick Morrissey, Mullen seems totally en rapport at all times. There first recording date (4), is high on real mutual inspiration. And 'ince Morrissey-Mullen came together, the guitarist's playing has continued to grow in strength and mobility. In live performances with the band, Mullen produces solos containing great excitement and emphatic swing. On Morrissey-Mullen LPs, his solos are more pithy, but no less arresting, as evidenced by individual cuts like *Takin' Time* (7), *Bladerunner* (8), *Ol' Sax & Captain Axe* (8). Mullen's first solo album (9) gives him the chance to demonstrate more versatility than usual, as he essays diverse material by such as Wayne Shorter, Mike Mainieri and Stevie Wonder. And the inclusion of an all-too-brief version of Thelonius Monk's *Crepescule For Nellie* means one might not unreasonably expect to hear much more of Jim Mullen, acoustic guitarist, than hitherto.

reedman Dick Morrissey (1975) — an event of signal importance. Lived, worked in US 1½ years during which time toured with Average White Band, spent six-months period with flautist Herbie Mann, then returned to UK.

Morrissey-Mullen Band formed (1977) — and has been continuing, with increased recognition through the succeeding years, ever since. Outside of Morrissey-Mullen, latter enjoys working straight-ahead jazz gigs, such as those with organist Mike Carr, with whom first worked in 1980. Since returning to the London jazz scene full-time, Jim Mullen's development as a player has been remarkable. To-day, he is recognised widely as one of the few truly original jazz guitarists in the UK. Mullen, who uses his right thumb for picking very much in the manner of Wes Montgomery (q.v.) — one of his acknowledged idols — is an especially strong blues player, whose hard-driving work with the fine Morrissey-Mullen Band continues to endear him to a steadily-growing number of local and European fans.

That he is readily adaptable can be judged from his contributions to (1), (2), (3). He sounds particularly happy in the context of organ-guitar, which is probably why (2) contains some of his finest playing on record. His idiomatic solo on the bebop classic *Shaw 'Nuff* is brilliantly sustained.

SELECTED DISCOGRAPHY

1 **Benny & Us** (Ben E. King, Average White Band) (one track only) ATLANTIC
2 **Mike Carr...Live At Ronnie Scott's** SPOTLITE
3 **Big Blues** (Jimmy Witherspoon) JSP
4 **Up** (with Dick Morrissey) ATLANTIC
5 **Cape Wrath** (Morrissey-Mullen) HARVEST
6 **Badness** (Morrissey-Mullen) HARVEST
7 **Life On the Wire** (Morrissey-Mullen) BEGGARS BANQUET
8 **It's Aboute Time** (Morrissey-Mullen) BEGGARS BANQUET
9 **Thumbs Up** CODA

BENSON BY BENSON

THE FOLLOWING is the bulk of a previously unpublished interview granted the author by George Benson. The conversation took place during a visit to London by the great guitarist when he was appearing at the Ronnie Scott Club. This was at an intriguing period in his career, just prior to his tremendous popularity as a recording artist took him far beyond the usual confines of being just a jazz musician — albeit one with a loyal following.

Of particular interest, bearing in mind the extraordinary success to come, is Benson's final comment regarding his desire to continue singing — whether to satisfy the urgings of his female following or otherwise...!

A likeable man, George Benson was also disarmingly frank, about about his own playing (e.g. arriving in New York 'with a bad tone', as well as a put-down of his work during *White Rabbit*, one of his most successful pre-pop LPs, and his apparent disinterest in the basic blues field.

When your stepfather — himself a guitarist — first played you Charlie Christian records, what was it about this playing which communicated to you, even at seven years old?

I knew he was something special. I could hear right away. He *commanded*. He took over. When he started playing, it became his own. The name Goodman didn't mean as much to me as the name Christian did — because my father told me he was the one who played the guitar solos. So he stayed on my mind a lot. When I heard other guitarists later, they never came up to it. Not until way later — much later in my life — did I hear musicians who were comparable. People like Montgomery and Burrell; like Grant (Green), Raney, Tal Farlow, Kessel.

I first played guitar at about nine. I was a singer, actually, and I could hear very well and pick things up real good. I backed my own stuff with the guitar. Then, I went on to singing with groups and so forth... Sang R&B and ballads, solo; kind of soft. However, the reason I became a guitar player was because the guitar started to become very popular, and there weren't very many players in my home town at that time. The fact that I sang and played almost hung me up, because they wanted me just to play! And I wanted to sing *and* play.

They kept on to me so much about it. "Why don't you leave Pittsburgh, get with one of those bands and make some money? You're good enough". But I never wanted to leave. I wanted to stay, I was happy. I was young — and I was married, and I had responsibility. I never made much money but I was happy. What made me leave was I had a winter where I couldn't move around. My car was destroyed, and I couldn't make the jobs. So, I had to go out with somebody. I had an offer from Jack

McDuff, and I joined his group. I found out it wasn't easy as I thought it was going to be because I didn't know chord changes and things.

How did you manage to communicate, musically, with Jack because of your lack of musical education?

He liked the way I accompanied him. And, anyway, I had good ears. If I heard something I could play it... The only records that were popular amongst those in my home were organ records. So I knew what guitar players played behind organ players... I heard that he liked a certain type of guitar player, and I knew what this guitar player played like. I could mimic anybody. If I heard him play once I could do it. I heard that he liked Thornel Schwartz, who was the master in the organ-guitar thing. When he auditioned me, he didn't hear me play solos. I accompanied him, and he liked me so well. Because he couldn't find a guitar player who could play like Thornel Schwartz. Nobody else could copy him. I didn't want to be like Thornel Schwartz — I wanted to be myself. But Jack, he wanted a Thornel Schwartz...

I was 19, then, and I travelled with him two years. And when he found out I couldn't improvise, he had already hired me, we were 1,000 miles from Pittsburgh. He tried to fire me, but he couldn't find anybody else who would go for the same money. And at that time it was very difficult to find a guitar player who could play blues *and* jazz. You either played jazz or R&B or blues, or whatever. But the guys who could do more than one thing... there were only a few. Grant Green was one — he was about the first guy who could play with Muddy Waters and play with Charlie Parker if he had to. Kenny Burrell couldn't get down into the alleys. Anyway, Grant had already played with Jack McDuff, had left — and Jack couldn't get him back. And Kenny was into his own thing. He was makin' good money and McDuff couldn't afford him. So I learned the book...

He let me solo a little — just a little. That's why I play so hot, because in those days he only gave me one chorus. Whatever I had to say, I had to get into that one chorus. So I filled it up with notes, feelings, blues — anything... I was used always to striking in right away — I don't need to build. I don't have to wait five minutes to build up a solo.

After such invaluable groundwork, what happened next in your already developing career?

After that, I started my own group. And I went to New York. Because that's where I knew everything was. If you want to do anything, jump in the middle of the fire — don't

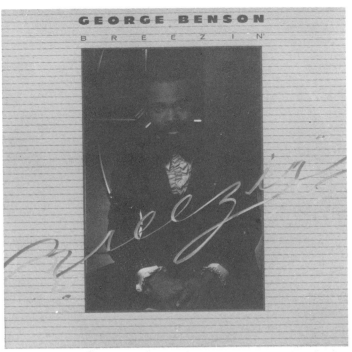

hang around the edges. If you want to get into Parliament, get into Parliament. Take all the beatings along the way — or the criticisms — because that's how you learn. Find out what your faults are.

So, what did you find out when you arrived in New York City?

That I had a bad tone and it needed working on. No nobody helped me with that. Tone is a thing that comes from hard work. So, I had to learn to hear myself, because I had had the impression that I'd the greatest tone in the world. But it was only my mind that made me think that; so I began to listen to my records, and I said: "Wow! They weren't wrong". The tone was horrible. I began to work on it, and I'm still working on it. I also discovered my playing tended to be too percussive. I'm a very *staccato*-y player, because I feel that way, but sometimes it gets to be too much.

When you were establishing yourself on the New York scene, did you ever use acoustic?

I used it once on a record date with (pianist) Jackie Byard. We did a fantastic record together called *Jackie Byard With Strings*. Also on that record date were bassists Ron Carter and Richard Davis, Ray Nance on violin, Alan Dawson on drums. I played an open- Martin guitar, which is almost a country or folk guitar. It had a very nice sound. The only thing is that when playing in clubs the music is so loud you can't appreciate it.

nowadays. It's become something that's accepted among people. They look for that sound — that plectrum sound. But I'm not in love with it. I think it's good if you want to play something extra-swift and with extra cleanness.

In your younger days, how influenced were you by the great blues guitars, like, say B.B. King?

It's like everything else — it's like learnin' to speak. Blues... that's all that was heard in my neighbourhood. Whenever I would go by a dance hall, there was no jazz. When I was a kid, all we heard on the jukebox was Jimmy Reed or B.B. King, and that kind of thing. I wasn't particularly in love with it. One thing I used to hate about blues music was that they kept repeating the words... they would say the exact same things, and I hated that. I didn't think it was a song, and therefore I didn't follow the melodic lines.

After your not inconsiderable involvement with the electric instrument, did you perhaps have to make any drastic re-adjustments in your playing?

No, no. I have a very natural knack for just picking up any instrument. It's a gift, if you wanna call it that. I don't believe that it's the instrument that makes the man. My father got me away from that years ago. I used to complain: "If only I had a better guitar..." IIe told me "It ain't the guitar, it's you! Django Reinhardt and them didn't have Gibson L5's, and their hands must have looked like branches..."

Even bearing in mind the fact you might have problems for club work, what about an all-acoustic LP?

Sure would interest me. I would probably want to switch over to classical guitar. But this takes years to build up to the same kind of dexterity that I have on the (electric) jazz guitar, and to switch from the pick to my fingers. It would take me a long time before I could come up to where I am now with the pick. But I could play it with the pick or with my thumb. I learned to play with my thumb first because I didn't know cats had picks in their hands for years — until somebody told me. I played for about five years before somebody told me: "Why don't you use a pick?"

Do I like a plectrum guitar? Not really. It's clear and it'll cut through all the volume the cats are using

Surely, though, you'd be aware of some great things going on, instrumentally?

I knew what was happenin', sure. I recognised some great cats. There's not very many that I'm crazy about, but B.B. King is probably the one. I haven't heard enough of someone like, say, Lightnin' Hopkins to tell you the truth, because I'm not a lover of blues music. I play blues? Sure. The thing is, it's a heritage thing. It's just been part of my ways, like a way of life. It's like corn bread. It just happens, you find it on the table. So, when you hear my playing (blues), it's very natural. If nobody had ever told me, I would never have known that was in my playing, because I

didn't search for it. But actually, I don't think I have the blues. I've never had the blues. I've always been a happy person...

By reputation, you are the kind of guy who manages to smile at adversity — at least you are very philosophical if things to wrong?

Yeah. It's hard to get me down. And life is strange. A record I cut I thought was the worst of all-time. Yet *White Rabbit* was the biggest record I ever had. I hated it. I told the producer, for every one record it sold I'd eat the second. When I first heard the playbacks on that, I hated it. I threatened to leave the company.

You seem to be so ridiculously versatile that, for some people, it might be a little too much. Especially, for instance, if someone wants you to play, someone else wants you to sing?

That's right. And how do you produce a person like that? And what sort of music should he play; and what is the best thing to do? In America if I played black clubs they'd want me to sing all the time — they'd not want me to play. If I play the white places, they don't want me to sing; they want me to play.

Nevertheless, you're certainly much better-known as George Benson, guitarist?

Yes. But women don't care what you're known for! They want to hear vocals. They like to be wooed. Once, it almost destroyed my career. I did some records, just singing, and it almost destroyed the disc jockeys because when they put my records on they automatically assumed that I was playing guitar... they'd put a record on — and no guitar, just singing. See, if I'd played a few notes it would have identified me. They were puzzled, you know — and it hurt. So, I had to leave that alone because the thing that's different, the thing that sticks out most about me, is my playing. It's me. It's more identifiably me.

Are you continuing to be interested in experimenting with your guitar-playing?

I'm not set in my ways — yet. I like inventing things, things that haven't been done. We found ourselves doing nightclubs — when I talk about 'we' I'm talking about myself and my fellow guitarist Earl Klugh — I found myself putting together little bits and pieces of things that are going to come together. I get bored very easily, so I constantly look for new things on my instrument. One day, I might be playing away at something that's very nasty and

funky, and the next day I could be trying something that's too sweet. It's like eating sugar out of a bowl. That's the way I feel...

When did you first realise you were really beginning to make it as a jazz guitarist?

When I received respectful comments from other musicians — the established musicians. When someone said of me: "Hey, man, that's Johnny Griffin!" "Who the hell is Johnny Griffin?" And, then, Johnny Griffin would come to me and say: "Hey, man, you George Benson? I'm so happy to meet you". That kind of thing. I'd never heard of him — and he was sayin': "You're great". And when some of these cats, when I was jumpin' up and down playin' rock 'n' roll, would say: "You've heard of Barney Kessel?" I would say "No". "You never heard of Barney Kessel, the guitarist? You're crazy!" And then they would take me and play me his records. Man, that was somethin' else. Hell, I thought, I'll never be able to play like that. Then, one day, a guy said: "Hey, man, would you like to make a gig with Barney Kessel and Jim Hall?" I just said: "Far out!..."

And when a guy like Tal Farlow says: "The reason I'm coming back out of here is because of you... 'cos I didn't know they had any young guys who were still interested in playing music anymore..." And you can't get over the fact that here is a man whose contributions to guitar music you can't even measure yet. My future? I'll just be tryin' to play my guitar better than I do now. But I won't be giving up my singin'...!

MARY OSBORNE

Mary Osborne: Born Minot, Bismark, North Dakota, 1921. Played violin in school symphony. Added guitar, bass, and played all three instruments — as well as occasionally singing, dancing — in three-piece combo at 15. As guitarist, was tremendously inspired to play jazz after hearing Charlie Christian (q.v.) with Alphonso Trent's band at Bismark club, although she's previously responded favourably to Eddie Lang (q.v.), Django Reinhardt (q.v.), Dick McDonough (q.v.). It was after hearing — and meeting — Christian, though, that she decided to amplify her guitar. Played year on Pittsburgh radio station KDKA. Building her reputation, subsequently toured with bands of Buddy Rogers, Dick Stabile, Terry Shand, Joe Venuti.

Between 1942-1943, worked with Russ Morgan, Gay Claridge, Winifred McDonald (with whose trio first came to NYC). After touring with latter, stayed in New York when group disbanded (1945). Found herself much in demand in and around 52nd Street; also made numerous record dates, with such as Mary Lou Williams, Beryl Booker, Mercer Ellington, Wynonie Harris, as well as recording under own name. Worked, recorded with Coleman Hawkins, but most familiar at Kelly's Stables on 'The Street' (it is said Django Reinhardt once came to Kelly's to hear Osborne play), leading own trio. Gradually got into freelance work — most productively, — until 1962 playing, recording with many top studio bands. In 1962, commenced five-year classical-guitar study in New York with Albert Valdes Blain. Moved with family to California (1968). Not too much is heard from her these days, but she still plays guitar on fairly rare occasions, and she is apparently active in both playing and teaching of classical guitar.

Strange, maybe, but there have been precious few lady jazz guitar players. Mary Osborne remains one of the very best. Her fluent, clean playing gained for her an impressive reputation even before her 52nd Street period of popularity. An unashamed Christian disciple, she nevertheless was hip to the newer sounds that were reverberating through this busy jazz thoroughfare on her arrival in the Big Apple and thereafter. The Christian-tinged-with-bop approach is intriguingly present on the precious few recordings she made under her own name during the period. Which included individual cuts for labels such as SIGNATURE (*Mary's Guitar Boogie; Blues In Mary's Flat*), ALADDIN (*What Will I Tell My Heart?; You've Changed*), and DECCA *Wonder Where's My Man Gone Tonight?*) Even in stellar company, such as with Coleman Hawkins' 52nd Street All Stars, she held her own (1), on *Allen's Alley, Spotlite*, etc. And her fleet guitar sits well alongside the leader's fine piano-playing during the pro-

ceedings of an all-female recording date by Mary Lou Williams' Girl Stars (1).

Sadly, Mary Osborne's own recording opportunities have been few and far between since the 1940's. The very rare (2) from 1959, is worth seeking out, with the lady's elegantly-swinging playing sympathetically supported by pianist Tommy Flanagan, drummer Jo Jones, and others, with especially rewarding moments coming during *I Let a Song Go Out of My Heart, These Foolish Things*, and an almost prophetic *Mary's Goodbye Blues*. Some of (2) resurfaced as part of the 1982-released (3) — together with even rarer gems in a selection of 1980-1981 recorded trio items. An event well worth repeating in the future...

SELECTED DISCOGRAPHY

The Greatest of the Small Bands, Vol. 2 (Mary Lou Williams; Coleman Hawkins) RCA VICTOR
A Girl & Her Guitar WARWICK
Now & Then STASH

JOE PASS

Joseph Anthony Passalaqua: Born New Brunswick, New Jersey, 1929. Studied in Johnston, Pennsylvania, with Nick Gemus (1939-1940). Played local gigs, plus appearances with Tony Pastor Orchestra while still schoolboy. Toured US fairly extensively as teen-ager, then spent year in Marine Corps. After being busted on drugs charge, moved to Las Vegas. Worked hotels, local joints, before again falling foul of the law (for which he spent 3½ years at the US Public Health Service Hospital, Fort Worth, Texas). Returned to Vegas, to resume commercial work. Toured, recorded with George Shearing (1955-1956). Subsequently, entered the Synanon drug rehabilitation centre, Santa Monica, California (1961). Since 1962, has become one of the most respected jazz guitarists anywhere. During 1960's, worked for some time on West Coast, involved in groups led by such as Gerald Wilson, Bud Shank, Earl Bostic, Les McCann, Richard 'Groove' Holmes, Carl Fischer (also accompanied singer Julie London). Won first poll victory (DOWN BEAT Readers' Poll — Talent Deserving Wider Recognition), in 1963. Same year, created favourable impression at Monterey Jazz Festival. Since when has appeared at most of the world's leading jazz festivals. During 1970's, under auspices of Norman Granz, began touring frequently — internationally as well as at home.

Visited Australia with Benny Goodman (1973). Worked extensively with Ella Fitzgerald, Oscar Peterson (1973-1974). Worked successful two-guitar partnership with Herb Ellis (q.v.) (1972-1974), and played first-ever London solo gig (at Ronnie Scott Club 1974), returning subsequently to partner Danish bassist Niels-Henning

Joe Pass

Orsted Pedersen, also visiting Europe. Has been a constant winner of the Readers' Poll of DOWN BEAT since 1977 (and to a lesser extent same magazine's Critics' Poll, too).

During the past 20 years, Joe Pass has continued to grow in stature. To-day, he is rightly acknowledged as one of jazz' major guitar-players, whose all-round technique, natural, flowing drive and warm, creative improvisations have together made him into an immensely popular figure, both with fellow players and fans alike. His period at Synanon is documented, interestingly, on (1). And the post-Synanon recordings of the 1960's show him to be an ever-improving performer whose versatile approach enables him to move smoothly and delightfully through small-group recordings such as (3), (4), (6) and, probably best of all (2). A big-band date with Gerald Wilson, (34), with Pass accorded a showcase role is a further rewarding revelation of his talents.

Since signing with Norman Granz' PABLO label in the early-1970's. Pass' recorded opportunities have soared, helping increase his popularity to hitherto unrealised proportions. An on-off association with Oscar Peterson, both in concert and on record, brought him to an even wider international audience, and as both (17) and (20) reveal, the pianist often pushes him into moments of dazzling guitar playing. That Pass can hold his own in the heaviest company is further evidenced during other recor-

dings ike (17), (18), (19), (28), (29), (34), (35). Both (25) and (26) contain much delightful interplay and solo work, with Pass' fluent guitar heard in tandem with just one musical associate. Similarly, his collaborations with bassist Orsted Pedersen — (21), (22) — have been never less than successful, especially the live recording.

But at this stage of his career, it is fast becoming obvious that to appreciate the artistry of Joe Pass at its very best, one must refer to those occasions when he is left completely alone to his own always-interesting devices. There is little to choose between (8), (9), (10), or (11) — each has admirable consistency in performance — with (9) probably taking the edge. Better still, though, is (27), which benefits from being taped in concert. Finally, not too many guitarists could have offered top-line singers such as Ella Fitzgerald and Carmen McRae the kind of sensitivity in accompaniment which the immensely gifted Joe Pass bequeaths to (31), (32), (33).

SELECTED DISCOGRAPHY

1 Sounds of Synanon PACIFIC JAZZ
2 The Complete Catch Me Sessions BLUE NOTE
3 Sign of the Times WORLD PACIFIC
4 Simplicity WORLD PACIFIC
5 12 String Guitar WORLD PACIFIC
6 For Django UNITED ARTISTS

7 Intercontinental MPS/BASF
8 Virtuoso PABLO
9 Virtuoso No. 2 PABLO
10 Virtuoso No. 3 PABLO
11 Virtuoso No. 4 PABLO
12 Portraits of Duke Ellington PABLO
13 Seven Come Eleven (with Herb Ellis) CONCORD JAZZ
14 Two For the Road (with Herb Ellis) PABLO
15 Jazz Concord (with Herb Ellis) CONCORD JAZZ
16 The Joe Pass Trio Live At Donte's PABLO LIVE
17 Oscar Peterson Big Six At the Montreux Jazz Festival 1975 PABLO
18 Jazz At the Philharmonic At Montreux PABLO LIVE
19 Dizzy Gillespie's Big Four PABLO
20 Tudo Bem! (with Paulinho de Costa, Oscar Castro Neves) PABLO
21 Northsea Lights (with Niels-Henning, Orsted Pedersen) PABLO LIVE
22 Chops! (with Niels-Henning, Orsted Pedersen) PABLO
23 I Remember Charlie Parker PABLO TODAY
24 Live In the Netherlands (with Oscar Peterson, Toots Thielemans, et al) PABLO LIVE
25 Blues For Two (with Zoots Sims) PABLO
26 Checkmate (with Jimmie Rowles) PABLO
27 Joe Pass At the Montreux Jazz Festival 1975 PABLO LIVE
28 The Trio (with Oscar Peterson) PABLO
29 Peterson & Pass a Salle Pleyel PABLO
30 Eximious PABLO
31 Take Love Easy (with Ella Fitzgerald) PABLO
32 Fitzgerald & Pass Again PABLO
33 Great American Songbook (with Carmen McRae) ATLANTIC
34 Moment of Truth (Gerald Wilson) FONTANA
35 Duke's Big Four (with Duke Ellington) PABLO

BUCKY PIZZARELLI

John 'Bucky' Pizzarelli: Born Paterson, New Jersey, 1926. Started on guitar at age nine. Taught by two uncles, Peter and Bob Domenick, both respected Paterson-and-district players, latter having worked with Joe Mooney, Mitch Miller. Nephew Bucky's first pro engagements were with local dance bands (1941). Promising career interupted by service in US Army (1944-1946), spent in Europe, the Philippines. Worked with Vaughn Monroe Orchestra on his return from service abroad (he'd worked with Monroe, briefly, just prior to induction), staying several years. Returned to Paterson (1952), still working occasionally with Monroe. During this period Pizzarelli, like Uncle Bob, gigged with Joe Mooney. Started regular work as NBC staffman (early-1950's), working for Skitch Henderson, among others. In late-1960s, switched to

ABC/TV. Took time off from studio work to tour with the Three Suns vocal-instrumental group (1955-1957). Joined Benny Goodman for European tours (1970, 1972, 1973, 1974 — also recorded with Goodman, in Stockholm).

During 1970's, often to be found in duo format, performing at Soerabaja's, New York. Played first solo concert in the city's Town Hall (1973 — his daughter, Mary, then 15, joined him for brace of duets, played a la Kress-McDonough). Had performed in two-guitar format with George Barnes (q.v.) for first time at beginning of 1970s; it was a situation to be repeated on numerous subsequent occasions. (The pair had met during Pizzarelli's period with Three Suns). Also worked in collaboration with Les Paul (q.v.), and as support for singers such as Teddi King, Jane Harvey (17). Participated in successful recreation of Jean Goldkette Orchestra, at Carnegie Hall (1975).

Since mid-1970's, Pizzarelli has continued to be much-employed, both in a purely freelance context, or as welcome accomplice to a variety of jazz musicians, principally those working in and around NYC. Pizzarelli's eloquence and flexibility of approach enables him to slip into most jazz situations, easily and unobtrusively. Using a modified seven-string Van Eps guitar — with an additional bass string below the usual E string — Pizzarelli's accompaniments often are as elegant as his solos. His only failing as a soloist seems to be a lack of real impact and excitment.

Nevertheless, there is much to admire in his playing. Pizzarelli seems to have a natural affinity with tenorist Zoot Sims. Their records — with Sims invariably taking the dominant role — are full of moments of sheer musical delight, with understatement a principal element. Both (7) and (9) are excellent; (8) is beyond reproach. There are similarly rewarding results on the guitarist's record date with another veteran tenorman, Bud Freeman (11). The laid-back approach of Pizzarelli sits well as a perfect foil for the extrovert approach of violinist Joe Venuti (10), (15); a collaboration with Stephan Grappelli (13) is more emotionally compatible.

Of his own recordings, Pizzarelli's solo LPs offer most conclusive proof of his undoubted abilities. (18) is merely very good; (19) is just superb...

SELECTED DISCOGRAPHY

1 Nightwings FLYING DUTCHMAN
2 Bucky Plays Bix & Kress MONMOUTH-EVERGREEN
3 A Flower For All Seasons CHOICE
4 Bucky's Bunch MONMOUTH-EVERGREEN
5 Guitars — Pure & Honest (with George Barnes) A&R
6 2 · x 7 = Pizzarelli (with John Pizzarelli) STASH
7 Nirvana (with Zoot Sims) GROOVE MERCHANT
8 Zoot Sims & Friend... CLASSIC JAZZ

9 Summum (with Zoot Simms) AHEAD
10 Joe & Zoot (with Joe Venuti & Zoot Sims) VOGUE
11 Buck & Bud (with Bud Freeman) FLYING DUTCHMAN
12 Them There Eyes (with Ruby Braff) SONET
13 Duet (with Stephane Grappelli) BLACK & BLUE
14 Dialogue (with Slam Stewart) SONET
15 Sliding By (with Joe Venuti) SONET
16 Town Hall Concert CBS
17 Jane Harvey RCA VICTOR
18 Green Guitar Blues MONMOUTH-EVERGREEN
19 Love Songs STASH

JIMMY RANEY

James Elbert Raney: Born Louisville, Kentucky, 1927. His father a prominent newspaperman, Raney studied guitar with A.J. Giancolla, Hayden Causey (latter recommending him as his own replacement with Jerry Wald Orchestra). Moved to Chicago, working there with many local combos, including pianist-vibist Max Miller, pianist Lou Levy. Joined Woody Herman (1948), though solo opportunities were limited. Then, became member of Al Haig Trio, moving on to Buddy De Franco Sextet. Played, on and off, with Artie Shaw Orchestra (1949-1950). After two months with vibist Terry Gibbs, gained international prominence as member of Stan Getz Quintet, between 1951-1953. Spent one year with Red Norvo Trio (1953-1954), including trip to Europe, in '54. Latter year, also worked with dance bandleader Les Elgart. Worked with Jimmy Lyons Trio, at Blue Angel, NYC (remaining until 1960).

Worked with multi-instrumentalist Don Elliott in Broadway production of *Thurber's Carnival* (1960). Rejoined Stan Getz (1962-1963), recording (two as yet unreleased LPs), touring. After which, was heavily involved with recordings, private teaching, TV jingles. Around mid-1960's, also worked with various singers, and on other Broadway shows. Returned to Louisville (late-1960's) for more teaching, a little playing — and some strictly non-musical jobs. Revisited NYC (1972), playing at The Guitar Club, likewise at Bradley's Gulliver's, New Jersey. Played Carnegie Hall recital with old friend, Al Haig (1974). Began recording again — including with Haig, and own groups. Son, Doug. Raney — a most promising jazz guitarist — began playing gigs with father; pair also recorded as duo (25), as well as visiting Europe, playing to receptive audiences. The importance of Jimmy Raney in the context of post-Christian guitar-playing should never be under-estimated. Indeed, there is much to be said that he should have been included in the Top Twelve jazz guitarists. His technique is well-nigh flawless. His harmonic and melodic skills are never less than exceptional. In terms of transferring the bop language to the guitar, there has been no-one more talented. In fact, the only — most important — aspect of bebop that Raney fails to transmit is in noble art of emotional projection. His is an essentially low-profile approach to jazz — gentle, even, with the accent on subtlety in performance, enhanced by superb articulation, rather than one of red-hot blowing.

Raney's contribution to the Getz Quintet was impressive. He complemented the tenorist's own mellifluous lines beautifully, and the pair often engaged in counterpoint, with delightful results. Raney, in person, often sounds more inspired, more adventurous, as evidenced by (5), (7). Best of all, though, throughout (6) *Budo*, his own compositions *Rubberneck, Signal*, on Vol. 2; *The Song Is You, Move, Parker 51* (another Raney original), Vol. 1. His empathy with Lester Young-derived tenor players is further illustrated with fine recordings in company with such others as Zoot Sims (16), Al Cohn (29), Bobby Jaspar (28), not forgetting (2), which combines the talents of the two first-named, plus Getz.

Raney's rapport with pianist Al Haig was always much apparent during their period as joint sidemen with the Getz Quintet. It is also much in evidence during other, non-Getz recordings like (1), (23) and, in particular, the elegant (20). Of his earlier record dates, Raney's contributions to a Teddy Charles session (10) are exquisite. Both *A Night In Tunisia* and his own intriguing *Composition for Four Pieces* contain some of his very finest playing. So, too, does (3), a 1953 date with Getz — Raney is the leader here — with both men in top form during another version of *Signal* and a classic interpretation of *Round Midnight*.

As much more recent recordings reveal — not to mention his eagerly-anticipated live appearances — Jimmy Raney's is still a major talent on jazz guitar. An important contributor to the evolution of jazz guitar, and one who ranks still with the best of to-day.

SELECTED DISCOGRAPHY

1 Mixes (with Stan Getz, Al Haig) MAINSTREAM
2 Brothers & Other Mothers (Stan Getz) SAVOY
3 Stan Getz & Friends PRESTIGE
4 It Might As Well Be Spring/The Complete Roost Sessions (Stan Getz) VOGUE
5 That Top Tenor Technician (Stan Getz) ALTO
6 Stan Getz At Storyville, Vols. 1,2 VOGUE
7 Hooray For Stan Getz SESSION DISC
8 Stan Getz Plays MUSIC FOR PLEASURE
9 Red Norvo Trio VOGUE
10 Ezz-thetic (Teddy Charles) XTRA
11 Stockholm Sweetnin'/Americans In Sweden 1949-1954, Vol. 2
12 Too Marvellous For Words BIOGRAPH
13 Revelation! (Bob Brookmeyer) XTRA
14 Jimmy Raney in 3 Attitudes ABC-PARAMOUNT

15 The Sweetstringers (with Jim Hall, Bob Brookmeyer) WORLD PACIFIC
16 2 Jims & A Zoot (with Jim Hall and Zoot Sims) MAINSTREAM
17 The Influence XANADU
18 Momentum MPS
19 Strings & Swings MUSE
20 Special Brew (with Al Haig) SPOTLITE
21 Live in Tokyo XANADU
22 Jimmy Raney — Solo XANADU
23 Strings Attached (with Al Haig) CHOICE
24 Here's That Raney Day AHEAD
25 Duets (with Doug Raney) STEEPLECHASE
26 Raney '81 CRISS CROSS
27 Point of Departure (Gary McFarland) IMPULSE
28 Guitaristic SWING
29 'Mr Music' (Al Cohn) RCA VICTOR

ERNEST RANGLIN

Ernest Ranglin: Born Manchester, Jamaica, 1933. Started playing guitar on regular basis in early-teens. Established healthy local reputation in Kingston, Jamaica, including regular work with 14-piece band fronted by altoist Bertie King. Had done much work in Bahamas in his early-twenties, where there were more opportunities to play jazz — his first love, always — than in his home country, where he had played all kinds of music, including calypso, ska.

Then, decided to move to Britain, where regular outlets for jazz-playing were even more plentiful. In doing so made the same move as fellow West Indians trumpeter Dizzy Reece, altoist Joe Harriot, altoist-flautist Harold McNair (with whom he'd worked regularly in the Bahamas), trumpeter-flugelhornist Shake Kane, in post-war years. Like his immediate predecessors, Ranglin created a highly-favourable impression on the London jazz scene when he arrived in the UK, at the end of 1963. His appearances at, say, the Ronnie Scott Club would be the signal for all local guitarists — jazz and otherwise — to call in to check him out.

But by the 1970's, Ranglin had left Britain permanently, to return to Jamaica. Sadly, he has rarely returned to Europe since that period, then only to make a rare recording date.

During the past dozen-or-so years, Ernest Ranglin has continued to keep something of a low profile, content to live and work in Jamaica (and for varying periods, it has been reported, in New York too). His absence from a British jazz scene, not exactly over-staffed by top-class jazz guitarists, is regrettable. For resources to the precious few recordings he has made during that same period demonstrates that he has lost absolutely nothing of his undoubted and superlative skills. His distinctive tone remains as lustrous as ever. His use of time and space is thrilling. His articulation, his infinite good taste, and his improvisational talents are all beautifully preserved. The proof of his enduring quality can be heard throughout both (1), (2), LP dates featuring primarily the keyboard talents of Monty Alexander, a friend of Ranglin's for many years and one of his biggest boosters. The running excitement he conveys during both *S.K.J.* and *Now's The Time*, from (1), typify his latterday excellence.

There is high-quality playing in abundance during both (2), (3), with Ranglin sounding especially joyous on the latter. But if there is one album — of the all-too-few jazz recordings under his own name — which illustrates all his assets best of all, then it must be (3). His impressive rhythmic powers and lovely changing harmonies stand out in the Caribbean-flavoured *Linstead Market*. His obvious admiration for Wes Montgomery (q.v.), ie his octave-playing, is demonstrated in *Angelina* and *Reflections*. And his overall superb relaxation really lifts a Kessel-ish interpretation of the standard *Just In Time*.

SELECTED DISCOGRAPHY

1 Love & Sunshine (Monty Alexander) MPS
2 Jamento (Monty Alexander) PABLO
3 Wranglin' ISLAND
4 Reflections ISLAND
5 Ranglypso MPS

EMILY REMLER

Emily Remler: Born New York City, 1957, but raised in Englewood Cliffs, New Jersey. Began on guitar — self-taught — at very youthful age. Played folk music between nine and 10 years — worked in folk group which also contained comedian Buddy Hackett's son. Next, became smitten with rock 'n' roll. Attended boarding school in Massachusetts; didn't find too much inspiration, academically, so opted for music school.

Enrolled at Berklee School of Music, Boston. Which is where she really became turned on by jazz (which she'd heard previously, without understanding too much). Not surprisingly, a major influence at that time was Wes Montgomery (q.v.) Graduating from Berklee, moved to New Orleans, where she found work a-plenty. Played with dance bandleader Dick Stabile at Fairmont Hotel; also at same venue as accompanist to singers Nancy Wilson, Ben Vereen. (Wilson subsequently asked her to appear at prestigious New York concert). In New Orleans, too, was member of R&B band, Little Queenie & The Percolators. During same period, also worked for Michel Legrand, Joel Gray, and started giving guitar lessons.

Met Herb Ellis (q.v.), in New Orleans. Ellis obviously impressed, recommended her to Carl Jefferson, president of Concord Jazz Records who, in turn, invited her to appear at his Concord Jazz Festival (1978). There, she appeared onstage with Ellis, Cal Collins, Barney Kessel (q.v.), Tal Farlow (q.v.), Howard Roberts (q.v.). Spent one more year in New Orleans, then moved on to NYC. Put together own trio for club dates. Played series of concert dates with singer Astrud Gilberto. Gave guitar lessons to Gregory Hines — who in turn invited her to Los Angeles to play on his show.

Created favourable impression at Berlin Jazz Festival (1981), also in floating jam session aboard ship to Hawaii. Worked for a while in Los Angeles, in stage musical *Sophisticated Ladies*. Chosen by critic-author Leonard Feather as 1981's Young Woman of the Year (in jazz).

Emily Remler's emergence during the 1970's as a fully-fledged, obviously talented player was one of the brightest happenings in the jazz guitar world of that decade. Harmonically, melodically, rhythmically, she appears to have little more to learn. Her sound is perhaps her most readily apparent attribute, crisp, penetrating, yet with a gossamer quality that gives it its attractiveness. Her recordings have been minimal in number thus far, but they evidence a promise of even greater things in the future. (2) is a highly satisfactory debut as session leader. Included amongst the many fine things are an admirably eloquent *In a Sentimental Mood*, a superbly articulated *Inception,* and an exhilarating *Movin' Along,* with Remler saluting her premier guitar influence by using her right thumb in solo, Montgomery-style. If (2) is a fine recorded example of Emily Remler's talents, then (3) is more than marginally superior. It is an album chockfull of highlights, including a version of *Cannonball* that oozes extra-confidence, a really hard-swinging treatment of Dexter Gordon's *For Regulars Only,* and some delightful finger-style chording during a fascinating working of Mongo Santamaria's *Afro Blue.* There seems little doubt that during the rest of the 1980's, the name of Emily Remler will figure prominently amongst the very best of the world's jazz pickers.

SELECTED DISCOGRAPHY

1 It's All In the Family (Clayton Bros.) CONCORD JAZZ
2 Firefly CONCORD JAZZ
3 Take Two CONCORD JAZZ

ALLAN REUSS

Allan Reuss: Born New York City, 1915. Fascinated by banjo at early age — and played first gig at 12, not too long after starting to play instrument . . . and apparently after but one lesson! Switched permanently to guitar, and by mid-1930's had become a fine, all-round-accomplished musician whose services were constantly in demand. Studied with George Van Eps (q.v.), who recommended him as his own replacement with Benny Goodman Orchestra (1935). Stayed for only three months, but rejoined year later, to remain on more permanent basis (1936-1938), adding much buoyancy, spring to band's rhythm section. After Goodman, freelanced widely, particularly as recording artist, and put together own guitar-teaching studio in New York. Worked with bands of Jack Teagarden, Paul Whiteman (8), in '39.

At beginning of 1940's, toured nationally with big bands of Ted Weems (1941-1942), Jimmy Dorsey (1942), before working for year with NBC studio band (1942-1943). Rejoined Goodman for further spell (1943-1944), before switching to rival Harry James Orchestra (1944-1945). During latter period, won readers' polls for both METRONOME, DOWN BEAT (1944). After James, led own trio in Los Angeles area. Then, sadly, drifted away from jazz scene almost totally, obviously preferring to concentrate on the lucrative pickings of local studio work. (Which as much as anything is how, in all probability, he came to participate in 1955 movie *The Benny Goodman Story* (10), appearing on-screen with big band and BG Octet *Slipped Disc* jam session). Also concentrated on more teaching.

A genuinely modest, somewhat retiring man, Allan Reuss seemed content for most of his playing career to take on the role of rhythm guitarist with numerous distinguished bands — big and small. A role which, incidentally, he fulfilled splendidly, at all times, perhaps never better than with James and Goodman. As a soloist, he performed in either an intensely rhythmic chordal style or in economic single-string fashion. One of his very rare solo outings — *Pickin' For Patsy* (7), which he recorded as a member of the Jack Teagarden Orchestra in 1939 — was highly-rated amongst fellow guitarists at the time. His solo style owes much to that of his principal influence: Dick McDonough.

As with the big bands, his recordings in a small-combo setting find him confined mainly to operating as rhythm guitarist. Amongst the most memorable sessions in which he participated have been those with Gene Krupa (2), Lionel Hampton (6) — including the rhythmically superior *Shufflin' At the Hollywood*, co-composed by Reuss and the leader — Teddy Wilson (4), (5), and Coleman Hawkins (9), last-named containing a delightfully chorded Reuss solo during *What Is There To Say?*

SELECTED DISCOGRAPHY

1 Benny Goodman, Vol. 5 (1935-1938): The

Fletcher Henderson Arrangements RCA VICTOR
2 Benny Goodman, Vol. 4 (1935-1939) RCA VICTOR
3 Jazz In the Thirties (Gene Krupa) WORLD RECORDS
4 The Teddy Wilson CBS
5 Teddy Wilson & His All Stars CBS
6 The Complete Lionel Hampton (1937-1941) BLUEBIRD
7 Rompin' & Stompin' (Jack Teagarden) Swing Era
8 Featuring Jack Teagarden (Paul Whiteman) MCA
9 Hollywood Stampede (Coleman Hawkins) CAPITOL
10 "The Benny Goodman Story" MCA
11 Harry James In Hi Fi CAPITOL

LEE RITENOUR

Lee Mack Ritenour: Born Hollywood, California, 1952. Raised in Palos Verdes, Calif. Began to study guitar from eight years. Four years later, was featured in 19-piece band The Esquires. Further guitar studies at 17 — with Joe Pass (q.v.), Howard Roberts (q.v.), classicist Christopher Parkening — but had already made record debut, on singer-songwriter John Phillips album. During high school days, recalls Ritenour, maintained a nine-hour-a-day practise routine, commencing when he returned home each day after school. In formative years, Wes Montgomery (q.v.) was greatest influence, but he was also inspired by B.B. King, John McLaughlin (q.v.), Charlie Christian (q.v.).

At 17, had first experience of playing with jazz combo — that of Craig Hundley. Left musical studies at USC to tour Japan with Sergio Mendes & Brasil '66. Biggest break back home came with regular Monday night (Guitar Night) gig at Donte's California. Locally-based guitarist John Pisano joined him for one night — shortly thereafter, and for period of about a year, they performed live as John Pisano-Lee Ritenour Duo. After which Ritenour put together own band. Participated in Guitar Summit — with Jim Hall (q.v.), Mundell Lowe (q.v.), Pass, Michael Howell — at '74 Monterey Jaz Festival. Worked for a while with fine combo, including also Dave Grusin, Harvey Mason.

During 1970's, became substantially involved with studio work. Together with Duke Miller, directed Studio Guitar Programme (teaching students guitar-playing, also how to help them choose a career, as teacher or studio musician). Following death of veteran guitarist-arranger Jack Marshall (1973), Ritenour took on tutorship of Marshall's guitar workshop at University of Southern California. Has worked with innumerable other top musicians, singers. Created favourable impression with own band at

UK Capital Radio Jazz Festival (1981).

During the past 10 years, Lee Ritenour has developed into one of the most skilled of all contemporary players. The possessor of dazzling technique — which allows him to execute practically any ideas he wishes, especially at the lightning tempos he often uses — Ritenour is alos a master of the wah-wah pedal and other electric guitar accessories. Perhaps Ritenour's superior technical skills will one day elevate him to the pantheon of the greatest jazz guitarists. But for all his impressive credentials, it must be said that those skills tend often to obscure too much real emotional commitment on his part; there are times when, for all his guitar wizardry, one yearns for qualities of real warmth and gut-level communication. Hopefully, that important omission from his otherwise splendid armoury will be forthcoming in the later years....

Certainly, Les Ritenour's recordings thus far have been superbly put together, right from the earliest (1), (2). His impressive all-round musicianship enables him to approach direct-disc recording dates such at (7), (8), (9), (10) with almost frightening ease, producing creative music of an extremely high standard. And, despite the aforementioned reservations about the music he produces, there is much to admire about the musical contents, format, and excellent recorded sound of others, like (3), (4), (5), and a particularly satisfying (6).

SELECTED DISCOGRAPHY

1 First Course EPIC
2 Captain Fingers EPIC
3 Guitar Player (two items only) MCA
4 The Captain's Journey ELEKTRA-MUSICIAN
5 Rit ELEKTRA-MUSICIAN
6 Rio ELEKTRA-MUSICIAN
7 Gentle Thoughts JVC
8 Sugar Loaf Express JVC
9 Friendship JVC
10 Gentle Thoughs (alternative takes of (7)) JVC

Lee Ritenour

HOWARD ROBERTS

Howard Roberts

Howard Mancel Roberts: Born Phoenix, Arizona, 1929. Mostly self-taught on guitar, but studied Schillinger system with Fabian Andre, at 17. Later, tutored by Shorty Rogers; previously had been taught by Horace Hutchett. As youngster, responded to the big-band sounds of Shaw, Ellington, Goodman; at 16, became aware of Bartok, Schoenberg, Hindemith, Stravinsky...and bebop. After only two years formal training, was playing with local dance bands and as member of high school band — while still at grade school. Moved to Los Angeles in his teens, and such was his progress managed to jam in and around that city with jazz greats like Bud Powell, Howard McGhee, Sonny Stitt, Dexter Gordon. Roomed for two years (from 1947) with Howard Hettmever, now classical guitarist. Commenced working with own groups, and with locally-based jazzmen like Bud Shank, Shorty Rogers, Buddy Collett, *et al.* Worked also as member of pianist Al Haig's Quartet, and with combo fronted by vibist Teddy Charles. And it was with pianist-singer Bobby Troup's Quarter over two years, that he began to really develop an impressive chordal style of playing. That 'new' sound first brought to public notice through recording dates with drummer Chico Hamilton's Trio (2). Made first recording dates under own name, 1956-1957 (7), (8).

Won DOWN BEAT New Star award (1955). Later, enrolled at USC to pursue further classical interests, becoming deeply involved with 14th-century music. Also made thorough study of its counterpoint form. His work with regard to formalised guitar technique led to his Howard Roberts' Guitar Book. Designed own guitar, embodying all best qualities of both acoustic and electric guitar. Result: the Howard Roberts Model electric guitar with re-introduction of arch-topped, round-holed design, similar to that of Spanish guitar. Played all solo guitar work on soundtrack of widely-popular movie *The Sandpiper*. Was one of the first combo leaders to play Californian jazz club Donte's (1966). From 1950's through 1970's, his superb musicianship, plus ability to sight-read anything, meant much of his playing time was confined to basically non-jazz studio work, though he has always endeavoured to play live jazz gigs whenever possible. During which time, appeared on literally thousands of album dates, most of which were non-jazz. The 1970's saw him increasingly more active in jazz circles, lecturing on guitar, at seminars and colleges. At the same time, developed an interest in writing original material.

Howard Roberts is recognised both by his peers as well as those who follow the fortunes of jazz guitar, either as critics or fans, as a consummate player whose each and every performance is high on music of superior quality and all-round interest. A musician, whose vast experience inside a hundred recording, TV, etc., studios has honed his talent close to perfection. Roberts, too, is acknowledged by fellow guitarists as someone who truly knows the technical aspects of his intstrument, obviously the result of his many years of dedicated study and total absorption in the subject.

Roberts progress through the years as a jazz player — from being a merely very good guitarist, as evidenced by recordings such as (2), (3), (7), (8), to a real individualist, who has added a genuine study both of rock and overall electronics to his armoury, as documented interestingly on such as (11), (13) makes for a rewarding story. A story that, in (12), has resulted in a remarkable performer, irrespective of era or style, whether he plays chordally or single-line...

SELECTED DISCOGRAPHY

1 **Julie Is Her Name, Vol. 1 (Julie London)** LONDON
2 **Chico Hamilton Trio** PACIFIC JAZZ
3 **Turning To Spring** DISCOVERY
4 **Group Activity (Bob Cooper)** AFFINITY
5 **Colour Him Funky** CAPITOL
6 **Guilty** CAPITOL
7 **Mr. Roberts Plays Guitar** VERVE
8 **Good Pickins** VERVE
9 **Velvet Groove** VERVE
10 **Movin' Man** ESP
11 **Equinox Express Elevator** IMPULSE
12 **The Real Howard Roberts** CONCORD JAZZ
13 **Antelope Freeway** IMPULSE

TERJE RYPDAL

Terje Rypdal: Born Oslo, Norway, 1947. Father, Jakop Rypdal, captain in a military band. Wife, Inger-Lise, pop singer, actress. Studied piano from age five; started on guitar at 13. First got into music in rock bands, early-teens. His premier guitar influence, then: Hank Marvin. First important jazz gig, with band of fellow Norwegian, altoist-sopranoist Jan Garbarek (1968). Also got to work with composer-arranger George Russell — also studying the American's Lydian concept — during same period when he also studied with Norwegian composer Finn Mertenson. Became deeply interested in classical music, but maintained ever-increasing interest in jazz — and, in particular, top US jazz guitarists such as Wes Montgomery (q.v.), Kenny Burrell (q.v.), Tal Farlow (q.v.), Charlie Byrd (q.v.).

First came to virtual international prominence during appearance at Baden-Baden free-jazz festival (1969). Returned to Baden-Baden (1971) to play with Violin Summit. Next year, fronted own trio at Berlin Jazz Festival — same year as he added flute, soprano-sax to his armoury. Put together own group — Terje Rypdal Odyssey in mid-1970's for touring, recording purposes. During which time he has also developed into a fine, interesting composer, having written extended pieces for symphony-size orchestras. Composed first symphony (1973), also Electric Fantasy, and music for theatre.

Terje Rypdal's emergence in the late-1960's as a highly-original guitar-player has coincided with growth of the ECM RECORD COMPANY, for whom the Norwegian has recorded for some time. Coincidentally, maybe, but Rypdal's crystalline guitar, impeccably played at all times, has in itself an ECM-like sound quality. To appreciate Rypdal's playing in-depth — likewise to trace his growth as a player — it is instructive to play his ECM albums in chronological order. His originality in approach is present during the eponymous (4), and (5), but the fully-developed Rypdal is more obvious when listening to recent recordings, especially how he interacts with other musicians, like Palle Mikkelborg and John Christensen on (9), and Miroslav Vitous, Jack DeJohnette on (10). For group rapport, though, both (6), (7), are hard to beat. From an earlier period, (1) finds Rypdal intergrating beautifully within a group of young forward-looking British jazzmen, including John Surman, Malcolm Griffiths.

Although there is much to admire in Rypdal's somewhat detached stance, and especially his enviable, pure technique, it is to be hoped that he will develop a more overtly emotional dimension to his overall playing. But, as of now, he remains a potent force to be reckoned with.

SELECTED DISCOGRAPHY

1 **Morning Glory** (with John Surman, Malcolm Griffith, et al) ISLAND
2 **Bleak House** POLYDOR
3 **Whenever I Seem To Be Far Away** ECM
4 **Terje Rypdal** ECM
5 **What Comes After** ECM
6 **Odyssey** ECM
7 **After the Rain** ECM
8 **Dream** KARUSELL GOLD
9 **Descendre** ECM
10 **To Be Continued** ECM

SAL SALVADOR

Salvatore Salvador: Born Monson, Mass., 1925, but grew up in Stafford Springs, Conn. The great talent that was Charlie Christian's first turned Salvador on to jazz in early-1940's. After which, became interested in acoustic players like George Van Eps (q.v.), Carl Kress (q.v.) Started correspondence courses with Oscar Moore (q.v.), Hy White: tutored by Eddie Smith. Began working as pro in and around Springfield (where he first met other jazz youngsters such as altoist Phil Woods, vibist-composer Teddy Charles). Moved to NYC (1949). Recommended by fellow guitarist Mundell Lowe (q.v.), for job as staff guitarist at Radio City Music Hall; also met, became friends with Johnny Smith (q.v.). Also played New York dates with such as Terry Gibbs, Mundell Lowe. Worked with Gibbs again after leaving Radio City (1951), then became member of The Dardanelles. Worked as house guitarist for COLUMBIA RECORDS during 1950's, accompanying such diverse vocalists as Tonny Bennett, Marlene Dietrich, Rosemary Clooney, Frankie Laine. Co-led quartet with Mundell Lowe before joining Stan Kenton Orchestra (1952-1953). Freelanced in NYC, then put together own quartet featuring Eddie Costa, vibes, piano, which attracted popularity amongst critics and fans. In late-1950's, fronted own big band for first time — something he continued to do, from time to time, until mid-1960's. Played well-received solo set at 1958 Newport Jazz Festival — subsequently appeared in sequence, together with saxist Sonny Stitt, in celebrated jazz movie from same Festival: *Jazz On a Summer Day.*

By mid-1960's, was leading small combos again. During 1970's, was heard much less in person, concentrating extensively on publishing activities. When he did make fairly rare appearances, was heard mostly in duo context with Allen Hanlon, the couple undertaking an even more rare event — an in-person recording, (10). During the 1950's firstly, with solo features with Kenton, like *There's a Small Hotel, Sophisticated Lady* (both 2), and *Invention For Guitar & Trumpet,* (1) — Sal Salvador looked

set fair to become one of the guitarists of the decade. His live appearances, not only with Kenton, but with Gibbs, Lowe, brought him plenty of wide exposure. A situation that prevailed with his own quarters and big bands. Yet, curiously and sadly, he didn't quite fulfil that initial promise and, by the 1970's, had all but faded from the jazz scene completely.

No innovator, but Salvador manages to maintain an enviable level of consistency, in all settings. As his records demonstrate. His first date as leader — (3) — find him in excellent form, especially during a sensitive, finely-wrought *Gone With the Wind*. And Salvador-Costa Quartet recordings like (4), (5), (6) — the latter with guests Phil Woods, Eddie Bert — show the guitarist inspired by the presence of his youthful co-leader. The big-band Salvadors are likewise interest-full. (8) is decidedly the best — (9) has many fine moments, but is less than 100% totally successful. The Salvador-Hanlon collaboration, (10), is refreshing, insofar as it produces cast-iron evidence that the former appears to have lost none of his admirable skills. And (11), taped at the end of 1982, is perhaps an even more positive re-affirmation of that fact.

SELECTED DISCOGRAPHY

1 New Concepts in Artistry in Rhythm (Stan Kenton) CREATIVE WORLD
2 Sketches On Standards (Stan Kenton) CREATIVE WORLD
3 Sal Salvador Quartet/Quintet BLUE NOTE
4 Boo Boo De Boop AFFINITY
5 Frivolous Sal BETHLEHEM
6 Shades of Salvador BETHLEHAM
7 Sal Salvador Quartet BETHLEHEM
8 Colours In Sound DECCA
9 Beat For This Generation DECCA
10 'Live' Duo /with Allen Hanson)

JOHN SCOFIELD

John Scofield: Born Wilton, Conn. 1951. Acquired first guitar at 11. Initially, dug music of such as the Beatles, Chuck Berry, Little Richard, John Lee Hooker, B.B. King, Otis Rush. First teacher, Alan Dean, also keen on same kind of music. The pair listened also to records of Pat Martino (q.v.), and with particular awe to Jim Hall's (q.v.) playing at a Greenwich Village club. By 15, Scholfield knew he wanted to became jazz guitarist. Enrolled at Berklee School of Music, Boston (1970). There, learned theory, also improved reading, and became all-round much more technically accomplished. While at Berklee, received invaluable assistance from Mick Goodrick (then guitarist with Gary Burton Quartet). His whole musical thinking was turned around after hearing the LPs *Extrapolations, My Goal's Beyond,* by John

McLaughlin (q.v.) When Goodrick had to pull out of Gerry Mulligan-Chet Baker reunion concert at Carnegie Hall (1974), he recommended Scofield to play guitar; that prestigious appearance documented by two albums of music (6). Two weeks later, was touring with exciting Billy Cobham-George Duke fusion band, staying two years, touring widely and appearing on best-selling records by the band. Worked for year with Gary Burton Quartet (1977) — though he doesn't believe his association with vibist's group was totally successful. But this led to sideman duties with top names, as expressive and as diverse as Charles Mingus (5), Tony Williams, Ron Carter, Jay McShann (7), Lee Konitz, Larry Coryell (q.v.), Joe Beck. Joined saxist Dave Liebman's band (1978). Even more inspiring, he recalls — working with own trio, completed by bassist Steve Swallow, drummer Adam Nussbaum (12). During last several years, has continued to visit Europe for approximately two months per year — including a trip to Poland, UK, etc (1983) as member of Miles Davis combo, to which he has contributed handsomely since joining in 1982.

Since the mid-1970's, John Scofield has continued to make most encouraging progress as a jazz-guitar stylist. Originally, showing many outside influences, Scofield's playing since the late-1970's has shown a marked individualism. An intensely creative player at all times, his technique is beyond reproach, his ability to string together choruses that are as logical as they are interesting marks him down as one of the most gifted of all guitarists of the present. His contributions to recordings by others are never less than apposite, ranging in styles and settings as, say, (1), (5), (6), and (17). As a duettist, his playing on (16) is supportive, sensitive.

His own records further amplify Scofield's consistency in performance at all levels, right from the very first — (9). (10), too, has much fine guitar playing, although in overall quality it is surpassed by both (11) and (13). The latter remains one of Scofield's finest dates. For the dedicatory *The Beatles*, he imparts a tonally-intriguing yearning quality; his lyricism illuminates *Spoons*; he oozes relaxation throughout *Looks Like Meringue*; and evidences a solo performance on *How the West Was One* that, rhythmically speaking, remains one of his finest.

As well as providing a unique challenge, Scofield's association with Davis has deservedly brought a major talent to perhaps an even wider audience than his hectic period with Billy Cobham. Certainly, his will be one of the dominant figures of jazz guitar throughout the present decade...

SELECTED DISCOGRAPHY

1 Funky Thide of Sings (Billy Cobham) ATLANTIC

2 Live On Tour In Europe (Billy Cobham) ATLANTIC
3 You Can't Go Home Again (Chet Baker) A&M HORIZON
4 Ivory Forest (Hal Galper) ENJA
5 Three or Four Shades of Blue (Charles Mingus) ATLANTIC
6 Carnegie Hall Concerts, Vols. 1,2 (Gerry Mulligan, Chet Baker) CTI
7 Solar Energy (Bill Goodwin) OMNISOUND
8 John Scofield Live ENJA
9 Shinola ENJA
10 Rough House INNER CITY
11 Bar Talk ARISTA/NOVUS
12 Who's Who? ARISTA/NOVUS
13 Live INNER CITY
14 Out Like A Light ENJA
15 Tributaries ARISTA NOVUS
16 Star People (Miles Davis) CBS

JOHNNY SMITH

John Henry Smith: Born Birmingham, Alabama, 1922, son of gifted banjo player. Self-taught as guitarist, even before moving to Portland, Maine (1935). Made professional debut with Fenton Brothers' country band (1939). Stopped off in Boston, led own trio (1940-1941) — already was attracting attention of fellow guitarists for his exceptional techniques. Played trumpet in US Air Force Band, violin, viola in concert band during military service (1942-1946). Also worked with Philadelphia Orchestra under Eugene Ormandy, this time on guitar. Became staff-man at NBC (1947-1954) as guitarist; also performed on trumpet with pop, symphony orchestras. While still at NBC, formed own jazz quintet. Recorded *Moonlight In Vermont*, together with tenorist Stan Getz, at own first-ever recording date. Attained unusual popularity, becoming one of 1952's two top jazz records. Voted top guitarist in New Star category by DOWN BEAT Critics' Poll. Topped readers' polls for DOWN BEAT, METRONOME in 1954, and with latter for following year.

Between 1953-1960, headed groups regularly at Birdland jazz club, NYC. During 1960's, supervised at own music store in Colorado Springs, only occasionally playing concerts, but participating in summer jazz clinics. Came to Europe twice as member of Bing Crosby's accompanying unit during last two years of singer's life; recorded at London Palladium with Crosby (10).

Johnny Smith has long been the envy of other guitarists for his awesome technical gifts. He remains one of the most articulate performers on his instrument, with a technique that allows him to accomplish practically any ideas, even at the most daunting of tempos. His sensitivity in approach is admirable, illuminating his ballad performances in particular. His taste, too, is impeccable. It is true to say, however, that Smith tends to lack both fire and attack, and a healthy commitment to basic jazz tenets. At his least effective there is a tendency to blandness.

The juxtaposition of Smith and Getz makes for delightfully lyrical, if rather low-key jazz (1). Low-key is a more-than-adequate way of describing the archetypal Johnny Smith small-groups recordings made at regular intervals during a lengthy association with ROOST RECORDS, that lasted from 1952-1962. Except for a selection of material to be found on (1) — including elegant, distinctive stylings of such as *It Might As Well Be Spring, When I Fall In Love, Deep Purple* — the majority of Smith's ROOST recordings have been unavailable for years. Best of which arguably are (2), (4), and (5), the latter being a solo date that is something of a masterclass for the art of Johnny Smith. Both (7), (8) benefit superior recording quality than the Roosts, and (7) might just be his finest-ever LP.

SELECTED DISCOGRAPHY

1 Moonlight In Vermont (with Stan Getz, Zoot Sims, et al) VOGUE
2 Johnny Smith Plays Jimmy Van Heusen ROOST
3 Johnny Smith Trio: Designed For You ROOST
4 Johnny Smith Plus the Trio ROOST
5 Man With Blue Guitar ROOST
6 Reminiscing ROOST
7 Johnny Smith VERVE
8 Kaleidoscope VERVE
9 Johnny Smith/Jeri Southern ROULETTE
10 Live At the London Palladium (Bing Crosby, Joe Bushkin Quartet) K-TEL

TERRY SMITH

Terence Smith: Born West Norwood, London, 1943. Acquired first guitar at 12 — the "economy" type, used by skiffle guitarists in early-1950's. First became of jazz through George Shearing Quintet — and jazz guitar through Shearing's guitarist Chuck Wayne (q.v.) But Django Reinhardt (q.v.) — 'my all-time greatest jazz guitarist' — created the first major impact. First professional job with Reg. Brookes dance band at Doncaster, Yorks., at 19; engagement lasted seven months.

Worked at London's Cool Elephant (1966), then at Ronnie Scott Club (1967). Became member of saxist Dick Morrissey's Quintet (1967-1968), then toured with singer J.J. Jackson, also recording (1). Major international recognition during lengthy period with If, highly successful jazz-rock combo; between 1969-1972, recorded, toured prolifically, including several lengthy US tours. Next, spent year with Zzebra, another highly-rated jazz-rock band (1975). Lived in Sweden (1975-1976); returned

to UK, put together own quintet, including Dick Morrissey (1976-1978), gigging frequently, including Ronnie Scott's.

In more recent times, has been enthusiastically involved with own Blues Band. Smith, who toured with both Scott Walker and the Walker Bros — including first-ever trip to Japan (1968) with the former — topped the MELODY MAKER Readers' Jazz Poll for three consecutive years (1966-1969).

From the mid-1960's, Terry Smith quickly became one of the most respected guitarists on the British jazz scene. His playing — heavily-influenced by the blues area of modern jazz — was ready made for If. Solo-wise, together with Dick Morrissey, his was the band's most expressive voice, and his consistency throughout If's first four LPs — (3), (4), (5), (6) — is admirable. And his blues-worthiness is exemplified by his fine support during (2).

Sadly, the Scott Walker-produced (11) remains Smith's only full-length showcase. The album presents him working with a studio big band, a concept that brings out the best in his playing, emphasising his all-round technical skills. Perhaps better still, however, are two trio tracks — *Early Morning Groove*, and the title tune, both Smith originals — which allow him to stretch out and produce probably his best solo work on record. Of special interest with respect to (9) is Smith's sensitive interpretation of his own *Para Mi Hijo*, his only recorded solo on acoustic guitar thus far.

SELECTED DISCOGRAPHY

1 The Greatest Little Soul Band In the Land (J.J. Jackson) POLYDOR
2 If I.... (Memphis Slim) BARCLAY
3 If ISLAND
4 If 2 ISLAND
5 Island 3 UNITED ARTISTS
6 Island 4 UNITED ARTISTS
7 Zzebra (Zzebra) POLYDOR
8 Mike Carr (Mike Carr) AD RHYTHM
9 British Jazz Artists, Vol. 2 LEE LAMBERT
10 Right Now! (Georgie Fame — one number only) PYE
11 Fall Out PHILLIPS

LES SPANN

Leslie L. Spann, Jr.: Born Pine Bluff, Arkansas, 1932. Studied guitar in high school, in Jamaica, NYC (1949). Between 1950-1957, became deeply immersed in the academic side of music, majoring in music education and flute at the Tennessee State University. During latter part of same period, played gigs with Tennessee State Collegians, and other bands, in and around Nashville. After finishing at the University, decided upon a professional career in jazz — he had become deeply interested in this music form at high school, and that interest had continued

Terry Smith

to grow strongly throughout his university years. First, worked with pianists Phinias Newborn (1957), Ronnell Bright (1958). But his major break-through came when be became member of one of trumpeter Dizzy Gillespie's finest small combos. Spann stayed with Gillespie from August 1958-August 1959, playing mostly guitar but also adding his solo flute from time to time, thus giving the quintet extra tonal colour. It was with Gillespie that Spann established an enviable reputation amongst fellow musicians — especially, not surprising, amongst guitarists. Toured, recorded with Gillespie, impressing audiences everywhere with his straight-forward, beautifully-conceived solo work on both his instruments. Chosen by Quincy Jones to join a truly star-studded jazz orchestra that was to have integral part of Harold Arlen stage musical *Free & Easy*, Spann visited Europe (1959-1960). When show failed to get off ground he, like other members of Jones orchestra, stayed in Europe, playing gigs in Scandinavia, France, etc., before, finally, orchestra disbanded. Continued to gig for some time later; then reported to have suffered from personal problems.

Since late-1960's, nothing has been heard of him, musically; and since 1970's, little if anything has been heard of the man himself...

The demise of Les Spann is one of the saddest jazz stories. For, not only was he a most accomplished flautist, but his always warm-and-swinging guitar playing made him one of the finest talents to emerge during the Fifties. Stylistically, he was deeply indebted to Wes Montgomery (q.v.), possessing similar tonal warmth and beauty, and often using octaves in a Montgomery-like manner. Like his mentor, he could play single-line or chorded jazz guitar, and by the end of the Fifties one could sense a serious attempt to become more his own man.

His playing on a small handful of recordings with the Gillespie Quintet (1) contrasted beautifully with work of the leader and pianist Junior Mance, and it was no surprise that producer Norman Granz asked him to appear on further dates for the VERVE label — like the Gillespie sessions, they all took place between February-April 1959 — involving other distinguished, long-established jazzmen such as Ben Webster (2), Johnny Hodges (3), (4), and Duke Ellington (4). Even in such august company, Spann acquits himself handsomely, playing in his thoughtful, un-demonstrative way, and showing a commendable consistency throughout. Spann's recordings under his own name were restricted to an LP date for JAZZLAND in 1960 and another, eight years later, for ATLANTIC, contents of which have never been issued. For (5), his contributions are divided evenly between flute and guitar. For the latter, there is much beautifully-felt playing spread over four numbers, that on *Q's Dues Blues* (an obvious dedication to his erstwhile employer Quincy Jones) and *There Is No*

Greater Love giving further credence to the high praise he had been accorded during a terribly short period in the limelight. Sadly, that immense promise was not to be totally fulfilled...

SELECTED DISCOGRAPHY

1 **The Ebullient Mr. Gillespie (Dizzy Gillespie)** METRO
2 **Ben Webster & Friends** VERVE
3 **The Smooth One (Johnny Hodges)** VERVE
4 **Blues Summit (Duke Ellington, Johnny Hodges)** VERVE
5 **Gemini** JAZZLAND

LOUIS STEWART

Louis Stewart: Born Waterford, Eire, 1944. Started on piano as child. Then, at 15, heard Les Paul and switched to guitar. Later, heard Barney Kessel (q.v.) on radio jazz programme — that decided which form of music he wanted to play on guitar. Decided also he wanted to become pro musician, and as youngster began to build an enviable reputation in the Dublin area, working with many local bands. Paid first visit to the US with one of the local outfits (1961). Worked regularly with Irish showband, after which joined Noel Kelehan Trio, playing in and around Dublin. During mid-1960's, worked in trio setting, often getting to work with big-name US jazz artists, like Gerry Mulligan, Lee Konitz. Received Press Award at 1968 Montreux Jazz Festival as Outstanding European Soloist (working with Jim Doherty Quartet). After which, decided to reside and work in London. Joined popular Tubby Hayes Quartet, thus giving him further exposure. His playing was brought to the attention of Benny Goodman; as a result, Stewart made three European tours by Goodman. Returned to Dublin (1971). Spent much time there working in TV, radio, recording. Began to write more at this period, including music for award-winning *A Week In the Life of Martin Cluxton*. Back to London, this time to become member of the Ronnie Scott Quartet (1975). But by the end of the 1970's, he had decided, once again, to return to his native Eire, where to-day he still works regularly, although he returns to the UK, and makes trips to Europe at fairly frequent intervals.

Louis Stewart remains one of the few world-class jazz musicians to emanate from Eire — and, most certainly, that country's foremost jazz guitarist. A superb technician, Stewart never allows his great skills to get in the way of his natural flair for improvisation. That he is indeed a most thoughtful performer should not obscure the fact that he can play with fire and drive. Stewart's first recordings prove that he was even then very much a complete guitarist, albeit one striving to attain his own identity. That he could achieve exhilaration in performance is

GABOR SZABO

Louis Stewart

Gabor Szabo: Born Budapest, Hungary, 1936. Took up guitar at 15 — but studied only three months. Turned on to jazz by tuning in regularly to Voice of America Jazz Hour. Practised assiduously to improve his playing, at same time developing own individual finger technique. Recorded with many local Hungarian groups — also accompanying singers — during teens; also played on movie soundtracks, worked regularly on Hungarian radio. Made tape of own work to send to Voice of America — it was broadcast by the station the night he left his native country just prior to the Soviet invasion. Arrived in US with joint refugee-cum-Freedom Fighter status. Interned at Camp Kilmer, before settling, fianlly, in Boston, Mass. Studied at local Berklee School of Music (1957-1959), also gigging locally with Toshiko Akiyoshi, and others. Featured with Newport International Band at Newport Jazz Festival (1958). Began to build healthy reputation on American jazz scene, a reputation that received even bigger boost on joining Chico Hamilton Quintet (1961). Stayed with the drummer over four years, becoming one of combo's strongest voices, and adding interestingly to its repertoire. Left Hamilton in 1965, worked briefly with writer-instrumentalist-bandleader Gary McFarland same year, then joined ex-Hamilton colleague Charles Lloyd (3). Put together regular working combo (1966-1968).

Disbanded 1969, taking six months off to re-think music philosophy and direction — during early-1960's had become deeply influenced by rock happenings. Next band showed particular emphasis on rock, blues. Provided sensitive accompaniments-solos for Lena Horne album (22), and also wrote score for Roman Polanski's controversial *Repulsion* movie. Formed band comprising former colleagues in previous bands, the Perfect Circle, playing a wide variety of music, acoustic and electric. Continued to write extensively, including film music for Gabor Kalman's *Farm Boy of Hungary*. Played major jazz festivals in the States, plus Lena Horne TV special, Flip Wilson Show. Participated in own Gabor Szabo (USA) TV special. Went back to Budapest to film *Jazz Podium*, 90-minute film, containing music, interviews, etc., with English-Hungarian dialogue. It was on further visit to his home town, in 1982, to produce an LP, that he died, quite suddenly...

The emergence of Gabor Szabo at the beginning of the 1960's gave jazz an important and wholly distinctive new voice. His influences were myriad, including American jazz guitar players of many persuasions, blues, rock and his own Hungarian folk-musical background — there was always a strain of the East European gypsy culture about this playing. Szabo's growth while with

shown during a series of recordings as member of the Tubby Hayes Orchestra (1), most notably during a freewheeling contributions to *Up, Up & Away*. And just how astonishingly mature he had become during the subsequent decade can be judged by his playing during (2). All his own recordings have numerous moments of filligree guitar work, with (4) being as good an example of super-relaxation combined with flair and imagination as any. (6) contains some of Stewart's finest writing — as indeed it contains some of his best playing — while his arrangement and performance of Faure's *Pavanne* is exquisite. (5) is very much an unhistrionic tour de force, while a live duet recording with flautist Brian Dunning (7) — recorded in Dublin, in 1979 — is full of subtle interactions, delightful twists and turns, and many moments of high-quality musical understatement.

SELECTED DISCOGRAPHY

1 The Tubby Hayes Orchestra FONTANA
2 Serious Gold (Ronnie Scott) PYE
3 Louis the First HAWK JAZZ
4 Baubles, Bangles & Beads WAVE
5 Out On His Own LIVIA
6 Milesian Source PYE
7 Alone Together (with Brian Dunning) LIVIA

Hamilton was astonishing. Tonally, he produced a beautiful sound at this time — something which he was to improve upon as the years went by — and the combination of tonal beauty, flawless execution and real depth illuminated performances of this period like *Who Can I Turn To?* and his own *Evil Eyes.*

Szabo's own recordings have encompassed a bewildering variety of sounds and techniques. He was possibly the first guitarist to try to reproduce on his instrument some of John Coltrane's own sound and harmonic approach. And he succeeded probably more than any jazz guitarist to incorporate devices from Indian music, even recording on sitar, (5).

Many are the recordings which amplify his uniqueness, but (11), (12), (9), (4), (14), (15), (16) and (18) rank with the very best. And his contributions to albums by such as Paul Desmond, (21), and Gary McFarland, (20) — containing marvellous Szabo guitar work — demonstrates his enormous versatility and highly-developed ability to empathise.

CTH 1001

SELECTED DISCOGRAPHY

1 The Further Adventures of El Chico (Chico Hamilton) IMPULSE
2 Passin' Thru (Chico Hamilton) JASMINE
3 Live with Charles Lloyd BLUE THUMB
4 Spellbinder IMPULSE
5 Jazz Raga IMPULSE
6 The Sorcerer IMPULSE
7 The California Dreamers IMPULSE
8 Greatest Hits IMPULSE
9 Memorabilia MCA/IMPULSE
10 Bacchanal Dreams SKYE
11 Gabor Szabo 1969 SKYE
12 Magical Connection BLUE THUMB
13 High Contrast BLUE THUMB
14 Blowin' Some Old Smoke BUDDAH
15 Mizrab CTI
16 Rambler CTI
17 Macho SALVATION
18 Nightflight MERCURY
19 Faces MERCURY
20 The Dedication Series/Vol. IX: The Great Arrangers (Gary McFarland) IMPULSE
21 Skylark (Paul Desmond) CTI
22 Something In the Way She Sings (Lena Horne) SKYE

MARTIN TAYLOR

Martin Taylor: Born Harlow, Essex, 1956. Started on guitar at age four. Basically self-taught, but given some little tutelage by father, guitarist-bassist with dance bands. Made professional debut at eight. Although an admitted average-only reader, managed to obtain ample work from 15 with cruise-ships plying between UK, the States. At 16, shared bill on QE2 Caribbean voyage with Count Basie Orchestra — even got the chance to sit in with band on several occasions. Also worked, at 15, with Sonny Dee dance band, year later with drummer Lennie Hastings' jazz combo. After three years working on boats, decided to return to London.

Began to quickly acquire enviable reputation on London jazz scene as guitarist with superior technique, and burgeoning all-round talent of his own. In late-1970's, worked in two guitar format with Ike Isaacs — a mentor and close friend — at London's Pizza On the Park venue, and was frequently heard in company only of bassist Peter Ind. Biggest break, however, came when asked by violinist Stephane Grappelli to join his combo. Subsequently, toured worldwide with veteran Frenchman, including no less than seven US trips, and appearances at major international jazz festivals like Newport, Playboy, Nice, Capital Radio (London). Also worked in duo setting with Grappelli in Switzerland, Scotland, London's Cafe Royal. In addition,. has worked with many other leading jazz artists, including Buddy DeFranco, Ruby Braff, Ronnie Scott, Al Grey, Peanuts Hucko, fellow guitarists Tal Farlow (q.v.), Barney Kessel (q.v.), and distinguished non-jazz figures like Yehudi Menuhin, Nelson Riddle.

Martin Taylor's emergence, at the tail-end of the 1970's, signified that, once again, Britain had produced a jazz guitarist of real international stature. His development since then has been little short of astonishing. His

technique has continued to be finely honed until to-day he can stand shoulder-to-shoulder with the world's leading players. Thankfully, though, Taylor doesn't use his admirable technique unwisely. In fact, is it true to say that his playing never has been of the pointlessly flashy variety. He develops his solos logically and with care to detail, yet he retains at all times that vital spark of spontaneity inherent in all the finest jazz playing. Taylor's is an acoustic guitar coupled with a floating pick-up, which accounts for the luminous, warm quality of his tone. (For recording purposes, he insists on a microphone apiece for both amp and guitar).

On record, Martin Taylor continues to shine, both at his own dates as well as those by such as Stephane Grappelli and David Grisman. Despite his jazz type sophistication, he seems to have a natural rapport with the good-time music of the latter, and there is much fine Taylor guitar work throughout the varied contents of both (9), (10). With Grappelli, he has forged an on-off partnership that compares with any other with which the violinist has been associated during the past 30-40 years. The live-ness of (3) makes that LP required listening, although the pair's first-ever date, (1), contains a plethora of musical excellence.

There is little or nothing at which to complain about Taylor's own recordings. The two albums recorded with Ind, (7), (8), especially the second contain many minutes of true jazz collaboration; the title tune of (8) shows just how superb a performer Taylor has become in more recent times. Of special interest, too, is the guitarist's (11), a solo album, recorded privately in 1983, which positively reaffirms his youthful mastery.

SELECTED DISCOGRAPHY

1 **We've Got the World On a String (with Stephane Grappelli)** EMI/ANGEL
2 **Vintage 1981 (with Stephane Grappelli)** CONCORD JAZZ
3 **At the Winery (with Stephane Grappelli)** CONCORD JAZZ
4 **After Hours (with Ike Isaacs)** JTC
5 **On The Road Again (with Stephane Grappelli, Teresa Brewer)** DOCTOR JAZZ
6 **Skye Boat** CONCORD JAZZ
7 **Taylor Made (with Peter Ind, John Richardson)** WAVE
8 **Triple Libra (with Peter Ind)** WAVE
9 **David Grisman's Acoustic Christmas** ROUNDER
10 **Dawg Jazz/Dawg Grass (with David Grisman)** WARNER BROS
11 **A Tribute to Art Tatum** MARTIN TAYLOR

TOOTS THIELEMANS

Jean 'Toots' Thielemans: Born Brussels, Belgium, 1922. First musical instrument — harmonica — at 15, while studying maths as college. Left Belgium early in World War II for France, but by the end of 1941 had returned to home country. In France, heard Django Reinhardt (q.v.). Which led him to buy own guitar; taught himself to play. Gigged at American GI clubs (1944). Paid first visit to US (1947). Appeared at Paris Jazz Festival (1949). Growing reputation enabled him to perform — on guitar — with Benny Goodman Sextet on European tour (1950). Emigrated to States following year.

Between 1953-1959, toured nationally as member of George Shearing Quintet, playing occasional harmonica, mostly guitar. As a result of the lengthy tenture with Shearing, was able to put together own combo after leaving the pianist. Because of his sight-reading ability, was able also to obtain extensive freelance studio work, mostly in NYC. Paid frequent trips back to Europe. Became particularly popular in Scandinavia (where he first recorded *Bluesette*, most famous composition).

Became regular staffman back in New York with ABC/TV (working mainly on widely-syndicated Jimmy Dean Show). From around 1969, became closely associated with Quincy Jones, playing on numerous movie soundtracks. Memorable appearance at Monterey Jazz Festival (1972); toured USSR same year with own quartet. During 1970's, continued to revisit Europe (including Belgium) on regular basis. Wrote songs, background music for Swedish animated film *Dunderklumpeu*, and composed theme music for highly-popular Sesame Street TV series. Broke it up with a memorable set during the Montreux Jazz Festival (1975). Since which time has continued to work at live jazz gigs, making jazz LPs, and operating in more commercial studio settings. In was in Sweden, in late-1950's, that Thielemans first introduced his unison guitar-whistling to a recording studio. If he'd concentrated on the one instrument, Toots Thielemans would have sustained a formidable reputation as a harmonica player — indeed, it is doubtful whether there has been a more gifted improviser on harmonica in jazz history thus far. But he is recognised too as a gifted guitar player, whose fluent, elegant style sounds at home in practically any setting. Originally a Django disciple, Thielemans was one fo the first post-war Europeans to respond to the delights of bebop.

His good taste and sensitivity stood him in good stead during his Shearing days, as recordings like (1), (2), (3) prove handsomely. In a more basic jazz setting, Thielemans — both on harmonica as well as guitar — responds in more freewheeling style. Especially when

caught in live performance, and together with distinguished players like Oscar Peterson, Joe Pass, Niels Henning Orsted Pedersen — (all 12) — or JoAnne Brackeen (10).

SNTF 822

SELECTED DISCOGRAPHY

1 **Lullaby of Birdland (George Shearing)** MGM
2 **The Best of George Shearing** CAPITOL
3 **The Shearing Spell** CAPITOL
4 **Man Bites Horn** RIVERSIDE
5 **Time Out For Toots** DECCA
6 **Spotlight On Toots** POLYDOR
7 **The Whistler & His Guitar** ABC-PARAMOUNT
8 **Too Much, Toots!** PHILLIPS
9 **Toots & Svend (with Svend Asmussen)** SONET
10 **Captured Alive** CHOICE
11 **Toots Thielemans Live** POLYDOR
12 **Live In the Netherlands (with Oscar Peterson, Joe Pass)** PABLO LIVE
13 **Gula Matari (Quincy Jones)** A&M
14 **Smackwater Jack (Quincy Jones)** A&M
15 **You've Got It Bad Girl (Quincy Jones)** A&M

RENE THOMAS

Rene Thomas: Born Liege, Belgium, 1927. Mainly self-taught, but did take some tuition between 10-11. Promising career as young jazz player interrupted by World War II. With cessation of hostilities, began professional life with freelance work in France, Belgium. Built up strong European reputation as jazz guitarist who understood bebop intuitively. Played Paris gigs with trumpeter Chet Baker (1955), and worked alongside numerous other visiting Americans. Then, decided to emigrate to Canada.

Visited NYC, during which time worked and recorded with the legendary Sonny Rollins — it was Rollins who at that time said of Thomas that he was 'better than any of the American guitarists on the scene to-day'. Later, returned to live, work in Europe.

Toured Europe with organist Lou Bennett, drummer Kenny Clarke, and with many other groups, including duo with Dutch drummer Han Bennink. Member of impressive Stan Getz Quartet (1969-1972), including also French organist Eddie Louiss; group toured Mexico, various European countries and playing unforgettable 1971 season at London's Ronnie Scott Club. Thomas returned to Montreal (1973), ostensibly to visit a relative there, but decided to continue to work in Canada again.

Rene Thomas — winner of the 1967 DOWN BEAT Readers' Poll, Talent Deserving Wider Recognition — will be remembered for all time as probably second only to Django Reinhardt, his original influence, as the finest guitar player to grace conventional jazz in Europe. A strongly-swinging player at all times, his improvisations were delivered with real emotional commitment and a fine sense of construction. Thomas was at least influenced by horn players as guitarists, probably more so. Which explains why he sounded so splendid in company with such as Sonny Rollins (6), Bobby Jaspar (3), Lucky Thompson (8). And it was with another top tenorist, Stan Getz, that Thomas produced some of the finest playing in his career. During which time he also contributed some out-of-the-ordinary compositions to the Getz Quartet's book. His empathy with group members Getz and Eddie Louiss, was readily apparent at all times, with Thomas' long, flowing lines and impressive attack gracing numbers like his own *Ballad For Leo, Theme For Manuel* (both 9, with *Manuel* repeated on 10), and *Ballad For My Dad* (9), latter co-composed with Louiss. (9) also contains *Invitation*, a flawless example of his exquisite ballad-playing; (4) has *West Coast Blues,* written by Thomas' only latterday guitar influence, Wes Montgomery (q.v.), and is a superior performance of the Belgian's unforced ability with blues.

SELECTED DISCOGRAPHY

1 **The Rene Thomas Quintet** VOGUE
2 **Guitar Groove** JAZZLAND
3 **Rene Thomas-Bobby Jaspar Quintet** RCA VICTOR
4 **Meeting Mr. Thomas** BARCLAY
5 **Thomas-Pelzer Limited** VOGEL
6 **Tenor Titan (Sonny Rollins)** VERVE
7 **Chet Baker Is Back** RCA VICTOR
8 **Song Book In Europe (with Lucky Thompson)** MPS
9 **Dynasty (Stan Getz)** VEFRVE
10 **Coleman Hawkins-Stan Getz-Don Byas** EUROPA JAZZ

RALPH TOWNER

Ralph Towner: Born Chehalis, Washington. 1940. From a musical family — mother, piano teacher/church organist; father, trumpet player. Began improvising at piano — at three! Played trumpet two years later. Studied theory/composition at University of Oregon (1958-1963). Undertook graduate work (1964-1966). Studied classical guitar with Karl Scheit at Vienna Academy of Music (1963-1964, then again, 1967-1968). Had played trumpet in dance-band at 13, in Bend, Oregon. Featured lute, guitar with Elizabethan Consort, Eugene Chamber Ensemble, Oregon (1964-1966).

In 1966, replaced Larry Coryell (q.v.) in Chuck Mahaffay band, in Seattle. To NYC (1969). There, jammed with such as John McLaughlin (q.v.), Airto Moreira. Played gigs with Tamba Four Latin-American band. With bassist Jimmy Garrison (1969-1970); then, consecutively with flautist Jeremy Steig (1969-1971); Winter Consort (1970-1971 — playing 12-string acoustic); Weather Report (1971, briefly); then vibist Gary Burton.

From 1971, his major pre-occupation was with Oregon, band that basically grew out of Winter Consort. Won DOWN BEAT Critics' Poll, Talent Deserving Wider Recognition (1974). During the past 10 years has been constantly in demand, recording, televising, and touring prolifically, at home and abroad. Ralph Towner's chart progress during the past decade has been little short of astonishing. Primarily, of course, a guitar player, he also acquits himself expertly on cornet, French horn, synthesiser, and assorted percussion. He is also a composer of extraordinary scope and versatility, able to move freely and naturally through different areas of musical expression like conventional and free jazz, classical, folk, and rock.

Towner's multi-talents have proved to be easily adaptable to the many different settings in which his playing has been featured, including the gently, classically-orientated Winter Consort, (12), the superior electric jazz band of Weather Report, (23), or conjoined to the shimmering artistry of Gary Burton, (13), (14), or the totally individual creations of pianist Keith Jarrett, (15).

Towner's has been a particularly deep involvement with actual sound reproduction that can be obtained from various guitars — electric or acousitc, 12-string or more conventional string size. Whichever particular model he chooses to use, he explores all avenues of expression, stretching the sound range to the maximum, yet never using devices or techniques that are anything but intensely musical.

Towner's participation in two-guitar collaborations have been just as successful as any others, more so than most. Which is why his on-record meetings with Larry Coryell, (21), and John Abercrombie, (16), (17); have resulted in much delightful music. In totally different ways, his recordings with saxist Jan Garbarek, (19), and the unique combo Azimuth, (20), have been highly successful, due principally to the guitarist's own playing and his shrewd guidance and musical thinking.

Towner's long-lasting involvement with the widely popular Oregon has been mutually beneficial. In person, the band established a notable reputation from its outset, something it has improved upon through the succeeding years. The Oregon recordings have been plentiful, and the overall standard of performance has been exceptional. But probably (2), (4), (6), (7) take individual honours for overall brilliance, highlighted by Ralph Towner's own astonishing creative performances that are high in terms of colour, dynamics and sheer virtuosity.

ECM 1250

SELECTED DISCOGRAPHY

1 **Music of Another Present Era (Oregon)** VANGUARD
2 **Distant Hills (Oregon)** VANGUARD
3 **Winter Light (Oregon)** VANGUARD
4 **In Concert (Oregon)** VANGUARD
5 **Out of the Woods (Oregon)** ECM
6 **Roots In the Sky (Oregon)** ECM
7 **In Performance (Oregon)** ECM
8 **Trios/Solos** ECM
9 **Diary** ECM
10 **Blue Sun** ECM
11 **Old Friends, New Friends** ECM
12 **Road (Winter Consort)** A&M

JOHN TROPEA

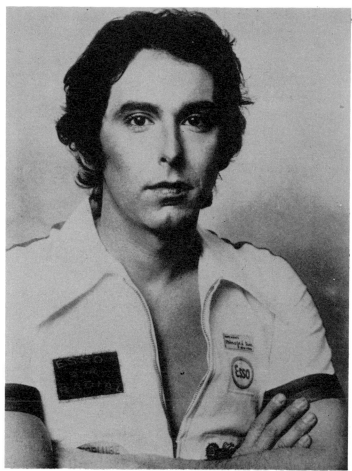

John Tropea

John Tropea: Born Manhattan, NYC, 1946, but raised from six months at Fort Lee, New Jersey. Very early interest in music enabled him to commence piano lessons at eight. Moved to guitar when 10 — thus fulfilling his original dream to be a guitarist (he had occasionally played banjo at four). Parents bought him his first guitar, a Stella acoustic. Started to teach himself, helped by a friend, immediately. Played in his first band during 7th/8th grades at school; he was youngest member of the school orchestra. Began studying classical guitar in Manhattan (1959); added mandolin studies at about the same time. Spent two years of study on both instruments with Giovannia Vicari. Also spent some time as student of Sal Salvador (q.v.), before enrolling at Berklee School of Music for three years. During this period in Boston, did some gigs as support for the Three Degrees.

After leaving Berklee, worked regularly in Broadway pit orchestra — even conducting on the odd occasion. Following which came the beginning of a non-stop involvement with studio work. And in 1969, began recording extensively and making jingles. After meeting producer Bob Crewe (1972), began working almost exclusively for him in recording studios, etc. Joined band put together by Brazilian instrumentalist-composer-arranger Eumir Deodato (1972), touring, recording, for approximately three years. Featured on international Number One pop hit recording of *2001* (7). After Deodato, it was back again for the most part of comprehensive studio work...

Because of his enormous capabilities in all manner of musical situations, John Tropea's true potential as a jazz guitarist cannot be said to have been fully realised. His contributions to non-jazz LPs by eminently talented musical persons such as Streisand, (13), Phoebe Snow, (12), Paul Simon, (11), and Laura Nyro, (8), (9), have been wholly splendid. During the Deodato period, he was the principal soloist for studio recording dates like (4), (5), (7). His solo work evidences an abiding interest in various forms — jazz, rock, blues, folk, Latin-American. To each idiom Tropea's contributions are structured in a telling, wholly appropriate way. Yet his full capabilities as a jazz improviser, working as a sideman, have only been hinted at, with *Tropea*, from (6), showing off his obvious skills best of all.

His own records have been noted for excellent overall concepts, plus superior playing by Tropea and fellow soloists, and superb production. (Tropea acts as his own producer, also being involved in arranging and/or orchestrating). (2) remains probably the finest all-round — including a beautifully-conceived solo on his own *Blue Too* — but both (1) and (3) are not far behind.

When John Tropea emerges from time to time from the recording studios to play a live date in and around New York, you can be sure that all available guitarists will try to be there too. Because of his much-in-demand commercial activities, he doesn't seem to be as involved with too much basic jazz for any real length of time. Both on record and as in-person performer, it is to be hoped that this eminently fine player gets many more opportunities to submerge himself in plentiful jazz situations, now and in the future. Then, perhaps, it will be possible to really ascertain his true position amongst contemporary jazz guitarists...

SELECTED DISCOGRAPHY

1 Tropea MARLIN
2 Short Trip To Space TK
3 To Touch You Again TK
4 Prelude (Deodato) CTI
5 Deodato CTI
6 Deodato/Airto In Concert CTI
7 2001 (Deodato) CTI
8 Nested (Lauro Nyro) CBS
9 Smile (Laura Nyro) CBS
10 Phil Upchurch MARLIN
11 Still Crazy After All These Years (Paul Simon) CBS
12 Second Childhood (Phoebe Snow) CBS
13 Songbird (Barbara Streisand) CBS
14 Who Am I? (David Ruffin) TAMLA MOTOWN
15 Star Wars (soundtrack, John Williams) 20TH CENTURY

JAMES 'BLOOD' ULMER

James Ulmer: Born St. Matthews, South Carolina, 1942. Played guitar from very early age (father also guitarist). Comprehensively involved with music — gospel, blues, folk, etc. At seven, commenced six-year association with Southern Sons gospel vocal group, but interested primarily in guitar. Went to live in Pittsburgh (1959). Gigged with local bands like Southern Sounds, Savoys, Jewel Brenner's Swing Kings; also got to jam with George Benson (q.v.), and to work in jazz-organ format with Jimmy Smith, Richard 'Groove' Holmes, Hank Marr (3). After high school graduation, moved on to Detroit (1967). In Detroit, first experimented with what was to become known as his harmolodic music (harmonic modulations).

After arriving in New York (1971), able to put harmolodic theories into practice through working with jazzmen of similar persuasions, most notably innovative Ornette Coleman, organist Larry Young, drummer Rashied Ali. In fact, studied for years in Coleman's Manhattan loft appartment, and played alongside Coleman until 1975. Worked also as leader of Minton's Playhouse house band for nine months. Appeared with Coleman at Ann Arbor Jazz & Blues Festival (1974), Newport Jazz Festival (1977). Gigged briefly with drummer Art Blakey (1973), and also worked in first half of 1970's with other top jazz musicians like pianist Paul Bley, bassist Charlie Haden, tenorist Joe Henderson, trumpeter Don Cherry.

The music of James 'Blood' Ulmer — he calls it his 'harmolodic diatonic funk' — comprises a seemingly unlikely synthesis of blues, electronics, gospel, atonality, with shock-wave, avant garde sound mixing freely — and sometimes confusingly — with basic, low-down funk. So personalised is Ulmer's music, it might seem impossible that his playing can be satisfactorily juxtaposed to others. But he certainly has acted as something of a catalyst to recordings by such as David Murray (9), Larry Young (3), Joe Henderson (4) — he is stunningly helpful to Henderson during Tress-Cun-Deo-La — and altoist Arthur Blythe (5). And Ulmer and Ornette Coleman are mutually stimulating on (6).

Ulmer's own recordings have all contained their own quantity of organic excitement and gut-level creativity, but none has been totally successful due in all probability to the knife-edge spontaneity of the man's very approach to his harmolodic diatonic funk. Of additional interest in assessing Ulmer — who also plays flute, but only rarely — is his singing, as raw, basic and compelling as his guitar playing. The lethal vocal-instrumental combination accounts most certainly on the success of his single release Are You Glad To Be In America? (12). But if one track does complete justice to the man who has been described as 'the most original guitarist since Jimi Hendrix', then it might well be Swing & Things, from (12), an apocalyptic display of his out-of-the-ordinary playing capabilities.

SELECTED DISCOGRAPHY

1 Hank Marr In the Marketplace KING
2 Accent On the Blues (John Patton) BLUE NOTE
3 Lawrence of Newark (Larry Young) PERCEPTION
4 Multiple (Joe Henderson) MILESTONE
5 Lenox Avenue Breakdown CBS
6 Tales of Captain Black (with Ornette Coleman) ARTISTS HOUSE
7 Black Rock CBS
8 Are You Glad To Be In America? (with David Murray, Oliver Lake, et al) ROUGH TRADE
9 No Wave (David Murray) MOERS
10 Freelancing (with David Murray, Oliver Lake, et al) CBS
11 Black Rock CBS
12 Odyssey CBS

PHIL UPCHURCH

Philip Upchurch: Born Chicago, Illinois, 1941. Pianist-father introduced him to ukulele (1952). Two years later, he bought his son a guitar. Basically self-taught, merged into the local Chicago scene during teens. Found a natural affinity with Chicago-style blues, and being equally gifted on guitar and electric-bass, became a familiar figure in the city's recording studios as a respected session player. Played guitar with diverse talents as Jerry Butler, the Spaniels, Porter Kilbert, and worked on scores of blues/R&B record dates with name artists like Muddy Waters, Otis Rush, Howlin' Wolf, et al. Upchurch's reputation was established between 1958-1962 — hectic years for his developing talents; although with constant

recording sessions, plus time off for touring purposes with various bands, there was too little time really to concentrate on his own thing for any reasonable length of time. First major break, though, came via recording the two-part *Can't Sit Down*, with singer Dee Clark, for whom he was working as accompanist. The record took off and in so doing helped focus attention, in part at least, on the guitar player.

Drafted in 1965, was posted to West Germany, where he managed to play jazz in various small combos. Discharged two years later, returned to his native city to recommence his prolific work existence, including gigs with such as altoist Cannonball Adderley, arranger-

TK Records 82542

composer-bassist Richard Evans, saxist Grover Washington. Through previous recording dates with the pianist, joined Ramsey Lewis Quartet (1970). Moved to California (1971) to work primarily with Quincy Jones in movies. But an earthquake sent him back to live in Chicago. Toured Japan with Jones (1972), then co-led band with singer-piant Tennyson Stephens. Was awarded National Academy of Recorded Arts & Sciences Governors' Award for his contribution to Chicago's music scene (1975). Since which time, he has continued to remain a much sought-after musician of genuine all-round skills, a professional to his very fingertips whose dedication to each and every job has long since made his something of a legendary name in the music business.

Probably as much due to his comprehensive involvement with the work of other people, but Phil Upchurch's own recorded output remains, numerically speaking, less

than satisfactory. Which is a shame because his guitar playing, deeply influenced by the blues at all times, is invariably a most satisfying experience. The lovely dark tone that invests his performance with such warmth and feeling is especially apparent during both sides of (8), with Upchurch in a more conventional jazz setting then usual. The title tune, together with *Muscle Shoal* and *I Want a Little Girl,* finds him in his very best form. Even with a somewhat unnecessary strings-and-horns backdrop, (9) is a further testament to his beautifully economic style and depth of feeling.

(12), a worthy legacy of the quintet Upchurch co-led with singer-pianist Tennyson Stephens in 1975, contains in *In Common* one of the guitarist's finest recorded solos; likewise, *Foolin' Around,* from (13), remains a particularly potent example of Upchurch's delightfully ambivalent style. 'I'm not really a jazz player', the notoriously modest Chicagoan once said. In a way, he is right. For basic blues is a more important ingredient of his musical make-up. But jazzman — and a fine one at that — he most certainly is...

SELECTED DISCOGRAPHY

1 **Stay Loose** (Jimmy Smith) VERVE
2 **The Special Magic of Stan Getz & Burt Bacharach** VERVE
3 **Bad Benson** (George Benson) CTI
4 **Body Heat** (Quincy Jones) A&M
5 **Light My Fire** (Woody Herman) CHECKER
6 **Heavy Exposure** (Woody Herman) CHECKER
7 **Them Changes** (Ramsey Lewis) CADET
8 **Feeling Blue** MILESTONE
9 **Grooving With the Soulful Strings** CADERT
10 **Upchurch** CADET
11 **Darkness, Darkness** BLUE THUMB
12 **Upchurch/Tennyson** KUDU
13 **Phil Upchurch** TK

GEORGE VAN EPS

George Abel Van Eps: Born Plainfield, New Jersey, 1913. Comes from noted musical family, including father Fred, noted banjo player of early part of century; brothers Bobby, piano arranger; Fred, trumpet, arranger; John saxes. Started on banjo (1924) — self-taught. Commenced gigging, on same instrument, at 13 (in brother Fred's band). Made first solo broadcast year later. Studied watch-making (1929-1931). Worked with singer Smith Ballew, after first touring with Harry Reser's Junior Artists, and Dutch Master Minstrels. Played guitar with dance band of Freddy Martin (1931-1933), then was heard successively with Benny Goodman (1934-1935), Ray Noble (1935-1941 — with period 1936-1939 spent freelancing in Hollywood). Topped METRONOME magazine readers' poll (1937).

Through following decade became active in studios, taking on extra occupation as engineer. (Van Eps, in 1954, completed what is thought to be the world's smallest fully-operating live steam locomotive).

During 1960's, continued to make appearances at concerts, including Aspen Jazz Festival (1964) — same year he announced his retirement from professional playing. However, didn't stop playing completely. Further inactivity followed a mild heart attack at the beginning of 1970's. Still played occasionally even after this, and he has been known to make a surprise live appearance in much more recent times.

George Van Eps remains one of jazz' great chordal exponents. His sound, too, is one of the most distinctive of all players, occasioned as it is by his adding an A string, below the E string, to the normal six-string set-up, and tuning the seventh string a fifth below its normal range. In addition, Van Eps has a great gift for reharmonisation, coupled with a superb built-in bass-line that gives his strictly acoustic approach the kind of running excitement of the great extrovert players.

A prolific recording artist during the first half of his career, Van Eps never really did get sufficient solo space. Nevertheless, his very presence added overall excellence to sessions featuring other master players such as Benny Goodman (1), (2), Jack Teagarden (2), (3), Eddie Miller (10). Half of (4) finds Van Eps offering a marvellously supportive, occasionally even subservient, contribution to what is basically a showcase for pianist Jess Stacy.

His own comparatively few recordings have not always done complete justice to his superior jazz talents, fine as most have been in giving the collector a chance to marvel at the man's great subtlety in performance. It would indeed be pleasing to have at hand, once again, items such as (7), (8), (9) — and best of all, the luxurious (6). On the latter, the ballads, in particular, like *Yesterdays* and *Dancing On the Ceiling*, have guitar playing that is sublime. (The more sprightly *I Never Knew* (5) originates from the old COLUMBIA LP from 1956).

Just how well-preserved the Van Eps skills remained in later years can be gauged by his two contributions to (13). A gorgeous chorded outing on *A Foggy Day* alone would have been sufficient to elicit the warmest praise for a talent so well preserved; but an exquisite duet performance of *The Shadow Of Your Smile*, with trombonist Murray McEachern, provides conclusive evidence...

SELECTED DISCOGRAPHY

1 A Jazz Holiday (Adrian Rollini) MCA
2 Benny Goodman, Vol. 4 RCA VICTOR
3 The Great Soloists/Featuring Jack Teagarden BIOGRAPH
4 Ralph Sutton & Jess Stacy: Piano Solos ACE OF HEARTS
5 50 Years of Jazz Guitar (one item only) COLUMBIA
6 Mellow Guitar COLUMBIA
7 Soliloquy CAPITOL
8 My Guitar CAPITOL
9 Seven String Guitar CAPITOL
10 George Van Eps 1949 (with Eddie Miller) JUMP
11 Pete Kelly At Home (Matty Matlock) RCA VICTOR
12 Pete Kelly Lets His Hair Down (Matty Matlock) WARNER BROS
13 The Complete 1970 Pasadena Jazz Party (Blue Angel Jazz Club)

CHUCK WAYNE

Charles Jagelka: Born New York City, 1923. Began on mandolin, with balalaika band; discarded the instrument when it warped, opted for guitar. Was employed as elevator operator when opportunities came to work with pianists Clarence Profit, Nat Jaffe on 52nd Street (1941). Served in US Army (1942-1944). The, back in NYC, worked with clarinettist/saxist Joe Marsala at Hickory House (1944-1946), Woody Herman (1946), Phil Moore Four (1947), pianist Barbara Carroll, and saxist Alvy West's Little Band (both in 1948). Gained widespread recognition during tenure with popular George Shearing Quintet (1949-1952). Left, eventually, to freelance — again, back in New York, mostly leading own combos. Toured as part of singer Tony Bennett's accompanying unit (1954-1957). Wrote for played music in Broadway show *Orpheus Descending* (1957). Became CBS staffman in 1959.

During 1960's, continued to lead own groups, as well as teaching guitar privately; also studied classical guitar. During decade played regularly on major TV shows (including Ed Sullivan), also undertaking innumerable diverse record dates — jazz and non-jazz. Worked on Broadway again — *The Nervous Set, Copper & Brass*. Rejoined CBS. Put together guitar duo with Joe Puma — (17) — in 1973, playing concerts, clubs, seminars, and long residency at St. Regis Hotel. Scored for documentary film *The Mugging*.

In a now long and distinguished career, Chuck Wayne has maintained a consistency in peformance few can surpass. Moreover, his sheer versatility, in practically any musical situation, has made his a much in-demand name in all media. An immensely gifted player, using a combination of single-line and chordal, Wayne's delightful flowing style makes him a firm favourite amongst his fellow musicians, and a guitarist to whom other guitar players looked to with admiration and respect. As one of the early bebop players, not surprisingly he associated freely with most of the leading figures, including Dizzy

Gillespie, (1), and Bud Powell, Lee Konitz, Buddy DeFranco, J.J. Johnson — all (8). But, of course, it was his filligree work with the Shearing Quintet in its finest period, (7), that most fans recall most readily.

Wayne never has been given half as many opportunities to record under his own name as his undoubted talents deserve. Which makes recourse to such as (9), (11), (12) a particular delight. If anything, (13) is even better — with Wayne playing the odd banjo solo to boot. His three contributions to (15) are as memorable as any other, while the most appropriately titled (14) — a series of delectable unaccompanied guitar solos — finds him at his most sensitive and most subtle.

SELECTED DISCOGRAPHY

1 Dizzy Gillespie: The Small Groups (1945-1946) PHOENIX
2 Swing Classics, Vol. 1: 1944/45 (Slam Stewart) POLYDOR
3 The Thundering Herds (Woody Herman) COLUMBIA
4 The Aladdin Sessions (Lester Young) BLUE NOTE
5 Jack Teagarden RCA VICTOR
6 The Greatest of the Samll Bands, Vol. 2 (Coleman Hawkins) RCA VICTOR
7 Lullaby of Birdland (George Shearing) VERVE
8 Tadd Dameron Big Ten & Royal Roost Jam/Jam Session BEPPO
9 The Memorable Claude Thornhill COLUMBIA
10 Claude Thornhill & His Orchestra 1947 LONDON
11 Into the Hot (Gil Evans) IMPULSE
12 String Fever VIK
13 The Jazz Guitarist SAVOY
14 Skyliner PROGRESSIVE
15 Tapestry FOCUS
16 Morning Mist PRESTIGE
17 Interactions (with Joe Puma) CHOICE
18 The Guitar Album (one track only) COLUMBIA
19 Jazztime U.S.A. (with Terry Gibbs; Billy Taylor; Oscar Pettiford) MCA CORAL

JACK WILKINS

John Wilkins: Born New York City, 1946. Grew up in intensely musical family circle. Father played tenor-sax, mother piano. Started — tentatively, he says — on old Kay guitar, playing folk, country music at home. Eventually, took guitar lessons (for two years), during which time also learned to read music as well. Occasionally, played with small combos, rock bands at school dances. But it was after hearing Johnny Smith (q.v.), that jazz beckoned. Graduated from high school, at which time, he says, he really began to take guitar-playing seriously. Accepted

further tutelage; jazz teacher John Mehegan helped immensely in his all-round development, but with particular regard to important individual aspects like chord voicings. Put together own combo (1965) — including a cousin... and Barry Manilow (Wilkins played vibes in this group — had studied this instrument, which he doesn't play anymore, with Terry Gibbs' brother).

Started playing in NYC clubs, then worked for just over a year with dance bands led by brothers Larry/Les Elgart, Sammy Kaye, Warren Covington. Quit to undertake studio work in New York; also appeared in pit bands for Broadway musicals such as *Promises Promises, Golden Rainbow*. Worked as accompanist for singers Morgana King, Pearl Bailey, Sammy Davis, and with top jazzmen Dizzy Gillespie, Stan Getz, Earl Hines.

Toured US, Europe, with Buddy Rich Septet (1973-1975), after working with bassist Michael Moore in duo. Wider exposure with Rich helped subsequent solo career enormously. The Rich period is documented interestingly by both (2), (3) — especially the latter, which benefits from being a location recording. Certainly, it is indicative of just how well-developed Wilkins had become since his first appearance on the local jazz scene. A more-or-less complete guitarist, in fact, with few, if any, faults in his make-up; a gifted performer who could handle blues, ballads, bebop, and all kinds of tunes, tempos, time-signatures.

Of Wilkins' all-too-few own recording dates, (6) is by far the most successful, both in terms of overall excellence, and in really serving as a true testimony to the man's undoubted talents. His superior tone, for example, is showcased throughout, particularly on his own *Fum*, and he displays a dazzling technique — using flawlessly-executed double-time runs and impressive octave-playing — during *Falling In Love With Love* and *Papa, Daddy & Me*. And he utilises the services of a steel-string acoustic guitar most effectively during a fascinating duet with pianist Jack DeJohnette on the latter's impressionistic *Brown, Warm & Wintery*.

SELECTED DISCOGRAPHY

1 Watershed (Paul Jeffrey) MAINSTREAM
2 Transition (Buddy Rich) GROOVE MERCHANT
3 Very Live At Buddy's Place (Buddy Rich) GROOVE MERCHANT
4 Sergenti Minstrel (Sonny Fortune (one track only) ATLANTIC
5 Windows MAINSTREAM
6 Merge CHIAROSCURO
7 You Can't Live Without It CHIAROSCURO

ATTILA ZOLLER

Attila Cornelius Zoller: Born Visegrad, Hungary, 1928. Comes from strong musical background, including father, a music teacher, conductor who taught his son violin from age four. Started playing trumpet at nine, using this instrument in school symphony orchestra for seven years. At almost 18, went to Budapest to become professional musician. Realised making a living on trumpet might be difficult, so switched to guitar. By 1947, had made such progress was playing in one of Budapest's top dance bands.

Because of growing political troubles, moved to Vienna (1948). Partnered local accordionist Vera Auer in leading a successful combo for five years. (Group won Top Combo prize at 1951 Vienna jazz contest — although its usual musical fare was dance, cabaret music).

By 1954, had decided on a jazz-only career. Moved to West Germany. Worked with pianist Jutta Hipp (1954-1955). It was with band of West German tenorist Hans Koller (1956-1959) that Zoller's reputation as jazz guitarist of international stature was established. Helped no little by sitting in with numerous visiting US musicians.

Decided to emigrate to US (1959). On recommendations by Jim Hall (q.v.), John Lewis, received scholarship for the Lenox School of Jazz, Mass. Worked for a while with drummer Chico Hamilton's combo. With flautist Herbie Mann (1962-1965), during which time won special German film prize for music for soundtrack of *The Bread of Our Early Years.* Put together own small group, with pianist Don Friedman (1965), which appeared at Newport Jazz Festival (1965). Played gigs with vibist Red Norvo in Canada (1966), then, briefly, with Benny Goodman (1967). From 1960, paid annual trips to Europe, for concerts, TV, radio, recordings.

With singer Astrud Gilberto's support band for Japanese trip (1970), returning following year, together with Jim Hall, Kenny Burrell (q.v.), as part of Guitar Festival. In 1971, granted patent for Bidirectional Pick-up device for guitar, electric-bass. Also credited with inventing first magnetic pick-up for vibraharp.

Since his emergence in top-flight US jazz circles at the beginning of 1960's, Attila Zoller has continued to be recognised as one of the most original guitarists around. With an absolutely first-rate technique, there seems to be nothing he cannot achieve on his chosen instrument. His basic approach to jazz guitar playing makes him very much an individualist — the only other performer whose style runs parallel to Zoller is the late Gabor Szabo (q.v.) Both have a keen harmonic sense, and a sound that sometimes evokes their East European background.

Zoller's contributions to recording dates of others are always helpful — together with the session leader's magnificent bass-playing, the guitar work to be found within (1) remains the single most memorable. In company of trombonist Albert Mangelsdorff and altoist Lee Kontiz, Zoller produces solos of real originality on (2), inspiring his two illustrious colleagues to give of their best, and being inspired in return. Of his own recordings, (4) is, all-round, probably the best, including in *Alicia's Lullaby,* a superior example of his ballad playing, a choice bossa nova styling in *The Birds & The Bees,* and a kaleidoscopic, wholly evocative extended solo that informs the intriguing *Gypsy Cry.*

Embryo SD 523

SELECTED DISCOGRAPHY

1 The Legendary Oscar Pettiford BLACK LION
2 Zo-Ko-Ma (with Lee Kontiz, Albert Mangelsdorff) MPS
3 The Horizon Beyond EM/ARCY
4 Gypsy Cry ATLANTIC/EMBRYO
5 Dream Bells ENJA
6 A Path Through Haze (with Masahiko Sato Trio) MPS
7 Katz & Maus (original film score) MPS
8 Heinrich Heine — Lyrik & Jazz PHILLIPS
9 Zoller-Zoller-Solal (with Hans Koller, Martial Solal) SABA/MPS

Understanding Tablature

Tablature is a system of music notation that has been developed specifically for guitarists. It takes place on six line staff, each line representing one of the six strings of the guitar. A number indicates which fret on the guitar is to be fingered. Rests and other musical symbols are basically the same.

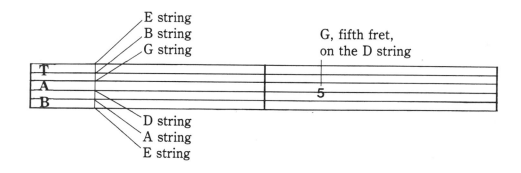

THE AUTHOR Born in Beckenham, Kent, Stan Britt has been writing on jazz and blues for over 20 years. He has written for publications as diverse as *Jazz Journal International, Billboard, Melody Maker, The Wire, Hi Fi Answers* and *Jazz*. An occasional broadcaster, he spent 15 years in various editorial capacities with two leading UK newspapers, and has also worked within the press offices of two prominent record companies. A devout record collector, Stan Britt is co-author, with Brian Case, of *The Illustrated Encylopedia of Jazz,* and contributed to *Sinatra & The Song Stylists.* He lives and works in South-West London.

AUTHOR'S DEDICATION For MEB (without whose inspiration this book, like life itself, would have been impossible)

THE MUSICIAN Chris Watson is a member of the National Youth Jazz Orchestra and a respected session guitarist.

With special thanks to: Ace of Clubs, Decca Record Co Ltd, Mamlish Records Inc, CBS, Embryo Records, TK Records, ECM Records, Sonet Productions Ltd, Milestone Records, Coda Records, All Life Records, Mood Records, Arista, Warner Bros, Pye Records, CTI Records, Mainstream Records, Marble Arch Records, for the courtesy of their album art.